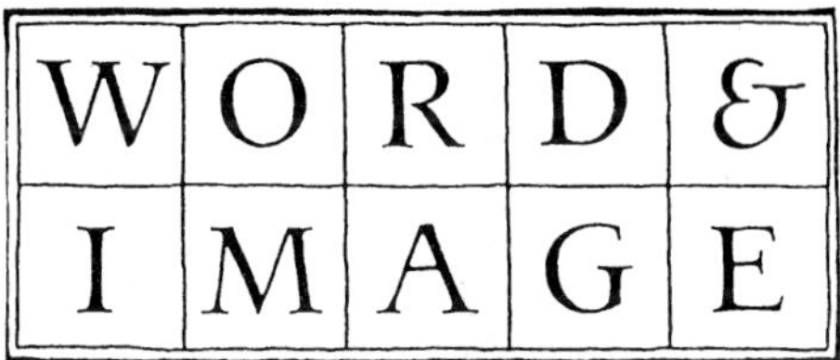

Series Editors
Leo Hoek and Peter de Voogd

In collaboration with

Studies in comparative literature 12

Series Editors
C.C. Barfoot and Theo D'haen

The Pictured Word

Word & Image Interactions 2

Edited by
Martin Heusser
Claus Clüver
Leo Hoek
Lauren Weingarden

Amsterdam - Atlanta, GA
1998

Cover design: Hendrik van Delft

ISBN: 90-420-0190-9 (paper)

The paper on which this book is printed meets the requirements of 'ISO 9706:1994, Information and documentation - Paper for documents - Requirements for permanence'.

Printed in The Netherlands

Table of Contents

Acknowledgments

My sincere thanks are due to my co-editors, Claus Clüver, Lauren Weingarden and Leo Hoek for their excellent editorial work. By the same token, I wish to thank Lucienne Droz for carefully proofreading and correcting the French manuscripts. Fred van der Zee at Rodopi and Cedric Barfoot (University of Leiden) have made many valuable suggestions in typographical and editorial matters.

I.A.W.I.S. very gratefully acknowledges its indebtedness to the Faculty of Letters of Vrije Universiteit, Amsterdam for their contribution towards the productions costs of this publication.

Martin Heusser

Reflections on Theory and Methodology

On Representation in Concrete and Semiotic Poetry

Claus Clüver

Among the phenomena of word and image relations that have moved to center stage in recent interarts studies is one that bears an ancient and yet widely unfamiliar label: ekphrasis. Over the last ten or fifteen years the label has been dusted off and even given new lustre in a few scholarly studies; the most exhaustive and illuminating among them is Murray Krieger's recent book *Ekphrasis: The Illusion of the Natural Sign* (1992).[1] But what exactly is, or should be, covered by that label in contemporary interarts discourse is still quite open to debate. In an article published in 1991 James Heffernan proposed to define ekphrasis as "the verbal representation of graphic representation" ("Ekphrasis" 299), where "graphic" is meant to stand not only for the graphic arts but also for painting and sculpture. This amounts to the most traditional position, even though it broadens the verbal aspect to include verbalizations of artworks in textbooks and critical reviews. Heffernan emphatically excluded as objects of ekphrastic representation all non-representational paintings and sculptures and all architecture.[2] I find that exclusion difficult to justify on theoretical grounds and impossible to observe in practice. In fact, I consider it most useful to define ekphrasis as "the verbal representation of a real or fictitious text composed in a non-verbal sign system". Once it is realized, however, that this extends the label to verbalizations not only of architecture but of dance and absolute music and all other non-verbal and non-visual texts as well, in a self-conscious but carefully pondered break with tradition and historical usage, my definition is bound to encounter opposition. I am quite prepared to defend it – but that is not my concern here.[3] In fact, for a moment I will instead look at precisely the tradition and the historical usage from which my own proposal so determinedly deviates.

That tradition has indeed to do with representation and has attracted most attention during periods when the mimetic impulse so peculiar to the West was dominant. It involves a concern with the kind of relation signs have to their referents, in particular, pictorial signs on one hand and verbal signs on the other. I use "pictorial signs" roughly in the sense Heffernan used "graphic": my term is likewise intended to exclude visual sign systems that are not normally employed to produce images or pictures of "nature" understood as the visually perceptible world. Among those other sign systems are most that are

Figure 1. Jiří Kolář (b. 1914), "Brancusi". 1960-61. From Williams, n. p.

currently used for the graphic notation of verbal language, no matter what their origin. For long periods in Western history, pictorial signs have been treated in critical and theoretical discourse as endowed with the capacity of resembling their natural objects to such a degree that looking at them was like looking at nature itself. The description of the same objects by words, on the other hand, was usually perceived to rely on signs that were arbitrary, no matter whether these signs were sounds or graphic marks. Nevertheless, such descriptions have held a central place in verbal discourse, especially in the discourse we call literary. And the mimetic impulse has always created a desire for descriptions to have the same vividness and impact on the senses as the signs displayed in space for direct visual inspection. There are rhetorical terms for this desired quality: the Greek *enargeia* and the Latin *evidentia* or also Cicero's *sub oculos subiectio*. In German it is *Anschaulichkeit*, a term which provides the title for an extensive recent study by Gottfried Willems "on the theory and history of word-image relations and the style of literary representation" (so the subtitle of the book; my trans.). Krieger considers "the semiotic desire for the natural sign" as one of the two basic "impulses" in literature, always in conflict with the fear of being deprived of "the freedom of our imagination and its flow in its arbitrary signs" (11). That desire has survived the realization that "natural signs" are likewise products of cultural conditioning and thus, in fact, conventional – although the debate over the semiotic status of iconicity has not been closed.

In view of that desire, Krieger sees among the motivations for producing verbal representations of pictorial representations the intent to exploit, for better effect, images already formulated by means of visual signs, as well as a competitive urge to equal or outdo the visual artist, and ultimately the attempt to establish the superiority of the verbal text by making it embody the pictorial, as it were, and at the same time allow the words in their temporal dimension to do what they supposedly can do better than visual signs.

These motivations may have had a dominant role in a specific poetic genre devoted to ekphrasis that has a long history but no agreed-upon name in English. In German it is called *Bildgedicht*, "picture poem" or "poem on a picture". The extensive work of Gisbert Kranz has shown that such poems serve an array of functions, and that the label may have to be kept elastic in order to cover the many different approaches to the task of representing visual artworks. One should note in passing that Kranz has encountered and included a sizeable number of poems on non-representational art and that for him the *Architekturgedicht* forms a subset of the *Bildgedicht.* But the great bulk of the thousands of titles he has collected comprises verbal representations of pictorial representations. Almost exclusively, these poems about pictorial texts do not themselves display unconventional visual features; a number of 20th-century *Bildgedichte,* however, have been conceived as visual Concrete poems.

Throughout its history, ekphrastic poetry has tended to celebrate the artist along with the work of art. In more recent times, certainly ever since the Romantic recasting of the artist as creative genius struggling to translate vision into form, poets have frequently represented visual works via their genesis in order to portray simultaneously the artist's mind at work, and to convey their own interpretation of the painting or sculpture as the artist's intention. That, too, is conceivably one of the potential strengths of the *Bildgedicht,* one of the ways in which it demonstrates its superiority over the visual text itself – especially in a culture that will equate the artist with his work and read his style as his signature. We recognize "a Monet" and "a Mondrian", and sometimes an artist is reduced in the public mind to a particular image or icon (which he may then in turn exploit as a trademark or logo, as Salvador Dalí did with his limp watches). When we see the image of the much reproduced *Bird in Space* (1925), we are likely to think automatically: Brancusi. So why not represent that mental habit literally as a *Bildgedicht,* as a text that is simultaneously image and poem?

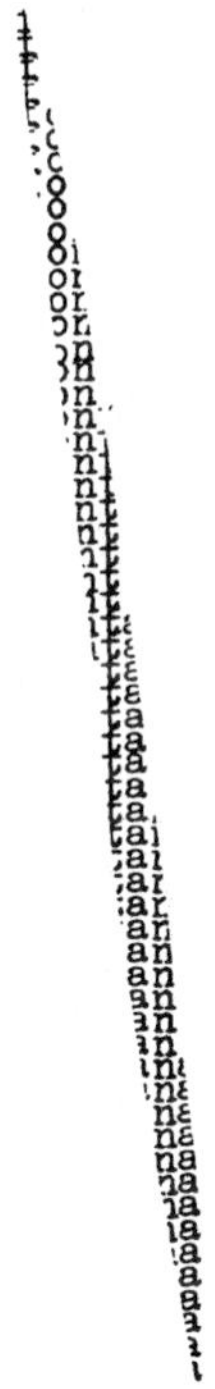

Figure 2. Jirí Kolár, "Fontana". 1960-61. From *Das sprechende Bild,* n. p.

A cut-out of a text composed of vertically aligned repetitions of the artist's name in the familiar silhouette of the sculpture, with the base formed by a stack of five complete "Brancusi's", inevitably becomes a representation of the sculpture, and the shape is perceived as identical with the name (fig. 1). But a very similar cut-out (fig. 2) will represent something quite different once we have deciphered the name that provides the verbal material: Lucio Fontana's most famous technique – his trade mark, as it were – is the slash in a tightly stretched canvas. But the cut-out may be a simplistic technique, even though in the case of "Fontana" the slashing of the name seems quite appropriate. More satisfactory is the discovery of a property of the graphic notation of a

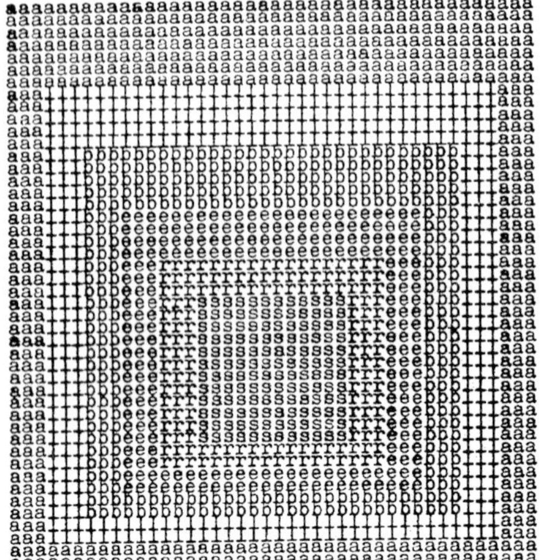

Figure 3. Jirí Kolár, "Albers". 1962. From Williams, n. p.

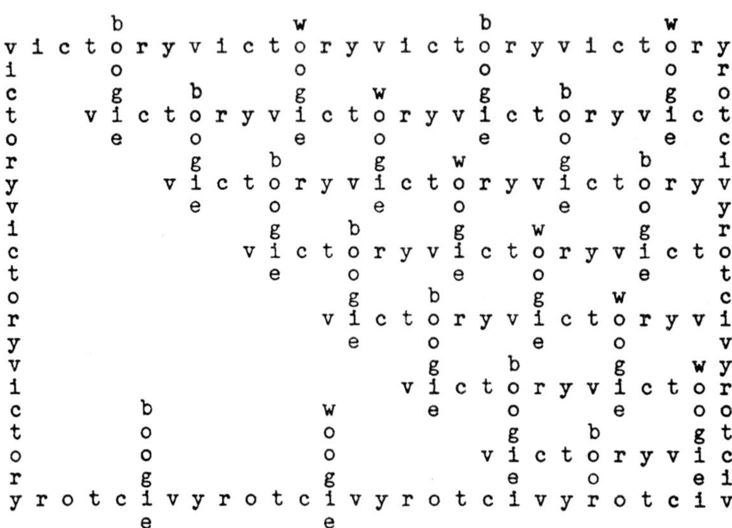

Figure 4. Ivo Vroom, "hommage à mondriaan". 1966. From Solt, 180.

particular name or title that allows the verbal material to be turned into a visual icon without mutilation. Josef Albers is best known for his series *Ehrung des Quadrats* (*Homage to the Square*). In the typewriter poem shown in figure 3, the Czech poet and collage artist Jirí Kolár, who also gave us "Brancusi" and "Fontana", has arranged the letters of Albers's last name so that they form the typical squares within squares, distinctly separated because of the differing density of the letters. Of course, Albers never created a six-square image; but that is a blemish, if one wants to read it as such, that Kolár accepted.

The same can be said of Ivo Vroom's typewriter poem "hommage à mondriaan" (fig. 4), which is constructed entirely out of the title of one of the painter's last, unfinished works: *Victory Boogie-Woogie.* We are likely to read the text as "a Mondrian" even though we do not associate the artist's work with horizontal rectangles; and it certainly does not imitate the painting whose title has provided its material in the same way in which Kolár's "Brancusi" imitates *Bird in Space.* But the poem, which is built according to very strict rules of its own, *does* offer visual traits that are characteristic of the final decades of Mondrian's work, and the emphatic diagonal is a reference to the series

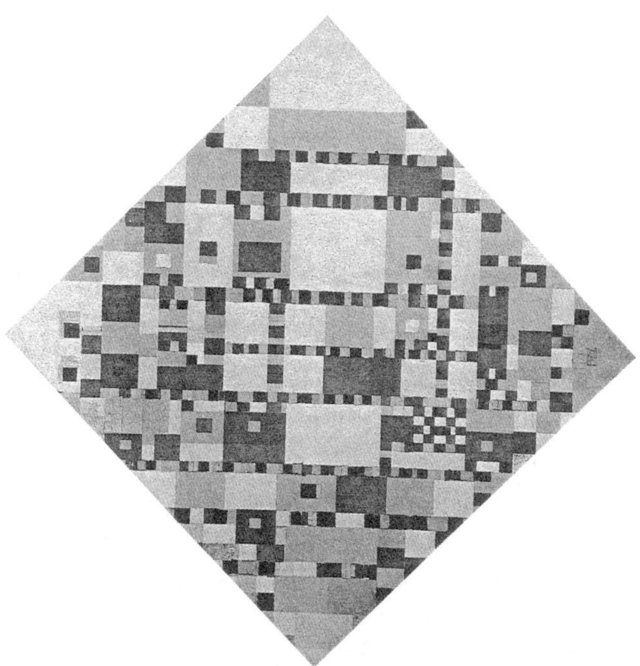

Figure 5. Piet Mondrian (1872-1944), *Victory Boogie-Woogie.* 1942-44. O/c with colored tape and paper, diagonal: 70¼ in. (178.4 cm). Coll. of Mr. and Mrs. Burton Tremaine.

of diamond paintings of which *Victory Boogie-Woogie* is the last (fig. 5).[4]

Bildgedichte like these, according to Gisbert Kranz the preferred manner of creating ekphrastic poems on non-figurative art, are late and special instances in the long tradition of Western writing that has developed varied forms of fusing signs derived from literary and visual systems of representation. Most of such hybrid texts are not ekphrastic in the sense the "Brancusi" and "Mondrian" poems are, and most, rather than engaging in a competition, appear to join the powers of visual and verbal representation while yet assigning the leading role to the word. Ulrich Ernst has recently published a compendious and impressive volume on the *Carmen figuratum* from antiquity through the Middle Ages that makes available, for the first time in such wealth and with such authority, many of the texts that establish that rich but much neglected tradition. Among the earlier examples are the shaped poems of Simias

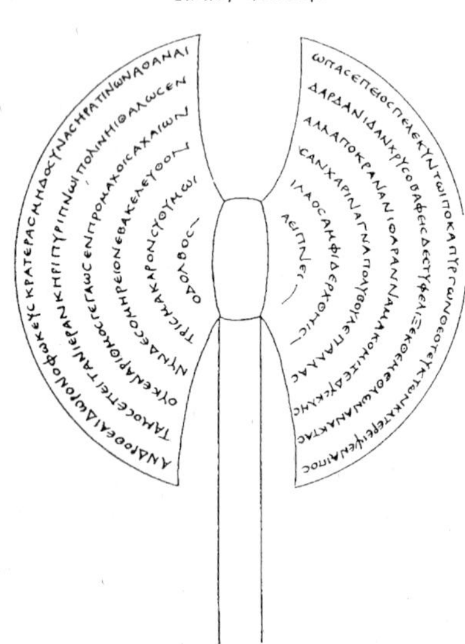

Figure 6. Simias of Rhodes (fl. 300 BCE), "Pelekys" ("The Axe"). Reconstruction by G. Wojaczek (1969). From Ernst, 71.

of Rhodes, who flourished around 300 BCE. Figure 6 shows his "Pelekys" ("Axe") in a reconstruction by G. Wojaczek, who assumes, along with others, that such texts were originally inscribed in the objects whose form they take, most likely within a ritualistic context. A high point, one millenium later, was the *Book of Praise of the Holy Cross* (*Liber de laudibus sanctae crucis*, early 9th c.) by one of the great Carolingian creators of Christian figured poems or "pattern poems",[5] Hrabanus Maurus, theologian, poet, and painter. Figure 7 shows the fifteenth of the book's 28 *figurae*, all of which were composed of a cross formed or marked by various kinds of colorful allegorial or symbolic images or

Figure 7. Hrabanus Maurus (784-856), Figura XV, *Liber de laudibus sanctae crucis.* Christ the Lamb and the four Evangelists. From Ernst, 284.

by large Greek or Roman letterforms; inscribed in these images or letterforms were self-contained texts, and the whole was woven into a textual grid made up of regular Latin verses that filled a square within colored borders (*versus intexti*).

An example from the eighteenth century (long past the period covered by Ernst's book), Charles-François Pannard's secular and much simpler poems in the shape of a bottle and a glass, shows once again the outline of an object created by the text that fills it, just like the "Axe" of Simias of Rhodes, but here composed on paper (figs. 8 and 9).

Provided we know the painter and his work, Jirí Kolár's text says "Albers" before we have had a chance to find out that it indeed also reads "Albers" (it belongs to a series of texts the Czech writer called "evident poems"). Depending on our familiarity with bottle shapes, Pannard's "Bouteille" signals "bottle" before we get close enough to read "Que mon / Flacon / Me semble bon!" We would be surprised if the text said anything else. There is a difference between the two poems, however, which on reflection turns out to be quite

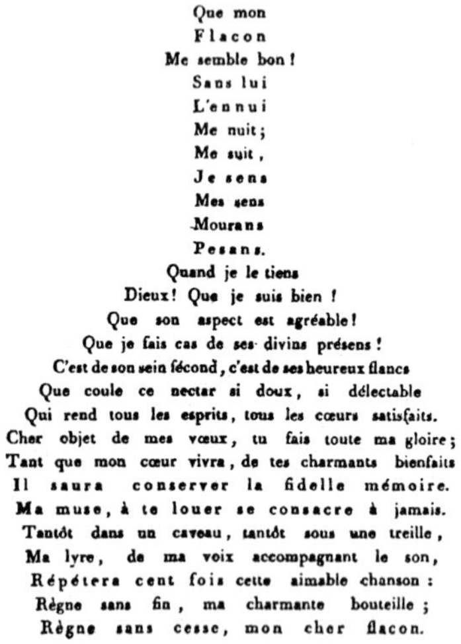

Que mon
Flacon
Me semble bon !
Sans lui
L'ennui
Me nuit ;
Me suit ,
Je sens
Mes sens
Mourans
Pesans.
Quand je le tiens
Dieux! Que je suis bien !
Que son aspect est agréable!
Que je fais cas de ses divins présens !
C'est de son sein fécond, c'est de ses heureux flancs
Que coule ce nectar si doux, si délectable
Qui rend tous les esprits, tous les cœurs satisfaits.
Cher objet de mes vœux, tu fais toute ma gloire ;
Tant que mon cœur vivra, de tes charmants bienfaits
Il saura conserver la fidelle mémoire.
Ma muse, à te louer se consacre à jamais.
Tantôt dans un caveau, tantôt sous une treille,
Ma lyre, de ma voix accompagnant le son,
Répétera cent fois cette aimable chanson :
Règne sans fin, ma charmante bouteille ;
Règne sans cesse, mon cher flacon.

Figure 8. Charles-François Pannard (1694?-1765), "Bouteille". From Peignot.

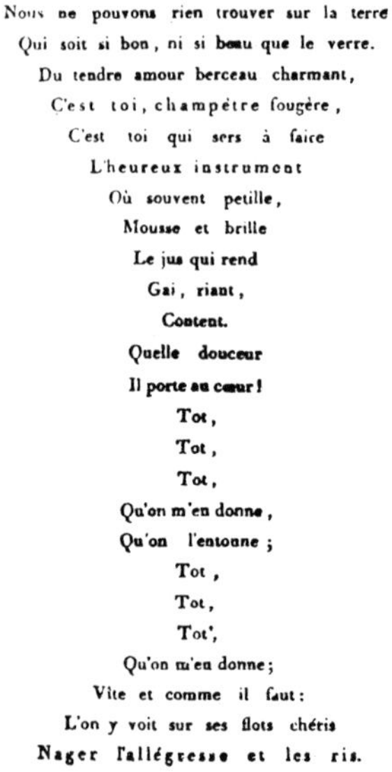

Nous ne pouvons rien trouver sur la terre
Qui soit si bon, ni si beau que le verre.
Du tendre amour berceau charmant,
C'est toi, champêtre fougère,
C'est toi qui sers à faire
L'heureux instrument
Où souvent petille,
Mousse et brille
Le jus qui rend
Gai, riant,
Content.
Quelle douceur
Il porte au cœur !
Tot,
Tot,
Tot,
Qu'on m'en donne,
Qu'on l'entonne ;
Tot ,
Tot,
Tot',
Qu'on m'en donne;
Vite et comme il faut :
L'on y voit sur ses flots chéris
Nager l'allégresse et les ris.

Figure 9. Charles-François Pannard (1694?-1765), "Verre". From Peignot

pfelApfelApfelApfel
pfelApfelApfelApfelApfelA
felApfelApfelApfelApfelApfe
ApfelApfelApfelApfelApfelApf
pfelApfelApfelApfelApfelApfel
ApfelApfelApfelApfelApfelApfe
pfelApfelApfelApfelApfelApfelA
ApfelApfelApfelApfelApfelApfe
felApfelApfelApfelApfelApfel
pfelApfelApfelApfelApfelApf
lApfelApfelApfelWurmAp
elApfelApfelApfelApfel
pfelApfelApfelApfel
felApfelApfelA

Figure 10. Reinhard Döhl (b. 1934), "Apfel". 1965. From Williams, n. p.

profound: the texts would be truly alike only if Pannard's "Bouteille" consisted in repetitions of the word (or of the letters contained in it) arranged to look like a bottle, which in this case could probably be best achieved by the cut-out technique used by Kolár to give us "Brancusi" and "Fontana". But figure 15. Here the descending diagonals are formed of identical letters: the magic word can be read both horizontally and in every ascending diagonal, completely so in the lines forming two sides of the triangle, and in the others by changing direction. Overtones of the power of such acrobatic verbal behavior are still heard in Finlay's poem (which, by the way, like ABRACADABRA, is *not* based on a palindrome); even as sound, "acrobats" shares some of the fascination of the enigmatic ancient word. Thus, while the text is certainly also an iconic intensification of the denotative meanings of the word that provides its material, the visual arrangement of "acrobats" introduces connotations and associations based on intertextual relations with much older verbivisual traditions and their cultural functions, connotations normally quite far removed from the semantic field covered by the word.

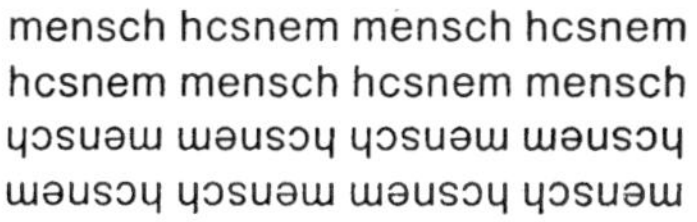

mensch hcsnem mensch hcsnem
hcsnem mensch hcsnem mensch
ɥɔsuǝɯ ɯǝusɔɥ ɥɔsuǝɯ ɯǝusɔɥ
ɯǝusɔɥ ɥɔsuǝɯ ɯǝusɔɥ ɥɔsuǝɯ

Figure 16. Eugen Gomringer (b. 1925), "mensch". 1960. From Williams, n. p.

"Mensch" is "human being". But Eugen Gomringer's very strict arrangement of four times four inscriptions of the word (fig. 16), forming a horizontal rectangle of four lines that also divides into four vertical columns, certainly does not create a visual image either of a human being's physical appearance or of any characteristic activity. What does characterize the text, besides the strict form, is the fact that the inscription is twice reversed: the first instance in the upper left corner gives its normal appearance, but the second instance, whether we read to the left or down, inverts the sequence of letters; and as we descend farther, we see the ordinary form of "mensch" upside down, in what one might at first take to be a mirror inscription. Completing the vertical descent, we encounter the expected inverted letter sequence of the upside-down form. Horizontally, we read in line one the word and its "inversion" and a repetition of both; line two begins with the "inversion" followed by the regular form, again repeated; the third line looks like the "mirror" image of the second; and the fourth completes the range of possibilities by offering the "mirror" image of the first. All of this sounds like an imitation of the basic structural treatment of the tone row in serial music, with its "mirror" and "crab" and the "mirror of the crab". But I do not know how to integrate that analogy into an interpretation that seeks to relate the formal arrangement to a representation of the word's referent. What the text does seem to be about is "human nature", and all the inversions are invitations for the reader to supply analogies, from his knowledge and experience, that would make this abstract structural scheme of "human nature" into something more concrete. The reader will also have to decide in which way, if any, the actual visual appearance of the text, including, size, typeface, and spatial arrangement, should be made a factor in the interpretation. We encounter here a verbivisual representation of something not directly accessible to the senses. Whatever is made *anschaulich* in this poem is beyond mimetic depiction, and graphic or sculptural representations of an allegorical or symbolist or nonfigurative kind would have to rely on verbal support, either by means of a title or inscriptions or of an ultimately language-based set of conventions, to suggest an appropriate reading.

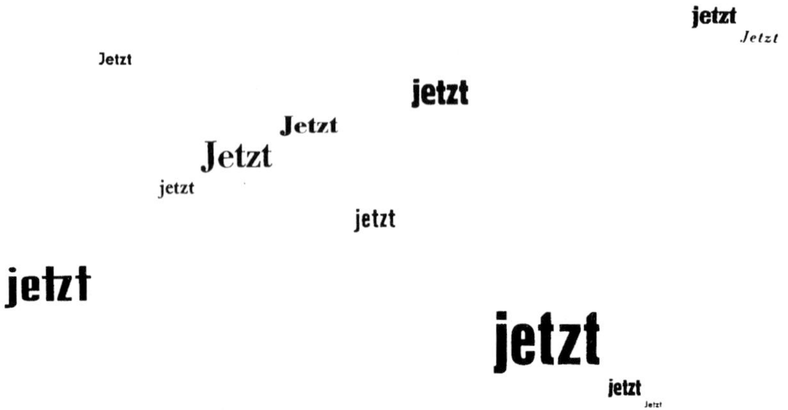

Figure 17. Gerhard Rühm (b. 1930), untitled. 1958. From Williams, n. p.

Gerhard Rühm's poem "jetzt" (fig. 17) is concerned with the iconization of time. It distributes tokens of the graphic notation of a temporal term, the equivalent of "now", over a two-dimensional spatial area. In many respects it is composed differently than most of the poems we have looked at so far. It is not a typewriter-generated text, and it does not aspire to a clear geometric shape, although it appears inscribed in a horizontal rectangle. Each of the twelve instances of "jetzt" is different from all the others, although there are affinities. The most obvious difference is in size, but there are also variations in typeface, five "jetzts" start with a capital letter, one is italicized, and their relative boldness is not identical. Their placement in the visual field follows no clear pattern, but there are some clusters, and all are placed on or near one of two intersecting diagonals.

There are at least two possible interpretations of the visual phenomena. Either we think of the visual field as strictly two-dimensional, which would translate into a simultaneity of all those "nows". Since one of them stands out, the reader is likely to identify it as signifying "now" for him, or perhaps even

Figure 18. Gerhard Rühm, untitled.
From *Gesammelte Gedichte*, 266.

"here and now". And he will then have to find a way of relating those other present moments to the most obtrusive one. It is possible to pursue such a reading further, but I find the alternative, which does not really cancel out the first approach, more satisfactory. It relies on conventions of visual representation associated with linear perspective, proceeding from the realization that a horizontal rectangle is the preferred format for landscape paintings. The most prominent "jetzt" is placed on the right near the lower edge, and another bold "jetzt" in nearly the same typeface but smaller is also near the lower edge, but not quite so close, all the way to the left. Almost all the other instances are higher up and smaller, and that fact, combined with the implied presence of the diagonals, suggests distance. Distance of temporal terms suggests distance in time: those present moments higher up and generally smaller are farther away, are "nows" now past, perhaps only remembered. It is true that the diminution in size is not progressive; but that activates a reading based on conventions in pictorial representation of three-dimensional space: objects bigger or bolder than other objects depicted in their vicinity are indeed larger and might be the largest objects of them all if they were brought into the foreground. Each of the more or less distant moments has its own character, and some stand out more clearly than others. Interestingly, the diagonal on which the largest "jetzt", the truly present moment, is located and which we read from lower right to upper left, is also continued in the other direction, to the very edge, which this reading has interpreted as the foreground; and the two "jetzt"s which we thus read as nearest to us diminish in size. The one very close to the big "jetzt" has been printed in exactly the same typeface and relative boldness, and the one furthest down, the smallest of them all, is almost illegible, but capitalized. If placement above the big “jetzt” is constructed to represent a moment of the past, then these two, which almost appear in its shadow, as it were, signify moments to come, moments already connected to and foreshadowed by the present “jetzt”.

Rühm has also given us an alternative version, which has a narrow vertical visual field subdivided by thin, equally spaced lines into horizontal rectangles (fig. 18). One of them is completely filled by a bold “Jetzt” in lower-case letters but with a capital initial, which avoids the *Unterlänge* of the lower-case j and results in the first, third, and fifth (last) letters touching the upper defining line. All the other rectangles, four above and three below, are empty. We read them as representing “Jetzts” of the past and of the future: but the prominent present stands here in utter isolation, flanked by ominous black vertical blocks.

The second “Jetzt” employs another sign not belonging to the alphabet, the straight line (also expanded into a wide rectangle), which we semanticize, along with the fields it creates, on the basis of the semantics of the poem's one verbal element.

There are, in fact, many modern visual poems that include such elements, and there are poems, or texts labeled “poems” and thus offered as such, that do not contain any verbal elements in their visual fields at all. One might for a moment think that the text in figure 19 by the Brazilian Pedro Xisto is such a

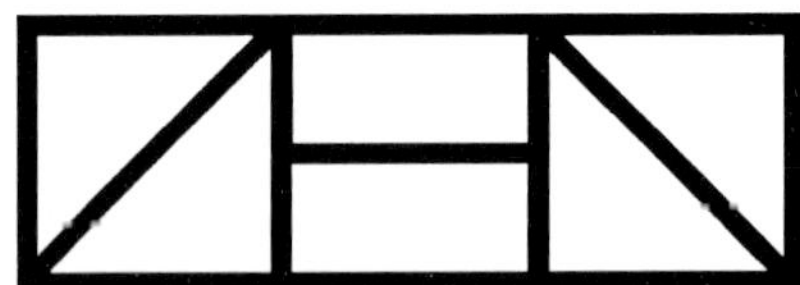

Figure 19. Pedro Xisto (1901-1987), “ZEN”. From *Logogramas*, 1966.

poem. But the accompanying title tells us that it is what Xisto called a “logogram” for “Zen”, and at the latest at that moment we recognize that it is indeed the word “ZEN” written in capitals and only slightly manipulated: three added lines close the squares in which the three letters have been inscribed and thus make visible the perfect bilateral balance of the structure, a structure based on sheer accidents in the formation of the three letters into which the far-Eastern term has been transliterated. Resembling in form and function the logos of commercial enterprises, some of which have been ingeniously designed, this sign stands as an icon for a concept and a worldview and mode of consciousness that elude representation perhaps even more than “mensch” or “jetzt”. It is crucial, however, that ZEN spells itself; if the transliteration were “SIM”, Xisto's logogram would make no sense, nor would it satisfy as a repre-

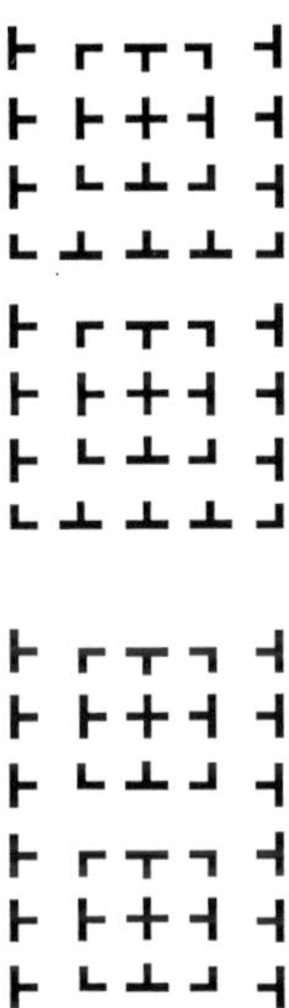

Figure 20. Mary Ellen Solt (b. 1920), "Moonshot Sonnet". 1964. From Solt, 242.

sentation of the concept if it were a purely visual design and not a constellation of letters.

But the poem by Mary Ellen Solt shown in figure 20 does not contain concealed letterforms, and its only verbal material is found in the title suggested by Ian Hamilton Finlay and accepted by Ms. Solt: "Moonshot Sonnet". The "sonnet" in the title makes everyone who remembers the formal rules of the Petrarchan sonnet recognize that these strange signs have been arranged in what one might concede to be an abstract though not particularly persuasive representation of the pattern of two quatrains followed by two tercets, and the fact that each "line" has five marks can be related to the iambic pentameter as the preferred meter of the English sonnet. The idea of representing an abstract convention of a literary system by means of visual signs may not be far-fetched; but this does not look like the ideal solution. We have, however, only dealt with half the title.

"Moonshot" contains "moon" and thus one of the cliché motifs of too many sonnets of the past; but the entire word, not in very active use in the nineties, refers to an activity quite different from sonneteering. In 1964, before astronauts had actually been shot to the moon, space researchers were busy photographing its surface, and those shots were frequently published in newspapers and magazines. Readers would find superimposed on the moonshots the same marks, apparently mapping devices, that constitute Solt's sonnet. Her text turns out to be a found poem, a reading of the scientists' marks as if they stood in the major lyric tradition of the West, or perhaps more precisely, the discovery that the sign system used by natural scientists in *their* manner of dealing with the moon need only be slightly manipulated in order to become a sign for the poets' and, by extension, the humanities' use of the moon as a fertile image. Thus perceived, the text may even be seen to symbolize a reunion of the "two cultures" into which Western consciousness has become divided, according to C. P. Snow.

These are high claims for a poem that may, in fact, no longer be very accessible. Encountered in a literary context, the wordless text will probably signal even without the title that it deals somehow with the sonnet, perhaps paying homage to the tradition while showing it simultaneously reduced to an empty formula. But in order to see the text as making a more significant statement, readers need to recognize the nature and function of the signs employed, and few will do that nowadays without the help of a footnote, when in the sixties the title provided direction enough.

The fate of relying on inaccessible signs seems to have been avoided, at least for turn-of-the-century Western audiences, in a text by the Italian semiotic poet Liliana Landi which, like Solt's sonnet, provides only the words of a title to direct the reading. The title is given in fine print in the lower right corner but has been cropped from the image shown here (it has been replaced by the caption; see fig. 21).

What do we make of the image without the title? It is not based on the codes of conventional Western pictorial representation, nor is it made up of signs belonging uniformly to any specific signifying system. An arrow, directional sign par excellence, red, thick, and short-stemmed, points upwards to an opening in a perfect circle formed by a thick black line. Directly above the arrow, and deriving from its pointedness a sense of movement, is a vertically oblong cloudlike formation of small red particles that appears to pass through the opening into the space circumscribed by the black line; on close inspection, these particles are small red letters. Most of the interior space is taken up by shapes that look like bands or ribbons, wider than the black line, straight and vertical but each folding over once or twice at a right angle and thus continuing horizontally; one side of the "ribbons" is colored purple, the other gold, so that they change the color displayed as they fold over.

With all its geometric properties the image nevertheless produces inevitably, almost at first sight, an organic, sexual association: that of sperm being released into a womb. It is intensified by the red color, which suggests blood, life blood, though there is no local color. In fact, the colors by themselves seem to belong to two ages and two types of signs: the gold and purple of the strangely folded bands inside have a hieratic and ancient quality, while the black and red are modern and more associated with publicity and advertizing. But if nevertheless the first association that asserts itself has to do with fertilization, then what are we to make of the small letters that compose the "sperm" and of the austere congested bands inside the "womb"?

The title of the piece is "Oh, Jerusalem!" As soon as we know that, we are enabled and motivated to construct our own interpretation, drawing on what we know about and associate with that name and what it stands for in our individual mental and emotional worlds. All readers are likely to make similar sense of the presence of the red roman letters, which on further examination turn out to be a topsy-turvy mix not only of capital and lower-case letters but also of numbers, punctuation marks, and even ampersands, with plenty of umlauts and other signs peculiar to the alphabets of European languages. And

Figure 21. Liliana Landi, "Oh, Jerusalem!"

my suspicion that the hieratic signs crowded into the interior of the walled-in space look almost like Hebrew letters has been confirmed by individuals able to read the language; I do not know if the same could be said of Arabic. Reading them like that does not cancel any other interpretation of the same signs focused by the title, in interaction with the text's other signs. It is exactly the avoidance of linking them with any specific signifying system that lends them their polysemous character. The relatively simple image is thus endowed with a wealth of interpretive possibilities, to be realized in accordance with the reader's imagination and his abilities to activate a variety of codes and handle a range of approaches, most of them relying on metonymy and metaphor. But any interpretation is likely to be directed and limited by the title, once it has been discovered. Landi's poem is thus perceived as an iconic representation of a complex reality. The meanings its readers will construct may vary widely, according to what they bring to the text. It is even conceivable that they will consider it a misrepresentation; but such a reading will only confirm the text's interpretability.

I shall conclude with two examples of semiotic poetry that employ a common device: while their texts consist only of non-verbal signs, these signs are accompanied by a key, like the Chinese character in Bory's "femme". In 1975, Mary Ellen Solt published a loose-leaf portfolio entitled *Marriage.* It is a very personal text and in some ways related to confessional women's lyrics and also to Ingmar Bergman's films of the time. But it is at the same time a highly formalized and visually beautiful text announced as "a code poem derived from the universal language of signs and symbols used from primitive times to the present day" (see fig. 22). Solt has divided the subject into eight categories: "I Pairings / II Conjugations / III Family / IV Home / V Relationships / VI Moods / VII Dimensions / VIII Conclusions," and for each of these she has supplied a set of keys, here exemplified by the keys for "Pairings" and "Conjugations" (fig. 23). The text itself consists of two tables composed of four interconnected quadrants, one dealing with the subjects named in categories I through IV (fig. 24), the other with categories V through VIII.

It cannot be of interest here to unravel even a corner of this semiotic web. But we should remark that the text not only makes *anschaulich* what as a verbal narrative might fill the space of a novel (or its variant, an autobiography), but that its employment of signs derived from so many conventional systems representing so many areas of human activity and knowledge links the private with the universal via a semiotic universe of signs.

Solt was in part inspired by the project announced a decade earlier by the Brazilians Décio Pignatari and Luiz Ângelo Pinto in an essay called "Nova linguagem, nova poesia". It was a plan for the creation of a semiotic poetry and had been illustrated by several examples. Of these, the most frequently reproduced is the untitled text by Pignatari shown in figure 25. All illustrations consisted in an interplay of geometric shapes, and these shapes were given new meanings in every example by means of a lexical key. Some seemed to border on the ridiculous, as if they had been written tongue in cheek. Pignatari's key is the most elaborate and incoherent. The black disk or ball is equated with "Pelé", still Brazil's most famous soccer player, a black; the rhombus is to be read as "a pátria é a familia (com televisão) amplificada" ("the country is the amplified family [with television set]"); and the horizontal rectangle is to signify "no fim dá certo" ("in the end it comes out right", which is not quite the same as "all's well that ends well"). The wordless text proper starts with the rhombus neatly placed in the rectangle but with parts of many disks filling the space surrounding the rhombus; and as we descend, there

M A R R I A G E

A code poem derived from the universal language
of signs and symbols used from primitive times
to the present day:
the alphabet
astrology astronomy botany
chemistry commerce engineering
mathematics medicine
meteorology music physics
punctuation runes zoology &c.

◆ *dot: secrecy origin of all signs*
◇ *diamond female anatomical symbol*
♡ *heart*
composite symbol
✡ *perfect marriage*
composite symbol
L *length (terrestrial) lambert: unit of brightness right angle: meeting of the celestial (vertical) and the terrestrial (horizontal)*
O *oxygen ocean blood type of husband and wife* October *(unofficial): husband's birth month*
V *potential energy velocity volume*
E *earth excellent*
LEO *husband's name*

Figure 22. Mary Ellen Solt, from *Marriage*. (1975). Title and general codes.

I Pairings

☿ *sun (old oriental symbol) source of all life*
⦶ *active male element saltpeter*
⊖ *passive female element earth (with equator)*
salt element: water
♂ *male male flower*
♀ *female female flower planet Venus*
mirror of Venus
▽ *male element: water*
△ *female wisdom godhead element: fire*
□ *male*
○ *female new moon unborn child God*
eternity element: fire
𝄞 *treble clef*
𝄢 *bass clef*
☉ *sun open eye of God element: air*
⊕ *earth creation: male plus female*
sun cross element: earth
=○= *equivalent*
△ *finite difference*
⬭ *whole note*
XX *double strength*
m+f = f+m *commutative law*
M—F *male implies female*
F—M *female implies male*

II Conjugations

⚳ *Ceres: goddess of earth's fertility*
♡ *love*
© *copyright*
⇔ *reversible reaction*
F° *degrees of heat warmth*
𝄐 *hold*
♮ *natural*
:‖ *repeat*
V *up-bow*
Λ *down-bow*
A *first class vessel*
X *kiss the unknown takes (chess)*
∝ *varies as*
→ *give*
℞ *take*
X *reactance*
R *resistance*
☾ *the moon's phases*
▷— *man & woman united: procreation*
⚲ *pregnant woman*
☆ *the five senses happy homecoming*

Figure 23. Solt, from *Marriage*: Key to Parts I, "Pairings," and II, "Conjugations".

Figure 24. Solt, from *Marriage* : Table I-II-III-IV.

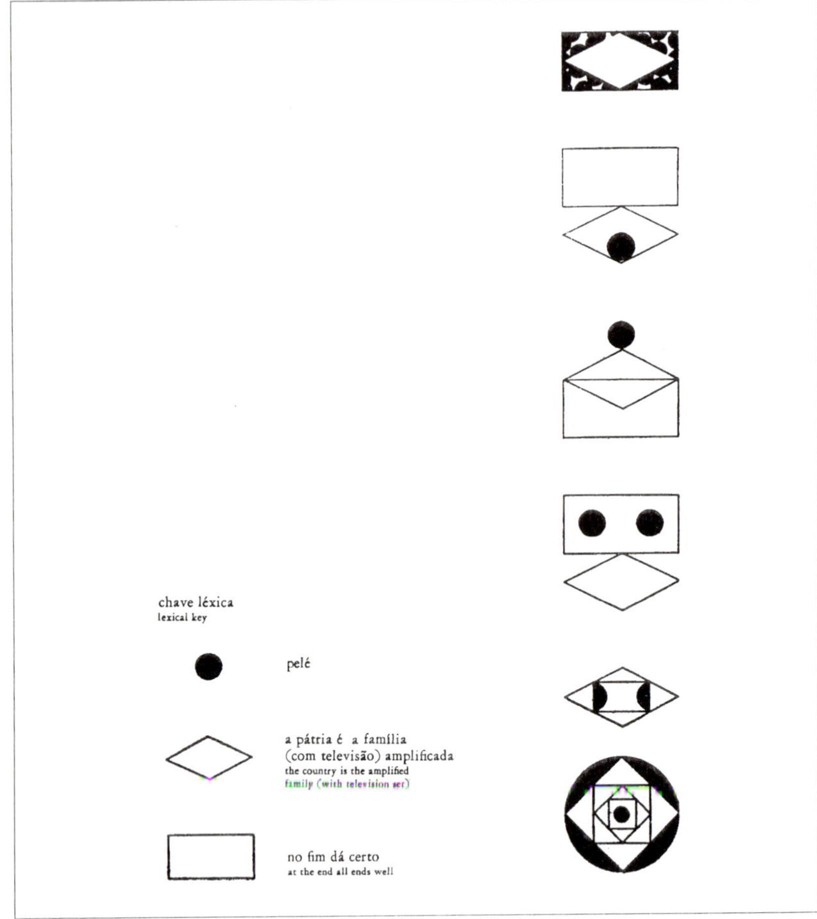

Figure 25. Décio Pignatari (b. 1927), untitled [semiotic poem]. 1964. From Solt,110.

seems to be a development, a kind of visual narrative, that changes the relative position of the three elements but never shows the disk inside the rhombus inside the rectangle, although that seems to be the goal. It is reached in an unexpected fashion in the final phase, where we see a figure of complete symmetry and thus stability, though achieved at the cost of changing both rhombus and rectangle into squares and with one black disk in the center and another containing the whole. But how is this visually satisfactory and perhaps also funny text to be related to the terms of its lexical key?

Even Brazilians are not certain. Possibly some were, in the sixties. And yet, they should all have recognized that there is another code at play here, that a disk inside a rhombus inside a rectangle compose the national symbol, the

Brazilian flag (fig. 26). It is ironic enough to suggest that the flag really represents a nation totally preoccupied with its successes as the world's soccer champion.[8] However, the text does not result in the (re-)constitution of the flag, but in its deformation, in a sign of stagnation that resembles a prison. Is it a coincidence that the poem was created soon after the "revolution" that brought a military dictatorship? It seems that any reference to the now hidden code might have run into the new censorship, which would have taken offence at the desecration of a national symbol even without noticing the political satire. If Landi's text is an icon of a city with a long and difficult history, the final image of Pignatari's text becomes a visual sign for the state of a troubled nation. In order to achieve that status it does rely on all the implications of the verbal key; and yet it will escape an even more pungent interpretation unless the reader is also aware of the presence of another, overruling semiotic code.

I began by placing this investigation in the framework of the traditional understanding of ekphrasis, and in particular ekphrastic poetry, as representing pictorial representation, and I referred to recent discussions like Murray Krieger's that place the ekphrastic effort in the context of the ancient rivalry between depiction and description. The first text I offered for inspection was therefore an ekphrastic poem that was also a shaped poem, its verbal material consisting in the artist's name and its shape imitating the shape of a well-known representational (though highly abstract) sculpture by that artist. Unquestionably ekphrastic even by Heffernan's definition, the poem derived its

Figure 26. Brazilian flag. The inscription reads "Order and Progress".

enargeia from its visual properties, but the dual function of its verbal material – naming the artist and serving as a title for his work – suggested that the object of its representation was ultimately not Brancusi's representation of a bird in space, but a much more complex issue having to do with the way we receive works of art. Its complexity contrasts effectively with the simplicity of the verbivisual text. The issue would be difficult to depict, and impossible to represent pictorially in such a condensed fashion; but that does not grant superiority to the word, for the pictorial code carries at least as much weight as the verbal in this hybrid text. Visually, the Concrete *Bildgedichte* on Fontana, Albers, and Mondrian were representations of non-representational forms of artmaking and thus not ekphrastic in Heffernan's terms, but otherwise hard to distinguish from the Brancusi poem, especially as regards their ultimate object of representation.

We then left the specifically ekphrastic mode but continued to explore in the following poems their representational aspects, emphasizing that in all of them except the semiotic poems an "iconic" quality had been superimposed upon the "symbolic" relation between the verbal signifier and its signified. While they are not *Bildgedichte*, all these poems are covered by the broader conception of ekphrasis proposed by Krieger, in a move he calls "beyond historical precedent" but which does not take him in the direction I would like to go with the term. He not only aims to "reconnect ekphrasis to all 'word-painting'" but to "include those other manifestations of the spatial impulse within poem-making that seek to ... work toward the illusion that it is performing a task we usually associate with an art of natural signs". In considering the case "when the verbal object would emulate the spatial character of the painting or sculpture by trying to force its words, despite their normal way of functioning as empty signs, to take on a substantive configuration – in effect to become an emblem", Krieger seems to refer directly to the kind of texts we have examined, with the exception of the semiotic poems. Somewhat surprisingly, however, he then calls "the representational attempt by the verbal art ... to form itself into its own poetic object" in parentheses "an ultimately vain attempt" (9).

What prompts Krieger's last judgment is his conviction that "the verbal art" will not succeed "to capture [both space and the visual] within its temporal sequence" (9). Krieger may not be writing about Concrete poetry after all, for the poems we have looked at succeed where he expects failure. They do so not only by increasing the visual, but at least as much by reducing "temporal sequence", largely by using very limited verbal material and, more importantly, by imposing a spatial syntax. When Krieger imagines "the verbal art ... form[ing] itself into its own poetic object" he is drawing an analogy to representational sculpture and painting, formerly thought of as "an art of natural signs". But in our examples the establishment or intensification of iconic relations between sign and referent by skillful exploitation of properties of the verbal material does not resuscitate any contentions about natural signs: if anything, it underscores the role of the arbitrary, of chance. Even more importantly, and the crux of our investigation: most iconic relationships we analyzed did not involve visually perceptible referents.

There are other ways of looking at these texts, and they have less to do with representation as ekphrasis in the way Krieger uses the term. And there are other Concrete poems that aim to be read much more emphatically than our examples as "poetic objects" in the way non-representational sculpture is read as text. I have not been concerned with that possibility here. Nor have I been explicitly concerned with the contention that many Concrete poems, especially the kind considered in this essay, are essentially metapoems, far more conducive to reflections about signifiers than leading to insights about the signified. What I have shown about some of the texts should have supported that view, while observations on others may provide arguments against it.

What I did emphasize was the potential of verbivisual intersemiotic texts to make concretely and vividly visible, *anschaulich*, what is verbally conveyed only by an abstract label, and to offer highly concentrated representations of referents that defy depiction. We have looked at examples constructed entirely of graphic notations of words and at others relying on verbal material only in their titles or lexical keys. I accepted the designation "semiotic poems" for these texts because I could show the governing function of the verbal components despite their exclusion from what appeared to be the text proper, and because the text proper did not primarily rely on codes of conventional pictorial representation. It should have become obvious even without detailed examination that, guided by the verbal clues, the reader would find those simple visual signs "saying" what it would take many words to communicate; and in a text like Pignatari's there is much that seems to defy verbalization altogether, in spite of the importance (as it turns out) of the lexcial key throughout. All the texts we have looked at may be poetry, but they all also appeal to our visual imagination and to non-verbal thinking – taking us, to use the subtitle of Mieke Bal's *Reading "Rembrandt"*, "beyond the word-image opposition".

Notes

1 Besides the studies by Krieger and Heffernan, see especially a number of contributions to Boehm and Pfotenhauer; cf. also the entries on "ekphrasis" in the annual "Bibliography on the Relations of Literature and Other Arts", *Yearbook of Comparative and General Literature* 36 (1987), and subsequent years.

2 In *Museum*, Heffernan has substituted "visual" for "graphic" (3) but reinforced the restriction to representations as objects of ekphrasis; his first loose definition, "the literary representation of visual art" (1), indicates a preference for keeping the ekphrastic discourse within the realm of verbal and visual "art".

3 I anticipate and counter critical objections in my "Ekphrasis Reconsidered".

4 For a more detailed analysis of Vroom's text and a comparison with Haroldo de Campos's poem "branco" read as a *Bildgedicht* on Mondrian see Clüver, "Painting Into Poetry". Kolár has also fashioned an "evident poem" out of Mondrian's name; for a reproduction, see Thomas [142].

5 This is the term preferred by Dick Higgins for this type of visual poetry created before the 20th century; see his anthology.

6 Jandl himself has provided a longer commentary along these lines for the inclusion of the poem in Williams's *Anthology*.

7 Like much of his later work, Finlay wanted this text displayed in a different dimension: "Properly, the poem should be constructed of cut-out letters, to occupy not a page but an entire wall above a children's play-ground". Comment in William's *Anthology*, n. p. A wall on a building is also the intended destination of the Garniers' "cinema".

8 Brazil first became champion in 1958, with a 17-year old Pelé, and repeated the feat in 1962, again with Pelé.

References

Bal, Mieke. *Reading "Rembrandt": Beyond the Word-Image Opposition.* The Northrop Frye Lectures in Literary Theory. Cambridge & New York: Cambridge University Press, 1991.

Boehm, Gottfried, and Helmut Pfotenhauer, eds. *Beschreibungskunst – Kunstbeschreibung: Ekphrasis von der Antike bis zur Gegenwart.* München: Wilhelm Fink, 1995.

Clüver, Claus. "Ekphrasis Reconsidered: On Verbal Representations of Non-Verbal Texts". To be published in edition of selected papers from the conference on "Interarts Studies: New Perspectives", Lunds Universitet, May 1995.

-----. "Painting Into Poetry". *Yearbook of Comparative and General Literature* 27 (1978): 19-34.

Ernst, Ulrich. *Carmen figuratum: Geschichte des Figurengedichts von den antiken Ursprüngen bis zum Ausgang des Mittelalters.* Pictura et Poesis 1. Köln, Weimar, Wien: Böhlau, 1991.

Goodman, Nelson. *Languages of Art: An Approach to a Theory of Symbols.* 2nd ed. Indianapolis: Hackett, 1976.

Heffernan, James A. W. "Ekphrasis and Representation". *New Literary History* 22 (1991): 297-316.

-----. *Museum of Words: The Poetics of Ekphrasis from Homer to Ashbury.* Chicago: University of Chicago Press, 1993.

Higgins, Dick. *Pattern Poetry: Guide to an Unknown Literature.* With appendices by Herbert Francke on Chinese Pattern Poetry and a comparative study by Kalanath Jha on the Citrakavyas of Sanskrit and the Prakrits. Albany: State University of New York Press, 1987.

Kolár, Jirí. *Das sprechende Bild: Poeme – Collagen – Poeme.* Mit einem Nachwort von Konrad Balder Schäuffelen. Sel. and trans. K. B. Schäuffelen and Tamara Kafková. Frankfurt/M.: Suhrkamp, 1971.

Kranz, Gisbert. *Das Bildgedicht.* Vol. 1: Theorie, Lexikon. Vol. 2: Bibliographie. Vol. 3: Nachträge. Köln: Böhlau. Vols. 1 and 2: 1981. Vol. 3: 1987.

Krieger, Murray. *Ekphrasis: The Illusion of the Natural Sign.* Emblems by Joan Krieger. Baltimore: Johns Hopkins University Press, 1992.

Peignot, Jérôme. *Du calligramme.* Dossiers graphiques du Chène. Paris: Chène, 1978.

Pinto, Luiz Ângelo, and Décio Pignatari. "Nova linguagem, nova poesia". *Invenção: Revista de Arte de Vanguarda* 4 (1964): 79-91.

Rühm, Gerhard. *Gesammelte Gedichte und Visuelle Texte.* Reinbek bei Hamburg: Rowohlt, 1970. [The two untitled "jetzt" poems are from the section "textbilder (1955-64)".]

Solt, Mary Ellen. *Marriage.* Printed at the Filial Press, Champaign, Ill. Bloomington, IN: Privately published, 1975. [Limited ed. of 50 copies.]

-----, ed. *Concrete Poetry: A World View.* Bloomington: Indiana University Press, 1970.

Thomas, Karin. *Bis heute: Stilgeschichte der bildenden Kunst im 20. Jahrhundert.* Köln: DuMont, [6]1981.

Willems, Gottfried. *Anschaulichkeit: Zu Theorie und Geschichte der Wort-Bild-Beziehungen und des literarischen Darstellungsstils.* Tübingen: Max Niemeyer, 1989.

Williams, Emmett, ed. *Anthology of Concrete Poetry.* New York: Something Else Press, 1967.

L'image pensée

Áron Kibédi Varga

L'étude de tout rapport présuppose l'existence d'au moins deux éléments différents et postule un lien possible entre ces deux éléments. Si l'on veut formuler au sujet de ce rapport des propositions ayant une validité générale, il faut que les éléments présentent une certaine stabilité. Or il se trouve que les deux notions de *texte* et d'*image* – les deux éléments dont notre congrès se propose d'étudier les rapports – ont considérablement changé de contenu au cours des dernières décennies, leur statut épistémologique s'est radicalement modifié. La question se pose dès lors s'il est possible d'étudier un rapport dont les termes ne cessent de se transformer. Ou faut-il peut-être dire que notre condition postmoderne consiste précisément dans l'obligation d'inventer et de manipuler un nouveau concept, celui des rapports *mobiles*?

On sait combien la notion de *texte* a subi des modifications au cours du 20e siècle. Les avant-gardes historiques des années vingt ont largement contribué à l'éclatement des genres littéraires, à la fusion des genres et à l'émergence d'un terme neutre, celui de *texte*, particulièrement favorisé par les nouvelles avant-gardes des années 70.[1] Le texte se trouve privilégié comme lieu de la rencontre difficile et du dialogue précaire, mais aussi et peut-être surtout, depuis Foucault, comme l'instance qui met en question le sujet qui parle.

Ce sont des impulsions d'une autre nature, me semble-t-il, qui ont modifié notre concept de l'*image*. L'esthétique se trouve depuis toujours, c'est-à-dire depuis le 18e siècle, plus directement liée aux objets visuels qu'aux produits artistiques de la temporalité: l'image est beaucoup plus couramment considérée comme un objet de l'analyse esthétique que le texte. Aujourd'hui, l'esthétique retrouve une place de choix dans la réflexion philosophique et, parallèlement, l'image devient un objet de questionnement théorique. Enfin, inutile de le dire ici, les découvertes technologiques, depuis celle de la photographie jusqu'aux installations vidéo et les images virtuelles, ne sont pas étrangères à la déstabilisation de l'image et à la difficulté croissante que nous éprouvons à la définir.

L'IMAGE ET LA PRÉSENCE

L'un des arguments classiques en faveur de l'image, au cours du débat séculaire du *paragone*, consiste à insister sur sa vivacité, sur l'impression forte et rapide qu'elle fait sur le spectateur. Selon Félibien – pour ne citer qu'un exemple parmi tant d'autres -, les images sont plus propres à susciter des émotions que les mots.[2] Pour le célèbre critique et théoricien du 17e siècle français, cet avantage se situe dans une perspective rhétorique: là où la parole l'emporte sur l'image sur le plan du *logos*, de l'invention des arguments, l'image en revanche triomphe sur le plan du *pathos*, des émotions qui doivent parachever la persuasion. Pour le fond, Gombrich ne fait que reformuler cette pensée en termes de la théorie de la communication lorsqu'il distingue l'information et son contexte pragmatique[3] : le texte est supérieur pour communiquer un renseignement précis, l'image pour nous le faire accepter.

Cette idée, que la critique d'art présente depuis des siècles en termes rhétoriques, sera reprise au 20e siècle pour subir, chez certains philosophes et poètes, une singulière métamorphose: de rhétorique, elle devient métaphysique. Depuis les Grecs, l'image a toujours suscité une réflexion sur l'être, sur l'identité et sur la chose. Cette réflexion ne se manifeste pas uniquement à l'intérieur du discours philosophique, elle est présente dans d'autres discours aussi, en particulier dans celui de la poésie moderne.

En effet, qu'il s'agisse des surréalistes ou de la génération de poètes qui les suivent, l'image est inséparable de la poésie du 20e siècle. Contrairement à ce qui se passe parfois dans le roman, en particulier dans le roman psychologique (*La Princesse de Clèves*, *Adolphe*), dont la continuité est rarement interrompue par l'irruption d'objets, la poésie ne saura se passer de choses.[4] Le roman, lorsqu'il se tourne vers les objets, les *décrit*; la poésie les *nomme*. Et nommer les choses, c'est créer des images ou des métaphores. Le roman représente, la poésie présente.

La poésie ne cesse ainsi de concurrencer la peinture, le précepte d'*ut pictura poesis* reste nécessairement et toujours actuel. Seulement là où les classiques situaient l'émulation sur le plan des procédés, c'est-à-dire de la rhétorique, la poésie moderne place ce principe au niveau, épistémologique ou ontologique, de la présentation: il ne s'agit pas de communiquer un savoir, il s'agit de l'inventer ou de le montrer. La métaphore surréaliste s'ouvre sur une connaissance neuve, l'image dépouillée de Ponge, de Du Bouchet, de Bonnefoy fait surgir, en le nommant, l'être des choses. La poésie entend se transformer en épiphanie.

L'image évoquée par les mots ne peut pas se substituer à la chose, elle ne saurait coïncider avec elle. Une distance les sépare, la poésie est le lieu où se manifeste la nostalgie de la chose. Et elle cherche à se rapprocher de la peinture parce qu'elle sait que l'image visible raccourcit cette distance. Lorsque l'on demande dans un entretien à Yves Bonnefoy la raison de ses préoccupations constantes avec la peinture, avec Piero della Francesca, Rubens ou Morandi, il invoque 'l'immédiateté' de cet art.[5] La peinture rend présent l'être des choses. Grâce à l'image, peinture comme poésie provoquent le choc de la présence, le choc de ce qui arrache à la continuité temporelle. Nous retrouvons une conception analogue de la peinture là où Lyotard fait observer, à propos de Barnet Newman: "Dans l'abandon du sens, la déontologie de l'artiste consiste à produire le témoignage qu'*il y a*, à répondre à l'ordre d'être. Il convient à la pièce à conviction que devient ainsi le tableau de ne rien offrir à déchiffrer, moins encore à interpréter". [6]

L'intérêt que la poésie postsurréaliste manifeste à la présence des choses et à l'immédiateté de la peinture semble rappeler le concept phénoménologique de la *présence* tel qu'il a été mis en lumière par l'existentialisme. Je pense en particulier à *Gegenwart. Eine kritische Ethik* d'Eberhard Griesebach. L'auteur insiste sur le caractère conservateur, quasi-réactionnaire des sciences, des sciences humaines en particulier, qui s'affairent pour organiser ce qui est déjà acquis, pour établir des classements à propos de ce qui ne peut plus surprendre, bref, qui nous réconfortent au sujet du *passé*, mais qui ne sont d'aucun secours au moment de la véritable rencontre, au moment où la rencontre inattendue, dans le dialogue, d'un être qui demande notre amour ou qui provoque notre angoisse, exige une réaction prompte, de caractère éthique, dans le *présent*. Le présent est le moment inquiétant de la *présence*, qui a lieu, qui advient, et devant laquelle l'homme est démuni.

L'apparition historiquement presque simultanée de ces deux notions n'est certainement pas un hasard, malgré les différences significatives: à la présence horizontale de l'existentialisme – la rencontre éthique d'autrui, grâce au dialogue – s'oppose la présence verticale de l'art – la rencontre métaphysique de l'Être, grâce à l'image. La première se manifeste de préférence dans les genres narratifs, comme le roman et le théâtre, la seconde dans la poésie et la peinture.

La présence peut se manifester aussi sous une autre forme, une forme "implosée", qui, loin d'être négative, propose une épiphanie peut-être plus contraignante encore: c'est la cécité dont parle Derrida, qui précède ou accompagne la conversion, chez Saint Paul par exemple, et qui rend clairvoyant.[7] L'ultime stade est atteint: on fait l'économie de l'image pour avoir directement accès à l'invisible. Cependant, la poésie et la peinture refusent cette économie – qui est celle de tout mysticisme – : elles se situent, grâce à leur matérialité, à l'exacte limite entre, d'une part, la cécité et le silence et, d'autre part, la mobilité de la vision ordinaire, narrative.

L'IMAGE ET LE RÉEL

Comment saisir, dès lors, le statut moderne de l'image? Elle nous frappe, rhétoriquement mais aussi métaphysiquement, par son épiphanie. En lui accordant un tel pouvoir, ne risque-t-on pas de conférer à l'image un statut essentialiste, de la réifier?

Nous savons que depuis Platon la réflexion occidentale déconsidère l'image, qui n'est que le double, que le reflet d'un original non-présent. La méfiance séculaire à l'égard de l'image s'explique selon François Dagognet par la peur du double: notre image nous échappe et nous multiplie.[8] Comment distinguer ensuite l'original et la copie, le vrai et le faux?

L'image se confond avec l'illusion, elle est mensongère. La religion se montre en général hostile.[9] La parole est d'origine divine, elle est bonne ou, après le péché, susceptible d'être corrigée, l'image est dangereuse, elle séduit. L'histoire de la littérature en est la preuve. Depuis Pétrarque, l'amour sensuel commence par le regard: "leurs yeux se rencontrèrent", c'est le titre du beau livre de Jean Rousset sur le thème de la naissance de l'amour en littérature. Le théâtre montre des images fausses, qui pervertissent la jeunesse, c'est pourquoi Bossuet et Rousseau le condamnent.

Le problème fondamental se laisse dès lors résumer ainsi: si l'image est suspecte, si elle n'est qu'une illusion, un double qui renvoie à autre chose, comment peut-elle acquérir un statut métaphysique, comment peut-elle avoir une valeur de présence, comment peut-on en vanter l'immédiateté? À cette question, plusieurs réponses sont possibles. Ces réponses ne se complètent pas, elles ont plutôt tendance à s'exclure.

La première consisterait sans doute à distinguer strictement *image* et *peinture*. L'immédiateté dont parle Yves Bonnefoy concerne la peinture, qui est une création artistique. Certes, pourrait-on dire alors, l'image est un double, mais la création artistique ajoute une valeur, fait que le double devient un original. Dans ce cas, la matérialité du tableau et le style du peintre seraient appelés à valoriser l'image et la présence métaphysique risque de devenir une fonction esthétique.

Une autre solution serait de nier le problème en l'enfermant dans le passé. La présence offerte par l'image serait une notion périmée, chère à la génération postsurréaliste mais dépassée depuis par l'évolution même de la notion d'*image*. L'image au pouvoir métaphysique, le sublime visible, a toujours été liée à l'image fixe, à la peinture toujours identique à elle-même. Depui l'invention du cinéma, et surtout depuis l'invasion de la télévision dans la vie privée, l'image fixe est en retrait, ce sont les images sérielles, les images mobiles qui nous enveloppent constamment.[10] L'image fixe nous arrêtait, parce qu'elle constituait une irruption de l'espace dans la continuité temporelle; l'image mobile ne nous arrête pas, elle épouse le temps afin de nous offrir des mondes et des vies parallèles à la nôtre et qui ne cessent pas de nous accompagner. Les thèses de Lessing perdent leur sens: l'image se fait récit, l'image devient littérature. Elle peut toujours émouvoir, faire peur, mais elle n'offre plus la sensation de l'épiphanie.

La société informatisée contribue d'une manière plus radicale encore à reformuler le problème signalé. Cette société, la nôtre, nous apprend à accepter la mise en question genéralisée du réel et en particulier de la réalité évoquée par l'image. La télévision et les jeux vidéo nous présentent en effet sans cesse des images qui ne sont pas des copies et qui ne renvoient à aucun original. Le concept de cette image déréalisée s'inscrit en deux scénarios opposés.

Le premier scénario est aujourd'hui encore le plus répandu: il est noir. Selon ce scénario, l'image déréalisée serait l'aboutissement logique de la "société de spectacle", pour reprendre un terme de Guy Debord, d'une société où tout est simulacre. Les forces qui dominent restent anonymes, le pouvoir est invisible, on ne nous offre que le faux. Une immense conspiration nous conduit vers une aliénation complète et heureuse, toute image est un leurre, le double, le spectacle se fait passer pour la réalité. La société est l'oubli du réel, et de l'original.

Ce scénario n'est acceptable que si l'on postule un réel immuable. Un réel issu de deux mille ans de réflexion philosophique et scientifique dont on déplore la perte et dont on garde la nostalgie. Un autre scénario devient cependant possible, un scénario éminemment postmoderne, dès que l'on accepte l'idée que le réel n'est pas nécessairement et exclusivement ce qui peut se laisser ramener à un état de repos et de fixité (comme l'épiphanie de la peinture traditionnelle).[11] Sous l'impulsion de la science contemporaine, un réel déréalisé et changeant, un réel imprévisible est en voie de se construire et de se laisser inventer. Le réel ayant changé, l'image déréalisée retrouvera son original, elle redeviendra réelle. Le tableau et le poème disparaissent, la société postmoderne consacrent leur déclin, mais elle ne tue pas pour autant ni l'image ni le sublime, qui a lieu. Mais ailleurs, dans la mobilité.

Notes

1 La valorisation du terme s'appuie d'ailleurs, à ce moment-là, sur les développements de la linguistique postchomskyenne et de la philosophie déconstructiviste: après le règne millénaire d'une linguistique du mot et de la phrase – une linguistique idéaliste et essentialiste – une linguistique transphrastique commence à s'imposer.

2 *Entretiens sur les vies et les ouvrages des plus excellens peintres*, vol. V, 324.

3 "The Visual Image: its Place in Communication", *Scientific American*, 1972; repris in: *The Image and the Eye*, Oxford, Phaidon, 1982.

4 Voir mon article "L'objet en poésie", in: *Mélanges Martinet, Word*, 1967, 537-552.

5 *Entretiens sur la poésie*, Paris, Mercure de France, 1990.

6 *L'inhumain*, Paris, Galilée, 1988, 98.

7 *Mémoires d'aveugle*, Paris, Réunion des Musées Nationaux, 1990, 24-37.

8 *Philosophie de l'image*, Paris, Vrin, 2e éd., 1986.

9 Cf. Daniele Menozzi, *Les images – l'Église et les arts visuels*, Paris, Le Cerf, 1991. Pour une vaste synthèse, voir Alain Besançon, *L'image interdite*, Paris, Fayard, 1994.

10 Cf., outre les travaux de Paul Virilio, le numéro spécial de *Art Press*: ("Nouvelles technologies: un art sans modèle?", 1991) et l'excellent petit livre de Miklós Peternák (*Uj képfajtákról*, Budapest, Balassi, 1993).

11 Cf. Gianni Vattimo, *La société transparente*, Paris, Desclée de Brouwer, 1990.

Art Historical Iconography and Word & Image Studies: Manet's *A Bar at the Folies-Bergère* and the Naturalist Novel

Lauren S. Weingarden

In this paper I want to show how a discursive art historiography offers word and image studies a means for expanding its field of comparative analysis. Following Michel Foucault's model of discourse analysis, I define a discursive art historiography as a method of viewing the work of art as an encoded articulation of a historically-bound, yet multi-faceted, matrix of social systems or cultural events.[1] It is within this matrix that word and image studies can view visual texts as reciprocal objects with verbal texts. To emphasize this reciprocity, I use the term "text" interchangeably for describing verbal and visual objects.

At first glance, iconography may seem adequate to this comparative project. However, in formulating a discourse-oriented method for art history, I realized the limitations of iconography as it was originally defined by Erwin Panofsky in 1932 and subsequently practiced by art historians.[2] According to the Panofskyian model, art historical iconography involves the description and classification of pictorial images as depictions of literary themes. This method, however, prioritizes the verbal over the visual text. In an attempt to correct this imbalance, I adapted semiotic and structural analysis to iconographic methods. Such a semiotic-structuralist revision of iconography offers two practical advantages. First, art history gains more precise descriptive and interpretive tools for comparing pictorial and verbal representation. Second, this adjustment unites iconography with formal analysis, the two methods Panofsky definitively bifurcated for twentieth-century art historians. In this paper I use Edouard Manet's *A Bar at the Folies-Bergère* (1881-82; fig. 1) as a visual reference for demonstrating my revisions of Panofsky's method. At the same time, I seek to use these revisions to extend and thereby reinforce art history's collaboration with literary theory in word and image studies. Manet's painting, then, provides an opportunity to show, according to a Foucauldian model, that both figurative and abstract modes of representation function as the rules or codes that form a certain number of concepts and relations in *épistémes* or other cultural phenomena.[3]

I have chosen *A Bar at the Folies-Bergère* as a visual object of word and image studies for two reasons. For one thing, Manet traditionally has been

Figure 1: Edouard Manet, *A Bar at the Folies-Bergère,* 1881-82. Courtauld Institute Galleries, London.

associated with Charles Baudelaire and Émile Zola,[4] literary writers who practiced art criticism and, in the process, defined a nineteenth-century discourse on modernity. For another, art historical interpretations of the painting reveal the traditional methodological tensions between formalist and iconographic analysis. For the formalist, the sketchlike technique and spatial distortion of *A Bar at the Folies-Bergère* initiate the development of modernist abstraction.[5] For the iconographer, the realistic depiction of socio-economic conditions in late nineteenth-century Paris, provides a visual counterpart to nineteenth-century naturalist literature.[6] However, because the iconographer prioritizes the verbal text, this approach fails to consider how the pictorial image, and the techniques for rendering that image, constitute a visual text which *independently* articulates a social and aesthetic discourse on modernity.

Such a textual reading of the visual imagery depends upon semiotic-structuralist strategies for determining how formal patterns function as carriers of artistic and extra-artistic meanings. Manet's broken brushwork, spatial and linear distortion, chromatic and tonal combinations comprise just such patterns. Viewed in this way, abstract formal features function as representations of values and concepts shared by image-makers and viewers. Here, pragmatics, as defined by social science and language philosophy, corroborates the union of discourse analysis with iconography as well as the union of iconographic with formal analysis. Pragmatics studies the relation of signs to sign-users and interpreters within specific social structures and practical situations; that is, it studies the *practical* effects and functions of signs.[7] Pragmatics can thus be used to render an historical account of the artist's *active* role in the production and transformation of signs and sign systems. Indeed, a pragmatist view of the artist as an active agent within his or her social or historical context assumes that image-makers (as speakers) are both skilled users and interpreters of the sign-systems that constitute a socio-cultural discourse. A pragmatic approach to formal analysis thus substantiates the visual dimension of discourse analysis and, in turn, enhances the cross-disciplinary tools of word and image studies.[8]

What are the limits of Panofskyian iconography that preclude such a discursive analysis and have therefore curtailed art history's interpretive role in word and image studies? To answer this question, we should review the status of iconography within Panofsky's three-part interpretative system.

In his 1932 essay on iconography, Panofsky divided his method into three separate but interrelated stages of description and analysis. He also illustrated these three stages as a diagram inserted within the written text. The first or "pre-iconographical" stage, is purely descriptive. Here we describe how technical or formal elements combine to represent figures, their gestures, attributes, and spatial distribution. While this formal analysis tells us what is depicted, it cannot tell us the meaning of that depiction. For this we must enter the second or iconographical stage of analysis. Such an analysis requires a knowledge of literary sources through which we can interpret the symbolic function of these figures and, in turn, the narrative content (or "subject matter") of the pictorial composition. For Panofsky, these literary sources are found primarily in classical mythology or in Old and New Testament texts. The third level of analysis is actually a synthetic process of restoring the painting and its iconographic content to its cultural context, to reveal its conformity with the world-view in which it was produced. Panofsky called this third level "iconology" and considered it the highest level of interpretation. Indeed, iconology reified the intellectual climate of a historical epoch as well as the historian's intellectual capacity for synthesizing his/her knowledge of all other cultural norms.

To be sure, iconology's contextual perspective facilitates an integration of art history and word and image studies. However, iconology refers to a transcendent and abstract concept which Panofsky himself identified with the notion of *zeitgeist*. Yet, it is just such abstractions (or "ready-made syntheses") that discourse analysis has taught us to mistrust. That is, a discursive event can only be discerned and described by the concrete relations between the artifacts, documents, techniques, institutions, or any other (written, spoken, or depicted) statements that make one or another discourse possible at any one time and place.[9] Ironically, it is just this materiality of discourse analysis that leads the art historian away from iconology and returns him/her to the object-oriented foundation of iconography. However, if iconography's more concrete data-base is to be adapted to cross-disciplinary strategies of word and image studies, we must keep in mind two deficiencies in Panofsky's method and their consequent effects. For one thing, he believed that formal elements and technical devices in themselves have no signifying functions. As a result, he not only excluded pictorial means of representation from iconographic study but modernist abstraction as well.[10] The second limitation of Panofsky's iconographic method concerns its humanist bias. Since Panofsky restricts his (comparative) literary stockpile to classical or biblical texts, he also limits subject matter to illustrating the didactic or allegorical themes of these texts. This limitation not only excludes abstraction from iconographic analysis, it also excludes the category of genre painting to which *A Bar at the Folies-Bergère* belongs.[11]

My discursive analysis of *A Bar at the Folies-Bergère* thus counters what Panofsky's method implicitly validates: that is, that the pictorial arts merely function to illustrate literature. As an alternative approach, a discursive method shows how Manet and the nineteenth-century naturalist writers *mutually* deployed a technical device to articulate a social and aesthetic discourse on modernity. Parody is just such a device. Here parody is viewed historically, as a culturally specific, interartistic strategy, and it is critically reviewed, as a technique that exposes the mutual exchange between the verbal and visual arts during modernism's formation. Historical interpretation thus complements critical interpretation. That is, since the modernist practice of parody is marked by deliberate artistic choices, it exposes the technical features distinctive to each medium. A comparative analysis of these medium-specific techniques reveals, in turn, patterns of discursive reciprocity between verbal and visual texts.

Returning now to Manet's *A Bar at the Folies-Bergère*, we can show that it *shares* a subversive narrative and formal structure with that of the naturalist novel, as it was codified by Émile Zola.[12] That is, both the artist and writer used parody as a technical device to subvert aesthetic expectations, and thereby articulate a cultural critique on contemporary social conditions. Here, then, a comparative analysis of parodic literary and visual forms suspends iconographic analysis of the image in terms of its (literary) subject matter. Instead, this comparison extends iconography to a *formal* analysis of the pre-iconographic elements—that is, the abstract elements of image-making—as signs and their signifying functions. As a result, a historical/critical interpretation of parody restores the integrity of abstract form and subject matter intrinsic to early modernism. Furthermore, when parody is considered as a technical device with non-mimetic sign functions, it provides an opportunity to demonstrate how a pragmatist method can be used to discern the artist's active role in meaning production. Indeed, parody depends on the artist's/writer's understanding and skill in using the conventional means of expression in order to subvert or displace them. This enables the viewer/reader, in turn, to skillfully decode referents to prior (parodied) texts encoded in the new text. (Of course, the naturalist writer's/artist's subversive means are also forms of convention. While the naturalists seek to suppress their conventions, just such forms enable the critical historian to decode parodic devices.)

As literary historian Linda Hutcheon shows, modern parody is inherently double-coded: it inscribes both "continuity" with, and "critical distance" from, the old text in the new text. Hutcheon further shows that, more often than not, *(situational) irony* is both the cause and effect of parody.[13] Indeed, irony itself is double-coded, it holds at least two entities or concepts in contrastive positions. Consequently, when parody produces a doubling effect between the new text and the old (parodied) text, this effect induces an ironic attitude or situation for the viewer/reader. This reciprocity of technique and effect is what constitutes ironic parody which, during the nineteenth century, became consonant with modernity.

Baudelaire's firsthand observations of Parisian culture and contemporary art expose just such a modernist paradigm. His critical writings therefore provide a discursive space in which the relationship between Manet's painting and the nineteenth-century naturalist novel can be reviewed. Indeed, this relationship is framed by a historical continuum between modern ironic parody and earlier nineteenth-century German Romantic irony, a romanticism to which Baudelaire was heir. As defined by the early romantic writers, situational irony consists of an active state of critical self-reflection upon the human condition.[14] That is, a condition of constant contradictions between the finite and infinite, the self and the non-self. This ironic state entails a self-induced mirroring effect, whereby the subject recognizes a double self, a process Baudelaire aptly called *"se dédoubler"* or *dédoublement.*[15] During the course of the nineteenth century, the locus of ironic self-reflection shifts from the internal, subjective self to the external medium of artistic representation. Likewise, the context of this self-criticism shifts from the metaphysical to the material ambient. At this later point, the ironic attitude becomes encoded in and, thus, subsumed by the formal techniques of parody.

Manet's parodic behavior can first be identified in the way he parodies museum masterpieces and academic techniques. In *A Bar at the Folies-Bergère* the painted mirror functions as a parodic device for both iconographic and formal ends. It triggers contrastive associations with the whole tradition of mirrored feminine beauty and with the academic finish in which this cultural ideal was portrayed. These include mythological types, such as Velasquez' *Venus with the Mirror* (1642; a.k.a. *Rokeby Venus;* fig. 2), Titian's *Woman at her*

Figure 2: Diego Velasquez, *The Toilet of Venus* (*"The Rokeby Venus"*), 1642. Reproduced by the courtesy of the Trustees, The National Gallery, London.

Toilet (1512; fig. 3), and Ingres's contemporary portraits of elegantly poised and fashioned aristocratic and bourgeois women, such as *Comtesse d' Haussonville* (1845; fig. 4).

On a strictly formal level, Richard Shiff's discussion of Manet's "technique of originality" helps to substantiate Manet's parodic intentions in *A Bar at the Folies-Bergère.* Shiff shows that Manet, like other avant-garde artists, formulated a means of expression (*qua* conventions) to signify firsthand cognitive experiences unmediated by routine academic techniques. These new techniques were thus conceived in direct opposition to academic conventions: compositional uniformity, sketchlike broken brushwork, flatness, chromatic modelling and spatial distortion replace compositional hierarchy, high finish, chiaroscuro, and one-point illusionistic perspective. [16]

Manet's parodic formal devices also conform to Baudelaire's celebration of modernism's multiplicity; that is, a state of incessant paradox, surprise, and change. In "The Painter of Modern Life" Baudelaire identifies the "double composition" of modern beauty and thus invokes the critical self-reflection of romantic irony. Modernity, he writes, is the constant contradiction between "an eternal, invariable element", and "a relative element" — "the age, its fashions, its morals, its emotions". The artist can achieve this aesthetic dualism and, ultimately, cultural renewal, by triggering in the viewer "the shock of

Figure 3: Titian, *Portrait of a Young Woman at her Toilet,* 1512. Musée de Louvre, Paris.

surprise". He does so by rendering the familiar unfamiliar and by presenting [in Baudelaire's terms] "the ever-new which eternally elud[es]", but still alludes to, "the rules and analyses of the school".[17]

We have already seen this shock effect in Manet's museum parodies. However, he also follows the more technical methods that result from the ironic self-doubling or *dédoublement* which Baudelaire prescribed for the painter of modern life. That is, during the creative process the artist first loses himself in

Figure 4: Ingres, *Comtesse d'Haussonville,* 1845. Copyright The Frick Collection, New York.

the flux of the modern urban ambience. He then critically distances himself to reflect upon the capacity of his medium to trigger the viewer's self-reflection upon the transitory, multifarious modern conditions. For Baudelaire, the fragment form and a technique of imperfection offered the best means to this end.[18] These are parodic formal means since they contradict expectations for the complete, finished work of art. Here again, Ingres's portrait painting typifies such nineteenth-century academic standards for finish.

In *A Bar at the Folies-Bergère* Manet depicts modernity by way of the fragment form and a consonant technical imperfection. First we encounter painterly fragments of tonal patches that do not *physically* cohere. Likewise, the mirror image is itself a fragment of an overall ambience and fragments the objects and figures reflected therein. The disconnected gazes between the foreground figures (as well as the viewer) add to the psychological fragmentation of the whole. At the same time, these painterly and figurative fragments do cohere as the mirror-image of the contradictory, ironic condition *apropos* of modern life. (Here the mirror-image is both an indexical sign of modernity and an iconic sign of the actual, reflected scene.)[19]

The sustained doubleness that ironic parody engenders, "through the playing with multiple conventions",[20] is what qualifies Manet's painting as a critical self-reflection upon painting as an illusionistic device. This parodic strategy not only joins the form and content of *A Bar at the Folies-Bergère*; it also situates the painting in a discursive space shared with the naturalist novel.

A structuralist analysis of form and function shows what is foremost among the parodic features and ironic effects that *A Bar at the Folies-Bergère* shares with the naturalist novel. In each case, the painter/writer enforces a mirroring dialogue between the viewer/reader and the art work. Whether or not actually present, the mirror-motif functions as a parodic device for critical self-reflection. That is, each medium invites the viewer's/reader's anticipation of conventional patterns or events such as spatial illusionism in painting or felicitous plot development in the novel — and then denies these same expectations. It is precisely the mimetic style of the earlier nineteenth-century Romantic novel that provides the naturalist novel with a mirror-motif for ironic inversions of its idealist narrative structure as well as heroic character types.[21] Parody is also the literary device for effecting such ironic conditions. As literary historian David Baguley observes, an ironic narrative effects "*contrast[s]* between a character's hopes, ideals, aspirations and ensuing plight". While the reader's expectations are met at the novel's inception, its "*banal* ending" subverts those expectations by denying resolution or redemptive closure.[22] In Zola's *L'Assommoir*, for example, the author incisively details the slow degeneration of the anti-heroine, who rises above her rural origins, achieves bourgeois prosperity in Paris, and finally succumbs to material indulgence, poverty and death by alcoholism and starvation.

Similar to the ironic effects of the naturalist writer's subversion of narrative structure, Manet produces an ironic situation by way of an ironic inversion of the pictorial structure as an illusionistic extension of our space. Here, as in the novel, the viewer is engaged in a visual "snare".[23] By painting a painting of a mirrored reflection Manet initiates and then disrupts a conventional way of "entering" the painting. The painted mirror frustrates the viewer by refusing to be an illusionistic extension of our space or of the painted objects' space. Likewise, the male figure is central to the viewer's ironic aesthetic experience. Although we see the male patron's frontal reflection in the right side of the (background) mirror, the direction of his gaze and the absent view of his back in the frontal plane deny our conventional expectations for entering an illusionary space by way of a mediating figure.

As we know from the social historians of art, such as T. J. Clark and Theodore Reff,[24] the mirrored cafe-concert scene depicted here, as it is in naturalist novels,[25] is a synecdoche of the modern city; the barmaid likewise stands in a reciprocal relation to the urban whole. As such, she recalls one of the most prevalent themes of the naturalist novel — the theme of the "fallen" women. For one thing, her lowly labor marks her as a displaced member of urban society; her inevitable degeneration is likewise marked by the very urban conditions in which she hoped to better herself. More often than not the anti-heroine succumbs to prostitution for material and social gain, as witnessed in Zola's novel, *Nana*. Such a course of events, what Baguley calls the "entropic" metatheme of the naturalist novel, narrates the moral, social, and ethical decay brought on by modernization. The narrative structure of entropy thus deploys the banal ending as a parodic strategy of inversion and subversion.[26]

Notwithstanding these verbal and visual analogies I've just reviewed, I must confess that I do not think that Manet completely endorsed the naturalist writer's entropic view of modern conditions. I do believe, however, that a discursive account can accommodate similarity as well as difference between verbal and visual texts. Because of the techniques and thematics Manet's painting shares with the naturalist novel, entropic associations are inevitably encoded in the network of visual forms — whether abstract or figurative. For example, the dematerialized ambience of the cafe-concert scene evokes an atmosphere of incessant decay and decadence. But this same ambience also evokes Baudelaire's celebration of the incessant flux and contradictions that modernity engendered. In short, I think Manet as image-maker shared Baudelaire's aesthetic affirmation of such modern phenomena as a source of cultural self-renewal. And so, as sign-user, Manet chose the technical means already inscribed in his medium.

In closing with this verbal-visual conflict, I would like to comment upon W. J. T. Mitchell's recent essay, "Against Comparison: Teaching Literature and the Visual Arts", in which he exposes "the emptiness of the comparative method".[27] Here he argues that literature often appropriates the visual arts to define its own "literal presence" (or Ekphrasis /"ekphrastic" presence; that is, "the verbal representation of visual representation"). To correct this imbalance of power, he argues that "we don't have to look for [literary texts] that betray formal analogies with the paintings that interest us: the paintings themselves, and what we can learn about their production and reception will tell us what texts are relevant to them". But in viewing verbal and visual texts as "significant others", Mitchell also recognizes that this relationship may not always be a symmetrical one; we may see "similarity" and "collaboration" as well as "domination" and "difference".

I would agree with Mitchell insofar as we accept interartistic co-existence, which includes complementarity as well as conflict. But to do so, we must release word and image studies from the "ut pictura poesis" model, or in the case of Panofskyan iconography the "ut poesis pictura" model. For indeed, when literature and the visual arts do converge in a discursive field, we can identify planes of convergence, be they of theory and/or technique. Word and image studies might then formulate models for what Mitchell calls "ut pictura theoria" and for what I call "ut theoria technica". With just such models we can better compare the *functions* of visual and verbal representation in relation to a discursive space they share. What I am arguing, then, is that the methodology of word and image studies is "always already" a discursive project. As such, it needs to move through and beyond iconography so as to contribute to and benefit from a discursive art historiography.

Notes

1 Here my methods issue form Foucault's early works, particularly *The Archaeology of Knowledge* (A. M. Sheridan Smith, trans. [New York, 1971]) where he treats discourse formation and discourse practice with a more descriptive, "positivist" method than his later critical interpretations of the "apparatuses" of power/knowledge that shape discourse. See note 9 below.

2 See Panofsky's explication of his method in "Iconography and Iconology: An Introduction to the Study of Renaissance Art", originally published in *Studies in Iconology* (1939); rpt. in *Meaning in the Visual Arts* (1955). Although Panofsky primarily attended to narrative representations in Renaissance art, as well as their classical sources and classicism's medieval transformations, his iconographic method has served as the paradigm for art historians of every period.

3 Foucault defines épistéme as "the total set of relations that unite, at a given period, the discursive practices that give rise to epistemological figures, sciences, and possibly formalized systems" of knowledge. *Archaeology of Knowledge,* 191.

4 As a Baudelairean "painter of modern life", Manet can be compared with other Naturalist writers "of modern life" in addition to Zola. However, I have limited my comparative study to Zola and his novels, dating from the late 1860s to 1880 when *Nana* appeared in book form. During the second half of the 1860s Zola became

Manet's primary critical spokesman. During this time the writer was developing his naturalist theory and practice and the painter composed his most radical parodies of academic masterpieces and their Renaissance legacy. Although Zola's support of Manet waned after this time, the two remained friends until the painter's death, at which point Zola wrote a biographical essay tracing Manet's (heroic) career. I would also argue that Zola's alliance with Manet during the 1860s helped to shape his naturalist imagery of Parisian sites and character types; indeed, his highly pictorial descriptions represent Manet's Baudelarian perception of modern urban people and places (see for example, note 20 below.) Literary David Baguley acknowledges the "pictorial aspects of Zola's novels" and links their "*subjects and techniques* with contemporary painting", namely with Manet's work, in *Naturalist Fiction: The Entropic Vision* (Cambridge and New York, 1990), 88. See also: T. J. Clark and Theodore Reff, note 6 below.

5 For a summary of the formalist approaches to Manet's work, see: Françoise Cachin, "Introduction", *Manet: 1832-1883* (New York, N.Y., 1983).

6 See for example: T. J. Clark, "'A Bar the Folies Bergère'", in *The Painting of Modern Life: Paris in the Art of Manet and his Followers* (Princeton, N.J., 1984); and Theodore Reff, "The Cafe and the Cafe-Concert", in *Manet and Modern Paris,* (Washington, D.C., 1982), 73-77.

7 See, for example: Robert Hodge and Gunther Kress, *Social Semiotics* (Ithaca, 1988), especially Chapters 1-4; and for language philosophies, Steven Davis, ed., *Pragmatics: A Reader* (New York, 1991).

8 Art history already has in place a methodology for adapting pragmatics. Ernst Gombrich has shown how formal or technical devices of representation function as conventional means of communication. Gombrich studies stylistic modes of representation as historico-cultural systems for depicting how we cognitively experience the phenomenal world. See: E. H. Gombrich, *Art and Illusion: A Study in the Psychology of Pictorial Representation* (1960). My own conversion (or de-psychologization) of Gombrich's method into a social semiotics of visual communication is based on Umberto Eco's cultural or "pragmatic" semiotics, as well as Roman Jakobson's structuralist analysis of linguistic communication. See: Eco, *A Theory of Semiotics* (1977) and *Semiotics and the Philosophy of Language* (1984); and Jakobson, "Linguistics and Poetics" (1958) in *Style and Language* (1960), ed. T. Sebeok, 350-77. David Summers has also adapted a structuralist approach to stylistic interpretations derived from Gombrich. See: Summers, "Conventions in the History of Art", *New Literary History* (1981): 103-125; and "Intentions in the History of Art", *New Literary History* 18(1986): 305-321.

9 Foucault refers to the materiality of his method as "a pure description of discursive events". See Foucault, *Archaeology of Knowledge,* 9, 22, 26-29, 122, 125. Paul J. Thibauld, who has adapted Foucault's discourse analysis to social semiotics, describes the phenomenological grounds of discourse "neomaterialist". As he puts it, "The social semiotic conceptual framework is a *neomaterialist* one that is concerned with the multilevel hierarchically and dialectically related social semiotic processes and relations and their embodiment in the prediscurisve material matter-energy exchanges through which the former are realized. Thus, textual productions, their contextualizations, and the social agent/discursive subject relations these produce

are always immanent in some patterned transactions of matter, energy, and information. The neomaterialist perspective therefore has no need of the material/ideal distinction" (*Social Semiotics as Praxis: Text, Social Meaning Making, and Nabokov's* Ada [Minneapolis, 1991], 7). Thibauld's concept of neomaterialism also provides a model for establishing a pre-discursive field, free of iconography's verbal textual bias, from which verbal and visual modes of representation coincidentally take shape.

10 While more recent art historians have rectified this exclusion, most notably in the cases of Mondrian and Kandinsky, they still interpret pictorial content as illustrations of specific texts (rather than reciprocal articulations).

11 Panofsky's primary concern was the rebirth of humanism during the Renaissance. Following the nineteenth-century academic tradition, which the Renaissance initiated, Panofsky upheld the hierarchy of worthy (albeit instructive) subjects for artistic representation. That is, mythology, religious and history painting received the highest status, while genre painting was assigned to the bottom rung of the ladder.

12 Of course, many of Zola's devices and techniques were shared by his older and younger contemporaries, from Flaubert to Maupassant. My historical approach to naturalist fiction and Zola's "codification" of naturalism generally follows David Baguley's account in *Naturalist Fiction: The Entropic Vision* (see especially pp. pp. 1, 5, 22, 24, 70, 74). While a reluctant Flaubert was "the major inspiration" of the naturalist writers during the early years (1864-69), Zola's theoretical tracts on and his overt practice of naturalism placed him at the center of the history of naturalism. Baguley thus includes Zola's *Térese Raquin* (1867), coincident with his earliest theoretical texts, as one of the three "founding texts" of naturalism, together with the Goncourt brothers' *Germinie Lacerteux* (1864) and Flaubert's *L'Éducation sentimentale* (1869). (While Zola's *Térese Raquin* acknowledges its debt to Flaubert's *Madame Bovary* [published in instalments in 1856 and in book form in 1857], it also critically distances itself from the earlier text. See Baguley, pp. 90, 96.) Following a hiatus of naturalist writing during the 1870s, Zola became identified as the leader of the naturalist movement, both internationally and among the younger French writers of the 1880s.

13 Linda Hutcheon, *A Theory of Parody: The Teachings of Twentieth Century Art Forms* (New York, 1985), 24, 34, 52-68. Hutcheon distinguishes between the verbal or semantic function of irony (antiphrasis) and irony as "an evaluative strategy that implies an attitude of the encoding agent towards the text itself, an attitude which in turn allows and demands the decoder's interpetation and evaluation" (53). Hutcheon's differentiation derives from D.C. Muecke's distinction (in *Irony and the Ironic* [London and New York, 1970/1982]) between "Verbal Irony as a semantic inversion" and "Observable Irony (things seen or presented as ironic)". Observable Irony, which includes ironies of events, of character (self-ignorance, self-betrayal), of situation, or of ideas", is a German Romantic development from ancient/classical "Cosmic Irony or General Irony." See Muecke, pp. 22-23.

14 As a general source of German Romantic Ironists, see: Kathleen M. Wheeler, *German Aesthetic and Literary Criticism: The Romantic Ironists and Goethe* (London and New York, 1984). Included in this anthology of primary sources are: Jean Paul; Ludwig Tieck, Karl Solger, and Friedrich Schlegel. See also Peter Szondi's study, "Friedrich Schlegel and Romantic Irony" (1954), in *On Textual Understanding and Other Essays,* Harvey Mendelsohn, trans. (Minneapolis, 1986), 57-74.

15 Charles Baudelaire, "On the Essence of Laughter", in *The Painter of Modern Life and Other Essays,* Jonathan Mayne, trans. and ed. (London, 1964), 154, 164. The dictionary translation of "*se dédoubler*" is "to be divided into two", and of *"dédoublement"* is "dividing [or splitting] into two" (*Cassell's French-English/English-French Dictionary,* ed. Denis Girard [New York, 1962].) In translating Baudelaire's term "se dédoubler" as "rapid self-doubling" (*"la force de se dédoubler rapidement"*), I am following Paul de Man's interpretation of Baudelaire's concept of irony. Furthermore, I borrow the term *dédoublement* from de Man, who uses it to explain the "reflective *activity*" connoted by Baudelaire's use of the infinitive verb form *se dédoubler;* that is as an activity of "self-duplication or self-multiplication". See Paul de Man, "The Rhetoric of Temporality", in *Blindness and Insight: Essays in the Rhetoric of Contemporary Criticism,* 2nd ed. (Minneapolis, 1983), 212-13. Jonathan Mayne, however, translates it as "self-dividing".

16 Shiff has examined this problem from a variety of theoretical positions. See for example: "Remembering Impressions", *Critical Inquiry* 12 (Winter 1986), 439-448; "The Technique of Originality 'Innocence and Artifice in the Painting of Corot, Monet, and Cézanne", *Studies in Visual Communication* 8 (Autumn 1982), 2-32; and "Representation, Copying, and the Technique of Originality", *New Literary History* 15 (Winter 1984), 335-363.

17 Baudelaire, "The Painter of Modern Life", in *The Painter of Modern Life and Other Essays,* 11; and "The Exposition Universelle" (1855), in *Art in Paris 1845-1862: Salons and Other Exhibitions,* Jonathan Mayne, trans. and ed., (London, 1965), 124-25.

18 See: Baudelaire, "The Painter of Modern Life", 9-10, 27-28; and "Salon of 1845", in *Art in Paris,* 25.

19 This scene, in turn, resembles a similar cafe-concert scene of figures blurred and fragmented by their rapid movement and interior gas lights in Zola's *L'Assommoir* (Chapter 11). See note 25 below.

20 Hutcheon, *A Theory of Modern Parody,* 6-7.

21 In the naturalist novel mimetic representation functions as a mirror-topos to effect a "generic foil"— that is, mimetic representation unveils idealist illusions and the veils of (bourgeois) respectability, fostered by the earlier romantic novel forms, in order to reveal life's sordid secrets. The mirror-topos also functions to reflect the truth of lived "reality" as opposed to the fiction of art. While seeking to hide (or unaware of) his own conventions, the naturalist writer exposes the artifice of the Romantic novel's conventions. The actual presence of mirrors in the naturalist text functions to reflect the decrepit reality of a character's appearance as opposed to the fictionalized life that the character has shaped for him/herself. Here the mirror inverts conventional social, cultural, and aesthetic values, producing an ironic effect. See: Baguley, *Naturalist Fiction,* 51, 75; and Baguley, "Parody and the Realist Novel", *University of Toronto Quarterly* 55 (Fall 1985): 99, 103, 104, 105.

22 On "parody" as a naturalist literary device and its ironic effects, see: Baguley, *Naturalist Fiction,* 142-163; 179-180 (here Baguley adapts Hutcheon's definition of modernist parody and its correlation with situational, as opposed to verbal, irony). See also Baguley, "An Essay on Naturalist Poetics", *The Journal of the British Neo-Formalist Circle* 12 (April 1987), 50.

23 See Baguley, "An Essay on Naturalist Poetics", 50.

24 See note 6 above.

25 For example, In *L'Assommoir* (1877): In Père Colombels bar called l'Assommoir (Chapter 2) the mirror behind the bar-counter reflects and refracts bottles and glasses as well as "the casks painted a gay yellow, bright with varnish, and gleaming with copper taps and hoops" which decorated the interior of the large bar-room. Manet's painting titled *Nana* depicts Nana before a full-length mirror, dressed in her underclothes, "painting" her face apropos the Baudelairean courtesan, under the gaze of her aristocratic patron. Baudelaire celebrates the Parisian courtesan as a character type who exemplifies the rapid transformations of modern urban existence. Manet's painting of *Nana* (1877) is a portrait of a prostitute Henriette Hauser. Manet titled the portrait "Nana" after the daughter of Gervaise Macquart of *L'Assommoir* (see Chapter 11), the novel which Manet highly esteemed. Subsequently, the painted scene of *Nana* was appropriated by Zola in Chapter 5 of the novel, *Nana* (1880) in which Nana is observed in her theater dressing-room by the Prince, her royal patron, and his friends, the Comte Moffat and the Marquis de Chouard. For the chronology of Zola's novel and Manet's painting see: George Holden, "Introduction" to Nana, trans. George Holden (London and New York, 1972), 8-9.

26 See Baguley, *Naturalist Fiction,* 209-210.

27 W. J. T. Mitchell, "Against Comparison; Teaching Literature and the Visual Arts", from *Teaching Literature and the Other Arts,* eds. J. P. Barricelli, Joseph Gibaldi, and Estelle Lanter (New York, 1990), 30-37.

On Intertextual Relations

Seeing and Believing in the Early Middle Ages: A Preliminary Investigation[1]

Giselle de Nie

Fourteen hundred years ago, in 594 C.E., France's first historian Gregory of Tours departed from this life. He had been bishop in a sixth-century Frankish kingdom that had arisen out of the desintegrated Roman Empire, and which combined Germanic with what was left of Gallo-Roman political and social forms. His *Histories* are the only full-fledged historiographical work that has come down to us from the troubled period in the west between the fifth and the late seventh century.[2] Almost the only other literature produced seems to have been saints' lives and collections of miracles, including those which Gregory wrote. His epithet for one of his saintly subjects – *sacer heros* (*Vit. patr.* 20.4) – may indicate that the stories about saints, in general, may have functioned in some ways as the equivalent of Germanic epics about mythical heroes.[3] They also show that the saint was needed as a supernatural protector and healer who was independent of the instable and arbitrary worldly authorities. But miracles, as we see them happening in Gregory's stories, were sought not only for practical reasons such as protection or healing. As manifestations of the presence of the just and powerful invisible reality taught by the Church, they were evidently also a much-needed legitimation for hope in what seemed to be a cruel and chaotic world.

This beneficent and powerful heavenly order, however, was admitted by all to be invisible. How was it possible, nevertheless, as Gregory says, to "look towards the things that are not seen (*respic[ere] ad ea quae non videntur*)" (cf. Hebr. 11:1; *Vit. patr.* 6.*prol.*)? Is he saying that one could, in some way, "see" the invisible?

The philosopher Paul Ricoeur has designated as one of the uses of imagination the envisioning of another possible reality to contrast with the existing one in order to evaluate and work on it.[4] From the anthropological angle, Clifford Geertz has analyzed the functions of "religion as a cultural system" in a seminal article with that title. He describes the seeing of "belief reality" of religion and the acting out of its rituals as a way of constructing a coherent view of the world that, among other things, makes evil and suffering endurable. About this way of seeing the world, he says:

> The religious perspective differs from the commonsensical in that ... it *moves beyond the realities of everyday life* to wider ones which correct and complete them .... And it *differs from art* in that instead of effecting a disengagement from the whole question of factuality, deliberately manufacturing an air of semblance and illusion, it deepens the concern with fact and *seeks to create an aura of utter actuality*. It is this sense of the "really real" upon which the religious perspective rests and which *the symbolic activities* of religion as a cultural system are devoted to *producing, intensifying* and, so far as possible, *rendering inviolable* by the discordant revelations of secular experience.[5] [emphasis added]

Inspired by Eugen Drewermann's work on the interpenetration of theology and depth-psychology, I should like to reformulate this as: religion uses the symbolic activities in which imagination is implicated as a means of what I shall call "divining" what is regarded as the hidden spiritual reality – that is, perceiving the "really real" in or under the phenomena of common sense experience.[6] The prime example of this is, of course, the liturgical transformation of bread and wine in the Eucharist. And, differing with what appears to be Geertz's view of art as purposely and *only* illusionistic without any claim to truth, I hope to show that there are indications that Gregory treated religious imagination as what we would call art: the creation of something like an illusion that nevertheless stands for – and thereby participates in – the real.

An analysis of a selected few of Gregory's stories, will show something of how this early medieval bishop presented what he regarded as the connections between believing the word taught by the Church and "seeing" the reality to which it referred.

"Eyes of the heart": "eyes of faith"

In a well-known story that will serve to reveal his premises, Gregory tells us how a holy Catholic bishop cured the spiritual – and suddenly also physical – blindness of a man who had pretended, for payment, to be blind, so as to be "healed" in public by a heretic bishop who was envious of his Catholic rivals' miracles. After the unfortunate man had been told that "If you believe, all things are possible to the believer" (Mk 9:23), and had thereupon proclaimed his adherence to the Catholic view of the Trinity beginning with the phrase "I believe ...", he was cured through the laying upon of hands, the sign of the Cross and the pronouncement of the name of the Trinity. To drive his point home, our sixth-century author makes the message of this miracle-story explicit:

> Through the blindness of this man, however, it was made most clear how the bishop of the heretics was covering the eyes of [men's] hearts (*oculos cordium*)

> with the miserable veil of his doctrine, so that no one would be able to contemplate the true Light with the eyes of faith (*ne veram lucem ulli liceret fidei oculis contemplare*). O wretch, who, ... in the depravity of his own heart, tried to extinguish the torchof faith (*facem fidei*) in the hearts of the believers! (*Hist.* 2.3)

Mental and physical states are here presented as two aspects of the same phenomenon: spiritual blindness becomes physical blindness because the light of understanding is the same as that through which the bodily eyes see. Understanding, then, is thought of as, and conflated with, physical seeing, and seeing as understanding. What, however, is seen?

The "eyes of the heart" become "the eyes of faith" when they are filled with "the light of faith". This "light" consists of the decision to accept the Triune God as He is preached by the Catholic Church and – in this case, in the hope of a cure – the trust that "all things are possible" to Him. What "all things", more specifically, are, is the whole of God's dealings with men as they are recorded in the Bible. The Christian tradition of allegorical interpretation discerned, in these biblical sayings and visible events, certain underlying dynamic spiritual patterns or "figures" that represented the real – spiritual – truth. Gregory speaks of this process of discernment as "spiritual understanding" (*In psal. prol.*).[7] I suggest that in his miracle stories this same strategy of spiritual understanding is transposed from texts to sensory phenomena – here, however, the underlying truth is not only imaginatively visualized, but often reported as actually "seen".

In late antique and early medieval religious texts, however, not only extraordinary events such as miracles, but all of sensory reality tend to be regarded as symbols of invisible truth. This is evident in a compendium such as that of the fifth-century Bishop Eucherius of Lyon, with which Gregory was almost certainly acquainted.[8] According to an authority on religious symbolism in this period, Gerhart Ladner, the phenomena of the sensory world itself, as symbols, and the invisible reality to which they pointed, constituted an analogical, gradualistic, participatory – even sacramental – whole.[9] Every visible phenomenon and event could thus become an image or a "figure" of some transcendent divine truth, adumbrating religious mysteries that could not be adequately represented by (philosophical) concepts.[10] Essential in this hierarchical world view is that the spiritual form or image was the higher, "real" truth, and the sensory likeness, in which it would be recognized, a weak derivative.[11] The real truth, then, was one that was *imagined*, and never more than partly perceived by the senses.

Thus the "eyes of faith" – and this is the crux of the matter – decide to see present visible events and phenomena through the biblical patterns as dynamic models of all-time truth. This is what Geertz called the "really real" beyond common sense reality. And this is what Gregory meant by the phrase tion in the act of "believing". As I hope to show in what follows, it is not too much to say that he is aware of this strategy of imagination as *an art of the real:* that of bringing out, for oneself and for others, the hidden but very much present and powerful dynamic dimensions of sensory phenomena and events.[20]

"Appear[ing] as though green": The Transformation of Perception Through Imaging an Empowering Symbol Upon Sensory Data

In the following brief story, we shall see that "believing" could bring out the patterns of invisible spiritual reality in visible phenomena:

> They even say that the thorns themselves of the Crown [of Thorns] appear as though green: if, however, their leaves would seem to have withered, they are nevertheless revived every day through divine power.
> *Ferunt etiam ipsas coronae sentes quasi virides apparere: quae tamen si videantur aruisse foliis, quotidie tamen revirescere virtute divina.* (*Glor. mart.* 6)[21]

Writing about what might be called the contact-relics of Christ in the East, Gregory is reporting hearsay. Although he has never seen the object in question, he is evidently prepared to believe the story (or he would not report it), and expects his readers to do the same. Yet the wording seems to suggest a hedge: the thorns are not said to "be" but to "appear as though" green. Surprisingly, however, the same holds for the opposite state: the possibility that the leaves "would seem to have withered" – suggesting that this appearance too is not in accordance with "reality". What, then, is this reality? Is it: that to some, the thorns "appear" fresh, and to others, "withered"? Or, more specifically: that though they have appeared as withered to unbelieving eyes, the "eyes of faith" have seen them to be fresh-and-green?

The next question goes to the heart of the matter: how can anyone see what is presumed by all to be a more than 500 years old crown of thorns as alive-and-green? and how can anyone believe that this antique object has been seen as such?

Gregory's wording suggests that the greenness is seen alongside the witheredness, or perhaps, as a transparent hue (as the images of imagination tend to be) over it, so that one could see the witheredness through it. In short, he may be saying that it was seen in another mode: that of the imagination – and that this imaginative vision of the believer represents the spiritual "really real" over against the dull opaqueness of mere sensory appearances.[22] Here again, he seems to be aware that "believing" needs a strategy of imagination – just as the strategy of "spiritual understanding": in other words, that it is an art of bringing out what is hidden in sensory appearances. But for him, and this is the crucial point, this imaginative strategy does not invalidate its truth. Quite the contrary: it is the only way to the truth.[23]

There is, however, again another way to look at this question. It has been shown that meditative vision – that is, perception uninhibited by practical concerns – can apperceive its objects and the space around them as vibrantly luminous.[24] I suggest that this sacred object, which had rested on Christ's head at the supreme moment of the Passion, is likely to be approached and perceived in such a manner: with deep, speechless awe. Elsewhere, Gregory himself insists upon reverence in everyone's dealings with objects in the religious sphere.[25] This reverence or awe, I suggest, would be for Gregory an essential element in what I have designated, less reverentially, as "a strategy of imagination".

But why should it, luminous or not, be perceived to appear as though green? What "reality" is pointed to in the "greenness" of five hundred year old thorns? As a contact-relic, the crown must have been thought of as participating in the life and power of the resurrected Saviour in heaven. And heaven was Paradise, always imaged as eternal youth in eternal spring. The latter is almost certainly the quality of life pointed to and transmitted by the sight of the greenness: what one perceived in this greenness was in effect, as Gregory says, divine renewal every day.

And this leads to the heart of the matter. Meditative seeing has been shown to decrease the self-object distinction:[26] one could thus experience the divine renewal through to some degree identifying with the holy object. This is another way of saying that, as we saw, associating such a symbol with an appropriate object and thus meditatively "seeing" it superimposed upon this object, can induce an analogous affective experience of this renewal in the perceiver. Seeing the symbol with "the eyes of the heart", then, is experiencing the empowerment it makes visible. The wish and the need for this must have been a strong influence upon perception. Gregory's wording, I suggest, seems to indicate that he sensed this, and regarded the conscious and controlled kind of imagination we have seen in this story as something like a legitimate kind of divinatory art – without, however, designating it as such.

Conclusion

What we have seen happening in Gregory's stories seems to be summed up by the words of a psychologist who has said: "The world we perceive is a dream we learn to have from a script we have not written".[27] The script of the dream is the Bible and its subsequent interpretations. The learning process is that of its visualization through mental images evoked by words. Once learned, the dream is imaged upon or recognized in sensory phenomena.

To be able to survive in early medieval society, the church had learned to play power politics along with everyone else. Certainly, miracles could be, and were, used to achieve and confirm socio-political status as well as to intimidate would-be predators with the power of the saintly patron in heaven.[28] It was clearly in the church's interest to convince all men of the dream's present and future reality. However, since it was able to tap immeasurable energies that directed lives, created institutions, alleviated misery and achieved innumerable cures, it is difficult to deny the dream's own extremely powerful reality.

Invisible and intangible, this reality seems to have been experienced as dynamic patterns of a generous cosmic energy which were representable to oneself and others only through the culturally determined imagination of the heart. One way of participating in these beneficent dynamic patterns was to let images of it, symbolized by and thereby "seen" as present in some phenomenon or event, cross the threshold of consciousness and initiate an analogous pattern of emotional energy within oneself.

The latter experience belongs to the essence of "believing" as we find it described everywhere in Gregory's writings about miracles. It was a *decision to see* intimations of a creative divine energy in all phenomena and events through the translation of spontaneous, or desired, affective experience into variations of the image-symbols taught by the church from its Scriptural tradition. In this way, religion or believing functioned, as Geertz has said, as a cultural system. But, over against Geertz, I hope to have shown that for Gregory it also functioned as a more or less conscious art of the real: a kind of "divination" that "saw" the empowering contours of spiritual reality through imaging them alongside or recognizing them in sensory phenomena.

Notes

1 This article was developed from a session of the international ERASMUS seminar "Word, image and reality in medieval texts", sponsored by the ERASMUS network "Nederlands in Europa", and held at the University of Utrecht on 27 January 1993.

2 The most comprehensive treatment of Gregory's life and works is found in Luce Pietri, *La ville de Tours du IVe au VIe siècle: naissance d'une cité chrétienne* (Roma: École francaise de Rome, 1983), 246-334. Gregorius Turonensis, *Historiarum Libri X* (*Hist.*), ed. and trans. Rudolf Buchner (Ausgewählte Quellen zur deutschen Geschichte des Mittelalters, Freiherr vom Stein-Gedächtnisausgabe 2 and 3) (Darmstadt: Wissenschaftliche Buchgesellschaft, 1967).

3 Gregorius Turonensis, *Vita Patrum* (*Vit. patr.*), ed. Bruno Krusch (Monumenta

Germaniae Historica, Scriptores Rerum Merovingicarum 1.2) (Hannover: Hahn, 1885), 661-744. See on this theme: Alison G. Elliott, *Roads to Paradise. Reading the Lives of the Early Saints* (Hanover-London: University Press of New England, 1987), 16-41 and 168-192.

4 Paul Ricoeur, "Imagination in discourse and in action", *Analecta Husserliana* 7 (1978): 3-22, here 15-22.

5 Clifford Geertz, "Religion as a cultural system", in: idem, *The Interpretation of Cultures* (New York: Basic Books, 1973), 87-125, here 103-118, 112.

6 Eugen Drewermann, *Tiefenpsychologie und Exegese* 2 (Olten-Freiburg im Breisgau: Walter-Verlag, 1985), 239, 330 and passim.

7 *In psalterii tractatum commentarius* (*In psal.*), ed. Bruno Krusch (Mon. Germ. Hist., Script. Rer. Merov. 1.2) (Hannover: Hahn, 1885) 873-877. On "figures" in this period, see: Erich Auerbach, "Figura", *Archivum Romanicum* 22 (1938), 436-489, here 450-474.

8 *Formulae spiritalis intelligentiae*, CSEL 16.1.

9 Gerhart B. Ladner, "Medieval and Modern Understanding of Symbolism: a Comparison", *Speculum* 54 (1979), 223-256, here 230, 252.

10 As Averil Cameron, *Christianity and the Rhetoric of Empire. The Development of Christian Discourse* (Berkeley etc.: University of California Press, 1992), 59: "For Christian language, like Christian art, was trying to express mysteries that were essentially inexpressible except through symbol".

11 W. J. T. Mitchell, *Iconology. Image, Text, Ideology* (Chicago: University of Chicago Press, 1986), 21.

12 Cf. Howard C. Kee, *Miracle in the Early Christian World. A Study in Sociohistorical Method* (New Haven-London: Yale University Press, 1983), 225-236.

13 Cf. Geertz, "Religion", 124, 112-113, 118.

14 See also Elliott, *Roads*, 73 and passim.

15 Silvan S. Tomkins, *Affect, Imagery and Consciousness* 1 (New York: Springer, 1962), 13. On the subject of mental imagery see now: Stephen M. Kosslyn, *Image and Brain. The Resolution of the Imagery Debate* (Cambridge, MA - London: MIT Press, 1994).

16 As Paul Ricoeur, *Time and Narrative*, vol. 3, Trans. Kathleen Blamey and David Pellauer (Chicago-London: University of Chicago Press, 1988),185.

17 Jan van Biezen and J.W. Schulte Nordholt ed., *Hymnen* (Tournai 1967), 9.

18 Compare Gerald Epstein, *Waking Dream Therapy: Dream Process as Imagination* (New York-London: Human Sciences Press, 1981), 18: "... images are the concretizations of emotions"; 149: "Imagination and will act interdependently".

19 As, for instance, Epstein, *Waking*, 18, and Roberto Assagioli, *Psychosynthesis. A Manual of Principles and Techniques* (New York: Viking Press, 1965) 177-189.

20 Compare on this view of art, Mitchell, *Iconology*, 39.

21 Gregorius Turonensis, *In gloria martyrum* (*Glor. mart.*), ed. Bruno Krusch (Mon. Germ. Hist., Script. Rer. Mer. 1.2) (Hannover: Hahn, 1885), 484-561.

22 Mitchell, *Iconology*, 17.

23 This understanding of Gregory's thinking about imagination as divination agrees with the way he very audaciously uses one of his own dreams as a diplomatic tool in *Hist.* 8.5. Cf. my *Views from a many-windowed tower. Studies of imagination in the works of Gregory of Tours* (Studies in classical antiquity 7) (Amsterdam: Rodopi, 1987) 285-287. See now also my "Gregory of Tours' smile: spiritual reality, imagination and earthly events in the 'Histories'", in: Anton Scharer and Georg Scheibelreiter eds., *Historiographie im frühen Mittelalter* (Wien-München 1994) (Veröffentlichungen des Instituts für Österreichische Geschichtsforschung 32) 68-95.

24 Arthur Deikman, "Deautomatization and the mystic experience", in: Charles T. Tart ed., *Altered States of Consciousness* (New York etc.: John Wiley and Sons, 1969), 23-44, here 32-33.

25 Compare *Glor. mart.* 5.: *admiratusque silui.* On proper reverence, for instance: *Glor. mart.* 47 and *Virt. Mart.* 1.35 (*De virtutibus Sancti Martini*, ed. B. Krusch (Mon. Germ. Hist., Script. Rer. Mer. 1.2) (Hannover: Hahn, 1885), 584-661. For a more sociological approach to *reverentia*, see P. Brown, "Relics and social status in the age of Gregory of Tours" (The Stenton Lecture) (Reading 1976). Reprinted in: Peter Brown, *Society and the Holy in Late Antiquity* (London: Faber and Faber, 1982), 222-250, especially 230-236.

26 Deikman, "Deautomatization", 33.

27 Tomkins, *Imagery*, 13.

28 As Peter Brown, *The Cult of the Saints. Its Rise and Function in Latin Christianity* (The Haskell Lectures on History of Religions, New Series 2) (Chicago-London: University of Chicago Press, 1981), 86-105.

La bible d'images de Saint-Marc à Venise

Else Jongeneel

C'est en inversant la célèbre métaphore proustienne du texte-édifice que Michel Butor, dans l'ouverture de *Description de San Marco* (1963), tente de présenter d'emblée la basilique vénitienne. A la suite de *Mobile. Etude pour une représentation des Etats-Unis* (1962), où Butor essaie de dresser la carte textuelle du continent américain, l'auteur s'ingénie ici à textualiser un des monuments les plus célèbres du bassin méditerranéen. Ainsi *Description de San Marco*, un hommage au lecteur "qui cherche à entendre et à voir",[1] offre un itinéraire de lecture commentée de la basilique, pendant lequel l'auteur prend le lecteur par la main pour lui montrer quelques "pages" resplendissantes du sanctuaire. *Description de San Marco* se présente à la fois comme une illustration et comme une description de la basilique, comme un itinéraire d'écriture et de lecture: l'auteur a abandonné l'écriture linéaire au profit d'une mise en texte figurative assez simple d'ailleurs, comprenant trois caractères typographiques et trois blocs textuels à marges divergentes. Par là, Butor joue sur l'échange curieux qui se fait entre les inscriptions et les images des mosaïques de Saint-Marc: tantôt, nous le verrons, l'inscription fournit un commentaire de l'image en question, tantôt le rapport traditionnel entre l'image-illustration et le texte-commentaire est inversé, de sorte que l'inscription remplit une fonction illustrative, alors que l'image se voit conférer le rôle de commentaire descriptif.

A l'encontre d'autres églises byzantines, où les mosaïques constituent des îlots isolés couvrant principalement les coupoles et les niches, Saint-Marc possède une ornementation extrêmement riche. Ses mosaïques qui couvrent plus de 4000 mètres carrés de parois, s'étendent sur toute la superficie du bâtiment. Elles s'alignent en une "bible d'images" (Butor/ Proust/Ruskin) qui défilent devant les yeux du visiteur. Quand il laisse glisser son regard sur les parois, les niches, les coupoles, les portes, c'est comme s'il tournait lentement les pages d'un livre. Chaque partie de la basilique ouvre un nouveau chapitre, invite le lecteur à poursuivre la lecture, ou, bien souvent, à revenir sur ses pas, à relire. Or, c'est en m'appuyant sur l'idée de l'édifice-livre telle que Butor la développe dans *Description de San Marco*, que j'aimerais proposer ici ma propre lecture – combien modeste et partielle pourtant! – de quelques cycles de mosaïques de Saint-Marc. Dans ce but je me propose d'esquisser à grands traits le dialogue entre textes et images dans trois cycles de mosaïques qui décorent le vestibule de la basilique, en faisant de temps en temps de brèves excursions à quelques séries disposées à l'intérieur. J'ai choisi le vestibule parce que, à part le baptistère, c'est l'unique partie de l'édifice qui mette en scène des histoires échelonnées sur un grand nombre d'épisodes. Ces cycles de mosaïques exhibent clairement la problématique de la transposition du texte (biblique) en image: la temporalité des histoires sérielles est comprimée en configurations spatiales assez restreintes de signes figuratifs juxtaposés.

Le plan de la basilique Saint-Marc est en forme de croix grecque. La basilique comporte cinq coupoles hémisphériques dont quatre s'élèvent aux extrémités de la croix, et la cinquième au milieu, à la croisée du transept. Elle possède une abside et une nef centrale avec un choeur surélevé qui surmonte la crypte où se trouve le cercueil de l'évangéliste saint Marc. Le long des bras de la croix s'étendent les bas-côtés surmontés de galeries. Un *atrium* ou *exonarthex* qui remplace le portique des deux basiliques antérieures entoure la base de la croix suivant une ancienne tradition liturgique (fig. 1). L'église actuelle date de la seconde moitié du XIe siècle. Il y a eu deux constructions précédentes, à partir du début du IXe siècle, à moitié détruites par des incendies. Probablement le plan de la basilique a été conçu sur le modèle de l'Eglise des Douze Apôtres de Constantinople, à moitié démantelée et pillée par les Vénitiens lors de la IVe croisade au début du XIIIe siècle.

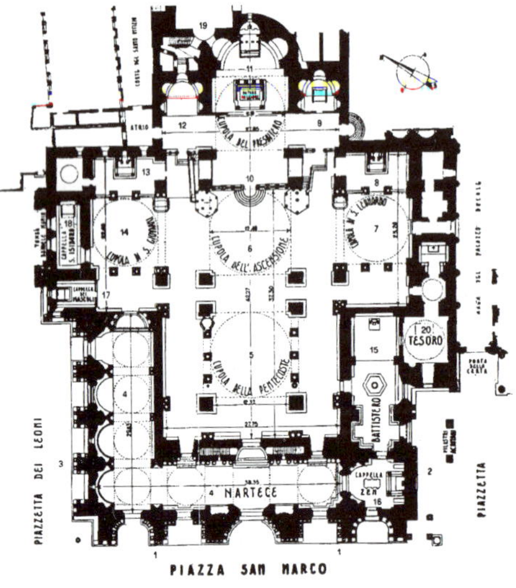

Figure 1. Plan de la basilique Saint-Marc.

L'iconographie des mosaïques présente un plan bien déterminé qui respecte en grandes lignes la tradition byzantine, entremêlée d'influences locales. Le vestibule représente des scènes de l'Ancien Testament (la Création du monde, l'histoire de Noé, la construction et la démolition de la Tour de Babel, l'histoire d'Abraham, de Joseph et de Moïse). Par contre l'intérieur est consacré entièrement à "la Parole faite chair", au Nouveau Testament: ses mosaïques figurent des scènes de la vie du Christ, l'Ascension, la Pentecôte, le Jugement Universel, et des épisodes de la vie de saint Marc et de saints locaux. Jusqu'à ce jour, on ignore qui fut l'architecte de ce riche plan iconographique. Certains historiens de l'art mentionnent Gioacchino da Fiore, mystique calabrais du XIIe siècle; pourtant cette hypothèse n'est pas corroborée par des documents.

Les mosaïques à l'intérieur, le sanctuaire de la "nouvelle alliance", illustrent toutes le thème de l'accomplissement de la parole, en mettant en relief, comme une sorte de mappemonde, le développement prodigieux de la communauté chrétienne en terre infidèle après la Pentecôte. Par là, la basilique confirme en même temps le miracle de sa propre édification, qui se fonde elle aussi sur un accomplissement de parole, à savoir l'annonce faite à saint Marc, une parole qui a été faite pierres. Cette interférence de la parole et de son accomplissement, répétons-le, ressort au prime abord du dialogue qui s'instaure entre les inscriptions et les images.

L'iconographie des mosaïques de Saint-Marc propose donc un parcours de lecture bien précis, qui commence dans le vestibule, l'Ancien Testament, et mène à l'intérieur, dans la crypte où repose le corps de l'évangéliste, le coeur du sanctuaire, sa raison d'être. Ensuite l'itinéraire ramène le visiteur à partir de la coupole du Choeur (qui raconte l'avènement du Christ tel qu'il est annoncé par les prophètes de l'Ancien Testament) via les coupoles de l'Ascension et de la Pentecôte vers la grande porte d'entrée, des deux côtés de laquelle est représenté le Jugement Universel. En face en haut, à travers la grande baie qui donne sur la terrasse sous le quadrige, le regard du visiteur est capté par le ciel de Venise qui remplace la représentation manquante de la Jérusalem céleste.[2] A travers cette substitution triomphante, la basilique se manifeste comme le lieu de glorification de la Sérénissime, de sa puissance politique et religieuse. Rappelons que l'édification de la basilique impliqua la répudiation du premier patron grec de Venise, saint Théodore, au bénéfice de saint Marc qui fut proclamé protecteur de la ville, et dont le symbole, le lion ailé, fut adopté comme blason officiel de Venise. Par la construction de leur basilique les Vénitiens attestèrent donc qu' ils voulaient s'affranchir de la tutelle de Byzance. Ils détruisirent la petite chapelle existante dédiée à saint Théodore et sur les ruines mêmes, ils élevèrent un nouveau sanctuaire en l'honneur de l'évangéliste.

La légende de l'arrivée des ossements de saint Marc à Venise, qui circulait au moyen âge dans les lagunes du Haut-Adriatique, est une histoire de vol habilement camouflée en hagiographie assaisonnée de chronique locale. Elle a joué un rôle capital dans la distribution de l'ornementation mosaïquée de Saint-Marc, et mérite donc d'être récapitulée ici. D'après cette légende, l'évangéliste, alors que, vers la fin du Ier siècle, il parcourait en barque la région pour prêcher l'évangile, aurait été surpris par une tempête. Après de longues heures de navigation, son embarcation vint finalement s'échouer sur la plage d'une île de la lagune vénitienne où le saint navigateur, épuisé, s'endormit. Pendant son sommeil, un ange lui apparut et lui adressa la salutation fatidique: "PAX TIBI, MARCE, EVANGELISTA MEUS". Selon la légende ces paroles auraient une valeur prophétique: après sa mort, l'apôtre ne trouverait la paix éternelle que le jour du retour de son corps sur l'île même de l'apparition. Mais laquelle parmi les centaines d'îles de la lagune allait avoir le privilège de conserver les reliques du saint? Persuadés d'être, eux, les élus du ciel, les Vénitiens décidèrent de donner un coup de main à la providence. Au début du IXe siècle, deux marchands vénitiens se rendirent à Alexandrie en Egypte, où ils réussirent à dérober aux infidèles le corps de saint Marc. Une fois les saintes reliques à Venise, on commença aussitôt les travaux de construction d'un sanctuaire, qui fut consacré en 832.

Les mosaïques du vestibule ont été réparties en cinq cycles dont chacun raconte dans l'ordre chronologique les aventures d'un voyageur célèbre de l'Ancien Testament, à savoir Noé (15 scènes), Abraham (19 scènes), Joseph (40 scènes), Moïse (10 scènes), à ne pas oublier Adam le premier colonisateur du monde (24 épisodes). Toutes les séries de mosaïques sont orientées de gauche à droite, dans le sens de la lecture. Elles pointent donc en même temps dans la direction du paradis perdu représenté dans l'extrémité droite du bras du vestibule qui court derrière la façade centrale. Le paradis perdu, c'est le lieu de refuge vers lequel s'envolent tous les rêves de l'homme, qu'il aspire ardemment à reconquérir. Pourtant le cours de l'histoire sainte est orienté à contre-courant, de droite à gauche. Il éloigne l'homme errant du paradis pour l'amener vers cette autre terre promise, Chanaan, pour laquelle le peuple élu s'est mis en route sous la direction de Moïse. La dernière scène du vestibule, située à côté de la porte d'entrée du transept, se trouve en face de la crypte où seraient conservés les ossements de l'évangéliste, et représente le peuple désaltéré par Moïse. Grâce à cette iconographie raffinée, l'entrée dans le sanctuaire de Saint-Marc devient une pénétration dans la terre promise. Cette substitution subtile[3] n'est pas un des moindres témoignages de l'orgueil vénitien.

Deux des cinq voyageurs que représente le vestibule ont été "retirés de l'eau", à savoir Noé et Moïse. Ils se rattachent donc à l'histoire miraculeuse de Venise, de sa basilique, et de son patron, sortis eux aussi des eaux, en ressortant encore régulièrement lors de la saison pluvieuse. Les deux parois de mosaïques relativement détaillées consacrées à la construction de l'arche postulent une comparaison entre l'habitacle flottant de Noé, construit sur commande divine et d'après les strictes mesures données par Dieu lui-même, et la basilique dont l'érection est elle aussi d'origine divine. De même que l'arche de Noé, la basilique/Venise est un lieu de refuge, une espèce d'arche sérénissime, le berceau du nouveau monde civilisé.

Parmi les voyageurs il y en a trois qui sont venus d'Egypte: Abraham, Joseph et Moïse. Ce sont des précurseurs (/préfigurations) de saint Marc et du Christ, dont les histoires sont représentées sur les mosaïques de l'intérieur. A nouveau l'histoire sainte est mise en un rapport de typologie avec l'histoire vénitienne. Dans la vie des voyageurs de l'ancienne alliance aussi bien que dans celle du Christ et de saint Marc, l'Egypte figure à la fois comme terre hostile et comme lieu de refuge. Chassé de la terre promise par la faim, Abraham a séjourné quelque temps en Egypte. A cause de ses propres manigances, il a manqué y laisser sa peau. De peur d'être tué par les serviteurs de Pharaon pour les beaux yeux de sa femme Sarah, Abraham feint d'être son frère. Effectivement Sarah ne manque pas d'être confisquée par Pharaon. Furieux lorsqu'il apprend la vérité, celui-ci se voit néanmoins obligé de bannir le couple d'Egypte lorsque Dieu punit la cour royale par une maladie pestilentielle. Pour Moïse également, l'Egypte fut la terre de l'exil, mais en même temps le tremplin vers le pays "où coulent le lait et le miel". Pour Joseph, l'Egypte fut à la fois le pays de l'affliction et de la gloire. L'histoire de Joseph constitue le récit sériel le plus amplement développé par les mosaïstes: elle comprend au total 40 scènes couvrant trois coupoles du vestibule. Cette illustration abondante pourrait s'expliquer par le fait que Joseph semble être la préfiguration parfaite du patron de Venise: Joseph, c'est celui qui apporte le pain, le sauveur de la vie, celui dont le corps a été transporté d'Egypte pour être finalement enseveli dans la "terre promise".[4]

A l'intérieur les mosaïques représentent des scènes uniques, ou bien racontent des épisodes connus du Nouveau Testament, répartis sur un nombre restreint d'images. Ici chaque image est représentative de toute une série de scènes que le visiteur est censé connaître (la passion du Christ par exemple).[5] Les inscriptions sont rares, ce qui s'explique bien entendu par les dimensions de l'édifice qui rendent difficile sinon impossible une lecture soutenue. Par contre dans le vestibule, les textes abondent. Le voisinage de mosaïques et d'inscriptions active un va-et-vient entre l'illustration et le texte biblique, échange plus raffiné qu'on ne le croirait à première vue. On voit que les histoires sérielles ont confronté les mosaïstes avec les limites de l'art figuratif qui par définition est un art spatial et statique et se prête donc difficilement à la narration soutenue.

Pour enchaîner plusieurs épisodes en un tout compréhensible, l'artiste a donc eu recours à des subterfuges qu'en général le lecteur réussit à décoder sans problèmes. Le procédé le plus simple consiste dans la répétition d'un objet, d'un personnage, ou d'un fragment du décor, que le lecteur routiné interprète automatiquement comme un rapport de durée ou de fréquence, et non pas comme un rapport de simultanéité. Témoin plusieurs mosaïques où il est question de récits *singulatifs* (= le récit respecte la fréquence de l'histoire), telles, à l'intérieur, la tentation du Christ, et la prière du Christ au Jardin des Oliviers (fig. 2), et dans le vestibule, la construction et le peuplement de l'arche (fig. 3), la navigation de l'arche sur les eaux du déluge (fig. 4) et le voyage de Joseph d'Hébron à Dothan. Les séries dans le vestibule expriment une certaine durée, ce qui constitue donc un plus grand défi encore à l'habileté de l'artiste. Souvent le mosaïste a utilisé un simple signe démarcateur du décor pour cloisonner une histoire qui dure, comme dans les épisodes de l'ivresse et de la mort de Noé, où de petits piliers sveltes indiquent les entrées et sorties des personnages et marquent par là la temporalisation du récit (Noé se dénude pendant son sommeil, ce que découvre Cham qui se moque de son père auprès de ses frères Sem et Japhet, qui en détournant le visage, recouvrent leur père endormi d'un manteau; Noé réveillé bénit ses deux fils et maudit Cham; le corps de Noé est enterré par ses fils) (fig. 5). Les mêmes piliers-cloisons figurent dans l'histoire de Joseph (fig. 6).

La continuité de l'histoire illustrée est également soutenue par la répétition des mêmes signes figuratifs dans des contextes différents, qui constituent une sorte de lexique imagé. Signalons à titre d'exemples le signe du songe et celui du trône (voir fig. 5). On retrouve le signe du songe, un personnage endormi couché dans un nid de couvertures, dans l'histoire de Noé, de Joseph et de saint Marc. Le songe qui à chaque fois remet en mémoire la préhistoire miraculeuse de la basilique, occupe une place importante dans l'iconographie de Saint-Marc. Le trône connote le lieu du commandement. C'est le siège du patriarche souverain, le double figuratif du narrateur, à partir duquel l'action est dirigée et canalisée. Le trône se substitue au "Dixit Dominus", à la main divine qui sort des nuages, dans le cycle de la création et dans l'épisode antédiluvien du cycle de Noé: l'homme chassé du paradis prend le relais du Dieu tout-puissant. Les signes du nid de couvertures sont donc à moitié icones et à moitié symboles. Les mosaïques de Saint-Marc, d'un étonnant réalisme d'ailleurs, ne comprennent presque pas de symboles purs, ce qui pourrait s'expliquer par le fait qu'elles ne sont pas des images autosuffisantes mais des traductions fidèles du texte biblique. En raison de cette fonction de citation, l'image doit être "transparente". Dans les cycles du vestibule, je n'ai repéré que deux symboles inventés par les décorateurs eux-mêmes, à savoir les anges symbolisant les jours de la Création (fig. 7), et la main de Dieu le Père qui sort du ciel étoilé symbolisant la parole divine (voir fig. 3).

Plus d'un historien de l'art a signalé l'influence de l'art de la miniature sur l'iconographie des mosaïques de Saint-Marc.[6] Par analogie avec les miniatures, le lexique des gestes constitue une des composantes les plus riches du langage figuratif des mosaïques. Ce sont surtout les positions des bras et des mains qui forment une nomenclature émotive très élaborée. Citons quelques exemples:

Figure 2. La prière du Christ au Jardin des Oliviers (détail).

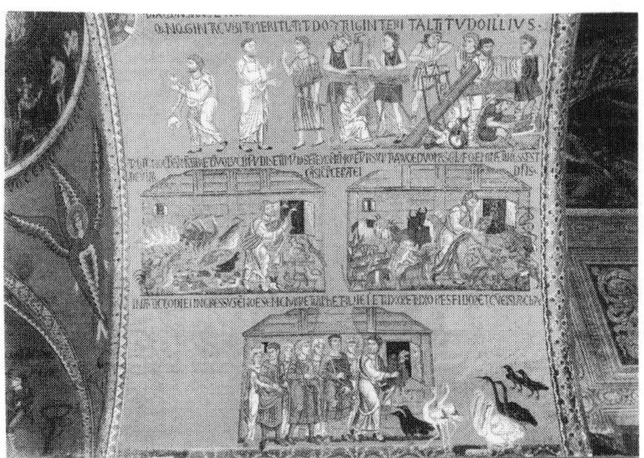

Figure 3. La construction de l'arche de Noé.

Figure 4. La navigation de l'arche.

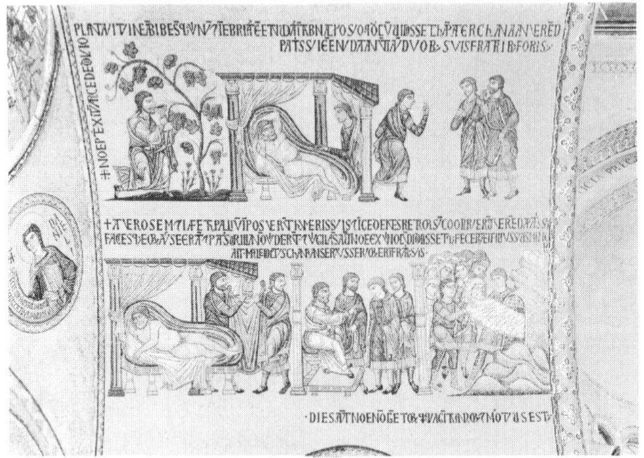

Figure 5. L'ivresse et la mort de Noé.

Figure 6. Histoire de Joseph (détail).

Figure 7. La création des astres.

– la main droite sur le coeur – crainte, vive émotion (fig. 5 Japhet écoutant les calomnies de son frère Cham)

– les mains en l'air – désespoir (Jacob apprenant la nouvelle de la mort de Joseph)

– la main droite soutenant le visage: profonde douleur (fig. 8 un frère de Joseph écoutant les explications que celui-ci donne de ses rêves)

– la main levée, les doigts légèrement écartés: jurement (fig. 9 Joseph jure fidélité à Dieu en refusant de céder aux instances de la femme de Potiphar).

La gestuelle des mains est d'ailleurs le moyen figuratif par excellence pour indiquer le dialogue, surtout dans la civilisation méditerranéenne qui fut celle des mosaïstes. Les gestes des mortels parlants sont des reflets affaiblis du geste impérieux signifiant la parole divine, que fait la main droite qui sort du ciel étoilé. Au début des cycles de mosaïques, le "Dixit Dominus" rythme la succession des scènes. La main droite de Dieu le Père, c'est la main qui crée, qui garantit l'accomplissement de la parole divine. Le Logos divin est à la fois parole et accomplissement de la Parole, la parole divine est la simultanéité de la chose générée. Ce n'est que dans la parole divine que le texte et l'image fusionnent, que *vox* et *res* coïncident. La tradition judéo-chrétienne est une tradition orale: c'est le Logos divin qui a créé le monde, c'est à travers la Parole que Dieu se fait connaître, finalement c'est à travers le Logos fait chair, le Christ, qu'Il se manifeste pleinement. Ainsi dans les mosaïques du vestibule se rapportant à l'Ancien Testament, donc au règne de la parole qui annonce, l'accent tombe sur la parole, ou mieux sur la consécration du texte biblique. Conforme à la rudimentaire fonction pédagogique que l'église catholique médiévale attribuait aux ornements de ses sanctuaires, les mosaïques y figurent comme des "livres des laïcs".

Cela est particulièrement clair dans la Coupole de la Création et dans l'histoire de Noé où ce sont les inscriptions qui viennent au premier plan. L'illustration fait écho au texte qui est sa source, son point de référence et son point d'aboutissement. L'histoire de la création du monde, telle qu'elle nous est racontée dans les premiers versets de la *Genèse*, évoque un rapport harmonieux sans faille entre texte et image, entre le mot qui nomme et la chose qui est. La parole créatrice de Dieu le Père coïncide avec son accomplissement, l'image est le prolongement naturel du texte, et ramène au texte qui la nomme: "Dieu dit: Que la lumière soit! Et la lumière fut. Dieu appela la lumière jour, et il appela les ténèbres nuit". Le premier chapitre de la *Genèse* est l'unique texte au monde qui évoque des images vierges de mots, des images incontaminées, et des mots qui génèrent leurs propres référents au lieu de les désigner.

L'histoire de la création du monde se lit en spirale descendante (fig. 10), de gauche à droite, de haut en bas. C'est l'unique histoire en spirale que possède la basilique. La spirale descendante pourrait renvoyer à la perte du paradis que

Figure 8. Histoire de Joseph (détail).

Figure 9. Hist. de Joseph (détail).

Figure 10. La Création du Monde.

racontent les dernières scènes de cette coupole. La disposition des images, je l'ai dit, respecte celle de la lecture, de gauche à droite. Cela vaut également pour l'organisation de l'espace figuratif: personnages, objets et animaux sont généralement tournés vers la droite. Les exceptions sont significatives, dans ce sens que le mouvement de droite à gauche exprime la contrariété, l'obstruction: dans le cycle de Joseph, le groupe des Ismaélites à qui les fils de Jacob vont vendre leur frère, s'achemine de la droite vers la gauche (fig. 11), plus loin Joseph s'évade des mains de la femme de Potiphar vers le côté gauche de la scène.

Dans l'histoire de Noé également, c'est le texte qui vient au premier plan. L'image est ici le prolongement du texte, son accomplissement. La disposition simple mais efficace des différentes scènes annonce la bande dessinée. La bande supérieure d'images illustrant la construction de l'arche, n'est pas subdivisée en scènes (voir fig. 3): la continuité de la représentation réfère à la longévité de l'épisode. La dernière image, l'entrée dans l'arche, clôt cette scène comme une conclusion. La position centrale de la mosaïque, comme une signature apposée au bas de la page, renvoie en même temps à un moment décisif de l'histoire de l'humanité. L'entrée dans l'arche déclenche le déluge qui marque la fin de l'Ancien Monde, ordonnée par Dieu qui a soin de verrouiller l'arche lui-même: "Puis l'Eternel ferma la porte sur lui" (*Genèse* 7:16).

Figure 11. Histoire de Joseph (détail).

Dans l'histoire de Joseph cependant le rapport entre texte et image s'invertit. Ici c'est l'image qui vient au premier plan, la succession rapide des images est commentée par des textes-légendes commençant par HIC. Néanmoins les images renvoient elles aussi à l'autorité sacrée, la bible. Les mots déictiques "Hic" soulignent le caractère instantané de l'image, et par là mettent en relief son inachèvement. L'image réclame une temporalité occultée et donc un récit qui la comble. Signalons aussi le grand nombre d'abréviations qui créent des trous dans le texte. Les inscriptions trouées proclament leur propre déficience: chaque texte abrégé est censé remettre en mémoire la plénitude de l'Ecriture Sainte, de même que chaque image atteste sa propre insuffisance d'instantané figé qui réclame la temporalité du texte. Jumelées, les images et les inscriptions fonctionnent comme des rébus qui génèrent le texte sacré. Parfois des mots-clés ont été incorporés dans la représentation figurative même. Le plus souvent il s'agit de noms propres ou de noms de choses qui permettent au visiteur de décoder sans faute des scènes sensiblement comprimées (le mot "Alexandria" par exemple, qui soutient l'architrave réunissant deux piliers surmontés de tourelles dans l'histoire de la translation du corps de saint Marc). Ces épigraphes sont des hybrides, à mi-chemin entre l'image (dont elles adoptent la moule et

Mots et images, écriture et espaces dans un roman français du XVe siècle

Pierre Demarolle

A l'occasion de ce Troisième Congrès International de *Texte et Image,* nous avons été invités à mettre en relief "l'interface, la fusion du mot et de l'image". Rien de plus étranger, matériellement parlant, que le texte d'un roman, constitué par une suite de signes dont le rapport avec la réalité désignée est arbitraire, et l'image, qui peut apparaître comme un reflet des choses vues. Pourtant, le contenu de la fiction romanesque n'appelle-t-il pas, dans l'esprit du lecteur, la formation d'images?

C'est précisément la notion même de contenu du roman que nous voudrions approfondir, à partir du *Jehan de Saintré,* qu'Antoine de La Sale écrivit aux alentours de 1456 (1).

Résumons-en l'intrigue. Au temps de Jean le Bon, roi de France, une cousine de la reine, que l'auteur appelle la Dame ou Madame, s'étant trouvée veuve après un mariage mal accordé, conçut par compensation l'ambition de "faire d'aucun josne chevalier ou escuier un homme renommé"; ayant jeté son dévolu sur un jeune garçon de treize ans plein de qualités, Jehan de Saintré, elle le prit en main et lui assura une carrière brillante dans le métier des armes. Tout alla bien jusqu'au jour où, au bout d'une quinzaine d'années, il décida de sa propre initiative de partir pour la croisade. Demeurée seule, la Dame trompa son jeune ami avec l'abbé d'un monastère voisin. De retour de la guerre, Saintré dut subir des humiliations de la part des deux amants. Il se vengea durement de l'un et de l'autre, avant de poursuivre une carrière qui ne lui procura que des honneurs.

Un tel résumé donne une idée fausse du roman, parce qu'il ignore à la fois les modalités du récit et l'organisation du contenu. Il n'a pas seulement le tort d'être synthétique; il offre une image du contenu arbitraire, et surtout non conforme à l'optique que l'auteur propose à son lecteur. La préférence donnée ici au déroulement de l'intrigue reflète une conception du roman qui n'est pas celle d'Antoine de La Sale. Il se trouve que *Jehan de Saintré* a fait l'objet, au XVIIIe siècle, d'une réécriture soumise à une optique déjà moderne, qui permet, de manière contrastive, de discerner les caractéristiques non seulement de la conception du roman médiéval, mais aussi de son contenu. Nous pensons à l'oeuvre du comte de Tressan (2). Celui-ci ne cache pas son irritation devant les développements didactiques qui nuisent, selon lui, à la marche de l'intrigue de ce qui est à ses yeux tout simplement une histoire d'amour.

En tout état de cause, il y a lieu de s'interroger sur l'utilisation du langage dans le *Jehan de Saintré*. Sous la plume d'Antoine de La Sale, les mots ne servent pas seulement à raconter ou à décrire. Ils nourrissent aussi la parole didactique de l'auteur, qui parle en son propre nom: c'est ainsi que nous apprenons, au cours d'un assez long développement (p. 3-5), que les Romains honoraient particulièrement les veuves qui, par fidélité à leur défunt époux, refusaient de se remarier. Même lorsque la parole de l'auteur se veut narrative, il est des moments où elle rapporte les propos tenus par un personnage, lequel ne recule pas devant des développements didactiques qui nous paraissent eux aussi interminables: avant de recevoir de Jean de Saintré l'engagement par lequel il la choisit pour sa Dame, la jeune princesse expose longuement à l'adolescent les dangers que constituent les sept péchés capitaux; cela occupe douze pages de notre édition. La prose d'Antoine de La Sale n'est pas d'abord une prose d'action.Or le contenu global du roman ne peut se définir qu'en fonction de la somme des éléments significatifs.

Si Antoine de La Sale avait privilégié l'intrigue, le déroulement dramatique de l'action, il aurait ainsi donné à son roman, outre un certain rythme temporel, un facteur d'unité. Or l'auteur de *Jehan de Saintré* n'a visiblement pas conçu son oeuvre dans une perspective unitaire. La lecture du roman montre que l'action se fragmente, et surtout qu'elle s'inscrit dans un certain nombre d'espaces qui ne sont pas seulement des cadres, mais des microcosmes comparables à certains égards aux "mansions" du théâtre médiéval.

On peut, dans un premier temps, définir ces espaces comme des lieux. Et puisqu'il s'agit de la conquête d'un jeune homme par une femme expérimentée, nous parlerons d'abord de l'espace dans lequel la Dame s'empare du jeune Saintré. C'est tout naturellement l'appartement de la princesse, situé dans une partie du palais du roi: passant par les galeries, le jeune homme est contraint d'entrer dans la chambre de la Dame, où celle-ci réunit ses suivantes, et où elle est maîtresse absolue; sorte de gynécée, ces appartements constituent un univers essentiellement peuplé de femmes, et c'est dans une atmosphère bien féminine que le jeune homme est l'objet de curiosités, d'indiscrétions concernant sa vie sentimentale. Profitant de sa supériorité sociale, de la différence d'âge, de son expérience, du soutien du milieu qu'elle préside, la Dame s'efforce de décontenancer et d'humilier l'adolescent pour le dominer, et aussi pour donner le change à ses suivantes, qui ne voient là qu'un divertissement un peu trouble qui ne leur déplaît pas. L'emploi par l'auteur de mots tels que *prisonnier* et *desprisonné* montre assez l'importance, dans une situation de sujétion, de l'espace dominé par la Dame. Le jeune héros, pour sa part, l'éprouve en quelque sorte physiquement: sorti de la chambre, "il commença tant qu'il peust a fuyr comme se il fust de cinquante loups chassiez." (p. 10).

C'est dans l'espace clos constitué par la chambre de la jeune princesse que celle-ci, seule à seule avec l'adolescent, lui fait prendre les engagements décisifs, portant à la fois sur la réussite sociale et sur la perfection morale, et fondés sur l'enseignement de l'Eglise, sur le respect des valeurs reconnues et sur la soumission à sa Dame. Nous avons dit que le roman ne privilégie pas l'action de manière exclusive; de fait, dans un univers déjà défini, et dont le cadre matériel passe au second plan, l'écriture n'est plus autre chose qu'un exposé pédagogique interminable: après l'examen des sept péchés capitaux, et les préceptes sur le "sauvement du corps", Jehan de Saintré se soumet et s'engage. La Dame reprend sans tarder son discours pédagogique, ponctué par l'expression "Encores veul et vous commande" qu'elle répète une quinzaine de fois; elle conclut par une promesse: s'il lui donne satisfaction, elle lui fera du bien et sera son amie.

Les appartements de la Dame ne sont qu'une partie du palais du roi. Le lecteur connaît aussi la galerie, lieu de passage où la princesse rencontre plusieurs fois le jeune garçon, qu'elle invite alors fermement à se rendre chez elle. Mais le lieu privilégié de leurs tête-à-tête est le préau de la Dame, le petit jardin dont elle lui remet un jour la clé parce qu'elle est contente de lui. Leurs relations devant rester discrètes, sinon secrètes, c'est là en particulier qu'ils se retrouvent lors des événements marquants de la carrière de Jehan. Dans les scènes situées dans le préau, le lecteur découvre quelque chose de l'intimité du couple, mais c'est là surtout qu'il est mis au courant des ambitions que la Dame nourrit au sujet de son protégé: c'est là que celle-ci remet au jeune homme, qui vient d'être nommé écuyer tranchant, l'argent nécessaire à l'achat de chevaux, et c'est là aussi qu'elle lui fait savoir qu'il est temps pour lui d'"entreprendre armes", c'est-à-dire de se faire connaître en défiant quiconque voudra l'affronter en combat singulier.

On voit que ces espaces ne sont pas seulement des lieux délimités matériellement. Comme les "mansions", ils sont en nombre restreint, et sont liés par un rapport direct et permanent à une partie de l'action, et à un certain nombre de protagonistes. Ils représentent des cellules sociales, caractérisées par les individus qui y pénètrent, par les relations qui existent entre ces individus, par le pouvoir qui s'y exerce, par des décisions et des actes, et par un certain type de discours. Le lieu, défini en termes géographiques, topographiques, voire en fonction du bâtiment dans lequel se déroule l'action, a aussi une signification sociale, relationnelle. Nous définirions un tel espace comme un milieu humain autant que comme une portion limitée de la surface terrestre.

De manière parallèle, le temps romanesque n'est pas identifiable avec un cadre chronologique donné a priori. Il est tributaire des événements dont l'auteur est censé nous faire part. Les événements introduisent l'espace, ou plutôt les espaces, parce qu'ils se produisent toujours quelque part, et généralement pas n'importe où. La "mansion" que constitue le domaine de la

Dame - et en particulier le préau - garde sa permanence; elle réapparaît chaque fois que l'héroïne et son ami s'y retrouvent en tête-à-tête. C'est l'un des relais du temps fictionnel de la narration.

Les espaces du roman ne se réduisent pas à ceux que nous venons d'évoquer. La carrière de Saintré l'oblige à participer à ces combats dont nous avons parlé, nés d'un défi porté souvent dans un pays lointain. L'action se situe alors dans d'autres espaces, eux aussi délimités matériellement et définis socialement. Tel est en particulier celui du champ clos dans lequel se déroulent les combats auxquels participe le jeune héros. Rien de plus fonctionnel que l'espace délimité par des lisses; rien de plus fidèle non plus à l'importance sociale de cette manifestation que l'organisation spatiale:

> "Et ce ordonné, le roy se part et s'en va sur son hourt qui a l'un des costez des lices estoit, tres richement tappissié de tous costez, et avec lui les princes, seigneurs et pluseurs autres chevaliers et escuiers de son conseil, et a sa senestre main la royne en son hourt, acompaignie de pluseurs princesses, dames et damoiselles de sa court et du royaume (...)" (pp.109-110).

En dépit des apparences, et à la différence de l'adaptation du comte de Tressan, *Jehan de Saintré* n'est pas d'abord le roman d'un couple. Dans l'univers de ce roman, les actes des personnages, leurs paroles, leur emploi du temps et le lieu où ils se trouvent sont constamment déterminés par leurs obligations sociales. Il n'est pas surprenant de constater que les héros sont toujours dans un espace qui leur est assigné par ces obligations. L'univers romanesque n'est pas autre chose, en définitive, que la somme de ces espaces juxtaposés. Dans chacun de ces espaces interviennent des actes, que l'on aurait peine à situer ailleurs; des paroles sont prononcées, qui ne sont pas simplement subordonnées à l'action, car la parole y est acte.

En d'autres termes, le roman est conçu comme un ensemble d'éléments relativement autonomes, caractérisés par la conjonction d'un espace, d'un temps, d'actes et de paroles qui font de chacun d'eux un univers soumis d'abord à sa cohérence interne.

S'il fallait schématiser cette organisation du contenu du roman, on serait certainement amené à représenter une sorte de nébuleuse, et en tout cas à réaliser un croquis utilisant deux dimensions. D'autre part, chaque espace fictionnel étant censé comporter trois dimensions, on aperçoit la complexité de l'organisation du contenu fictionnel du roman. En face de cette organisation complexe, quelles sont les ressources respectives du texte et de l'image?

Sous sa forme écrite, et en dehors de la poésie, tout texte en prose se développe dans un espace unidimensionnel, linéaire, qui correspond dans le domaine temporel à la succession des mots dans le temps de la lecture. Il n'y a normalement entre l'organisation fictionnelle en espaces et l'espace matériel du texte ni communauté de nature, ni relation systématique. Pourrait faire exception une écriture en "calligrammes", un "pavé" distinct étant affecté à chaque espace du récit. L'écriture acquerrait ainsi une seconde dimension, qui serait en outre utilisée pour créer un rapport nouveau entre signifiant et signifié. Mais tel n'est pas le cas dans notre roman. Le texte, parce qu'il appartient à l'univers du langage, ne saurait refléter matériellement la fiction romanesque, ni les cadres spatiaux dans lesquels elle s'inscrit.

En revanche, l'image, qui se situe dans deux dimensions, semble a priori devoir être considérée comme le moyen privilégié d'expression de l'espace, fût-ce de l'espace socialisé auquel nous pensons. Parce que nous sommes enclins à privilégier la vue dans notre appréhension des choses, nous avons tendance à concevoir les images comme le reflet le plus fidèle, et surtout le plus direct de celles-ci. Plus précisément, et puisqu'il est question d'espaces, nous sommes habitués à trouver dans les deux dimensions de l'image un reflet relativement fidèle de l'univers tridimensionnel dans lequel s'inscrivent les *realia*. En outre, puisque le contenu du roman comporte des scènes relativement statiques, une lecture appropriée ne requiert-elle pas que le lecteur cherche à concevoir des images, au lieu de nourrir uniquement son imagination d'actes ou de relations entre les personnages? D'un point de vue plus général, qui dit espaces - et en particulier espaces imaginaires - ne dit-il pas image, plutôt que langage (au sens étroit du terme)?

Reste pourtant un fait essentiel: pas plus que le langage parlé ou écrit, l'image ne saurait s'identifier au contenu romanesque, parce qu'elle est d'un autre ordre. En règle générale, l'espace imaginaire et l'espace iconique n'ont aucune raison de présenter des articulations parallèles.

Le contenu romanesque est pour nous un signifié, que nous appellerons paradoxalement une "réalité fictionnelle", et dont le lecteur admet l'existence et la cohérence en entrant dans le jeu de l'auteur. Ce signifié lui est rendu accessible par le moyen du système de signes que constitue la langue employée par l'écrivain. On doit le définir comme un contenu, et il a ses structures propres, parmi lesquelles l'espace, ou plutôt les espaces.

Certes, toute image, de son côté, s'inscrit dans un espace à deux dimensions, mais cet espace, purement matériel, ressortit au caractère de signe de l'image, et appartient au plan du signifiant. Autrement dit, si nous admettons que l'image est un signe, et non pas un facteur d'illusion, il existe la même distance entre d'une part le contenu exprimé, et d'autre part chacun des signifiants que constituent respectivement les images et les mots. En présence des images, il n'est pas question de faire l'économie d'une lecture iconique.

Certes, l'organisation des espaces dans le roman d'Antoine de La Sale peut rappeler certains moyens d'expression du Quattrocento italien, dont *Jehan de Saintré* est à peu près contemporain. Il n'en demeure pas moins que ce langage plastique, effectivement capable de donner accès à une telle conception de l'univers, demande à être interprété, et ne serait pas susceptible de constituer un reflet pur et simple du contenu du roman. En outre, d'autres langages iconiques pourraient sans aucun doute donner accès à ce même contenu par des moyens tout différents.

Nous ne croyons donc pas devoir attribuer à l'image un rapport privilégié avec les choses, et en particulier avec l'espace. Nous ne pensons pas non plus que l'imagination du lecteur doive nécessairement se nourrir d'images.

D'autre part, on n'insistera jamais assez sur la différence de nature qui sépare le langage de tout ce qu'il peut exprimer ou désigner. C'est peut-être cette différence de nature qui, paradoxalement, permet au langage de tout exprimer, au prix de la relation extraordinairement arbitraire qu'il entretient avec les *realia*.

Une dernière remarque de méthode s'impose. Dans la comparaison que nous avons faite entre les possibilités d'expression respectives du texte et de l'image, nous avons constamment pris comme référence le contenu romanesque, c'est-à-dire la somme des significations fournies par le texte. Or ce signifié, considéré globalement, ne correspond pas à un référent, puisque l'histoire est imaginaire.S'il est vrai que ce contenu procède des valeurs signifiantes du texte, de leur côté des valeurs d'expression plastiques permettraient à un artiste de transmettre par des moyens différents un contenu peut-être analogue, mais certainement pas identique. En effet, le contenu d'une oeuvre n'est pas une réalité préexistante qu'il s'agirait d'exprimer plus ou moins totalement. Un *Jehan de Saintré* écrit dans un "langage" iconique donnerait accès à un contenu différent. La permanence de l'intrigue ne changerait rien à l'affaire, car l'aspect dramatique d'une oeuvre n'est pas tout. Le contenu, considéré comme la somme des valeurs signifiées, dépend des moyens littéraires ou plastiques mis en oeuvre, dont on sous-estime l'importance en les appelant "moyens d'expression". Nous croyons avoir montré que ce contenu est pourtant d'un ordre différent de ceux-ci. De quelle nature est-il ? Indépendant du monde réel, constituant le signifié des "modes d'expression", c'est par excellence une "chose mentale", pour le créateur certes, mais aussi et surtout pour le récepteur. En y accédant, celui-ci entre dans l'univers du créateur, et dans les espaces selon lesquels cet univers s'ordonne. Mots et images sont à cet égard des médiateurs; mais s'ils ne donnent accès qu'à un monde fictionnel, il reste que ce monde est bien vivant dans l'esprit, par-delà les images et les mots. A ce niveau, ceux-ci ne se confondent pas: ils disparaissent les uns et les autres de la conscience du récepteur. Distinct du niveau du signifiant, privé de référent autre que lui-même, ce monde imaginaire est par excellence le résultat de la création, le lieu de complicité entre l'auteur et son lecteur; mots et images ne sont en l'occurrence que des interfaces oubliées.

Fallait-il, pour situer l'un par rapport à l'autre le mot et l'image, traiter de l'expression de l'espace? Ce choix nous a été au moins suggéré par la facture du roman. Nous ne le regrettons pas, dans la mesure où la notion d'espace concerne à la fois l'univers fictionnel et la matérialité de la succession des mots et du tracé des figures.

NOTES

1 Nous empruntons nos citations à l'édition suivante: Antoine de La Sale: *Jehan de Saintré,* éd. par Jean Misrahi et Charles A. Knudson (Genève, Droz, 1967, "Textes littéraires français"). Signalons une nouvelle édition, due à Mario Eusebi (*Saintré;* Paris, Champion, 1993-1994, "Les Classiques français du Moyen Age", n° 114 et 115, 2 t.).

2 Dans le *Corps d'extraits de romans de chevalerie, par M. le Comte de Tressan* (Paris, Pissot, 1782), l'adaptation du *Jehan de Saintré* se trouve dans le tome III, pp. 190 à 345.

Figure 2.

real identity only after he has shown his mettle as a knight, a moment marked by this same woodcut. For the reader unfamiliar with the provenance of the image, it is disjunctive. Gerard's recognition scene involves the young man, a hermit, and his white haired uncle, while Amadis is awakened to confirm his parents' growing suspicions and joy. The thematic content of the *illustration,* not its visual aspect, renders it appropriate for use in *Gerard.* The meaning of the image is accessible only to readers interpreting it commemoratively. Its placement here might have been a printers' in-joke if this were an isolated occurrence, but the repeated placement of woodcuts where they may be seen to serve a commemorative function strongly supports the notion that this image bears a message intended for all readers.[6] As this function of pictures is one to which modern readers are unaccustomed, it may be useful to examine the interactions of text and image used commemoratively by following the careers of a few of *Amadis'* woodblocks as they reappear both in successive volumes of *Amadis* itself and in other novels.

The two part scene of combat we considered above (fig. 1) is reused frequently in a thematic sense for situations involving single combat. That happens for the first time just a few chapters later (ch. 23) when Amadis is provoked into a fight to protect the dwarf. Unbeknownst to Amadis, the other knight this time is in fact his brother, Galaor. The double scene, the pines, the lances, are no longer appropriate; the image's relation to the accompanying text has been reduced to its thematic value as a scene of single combat on foot (with watching dwarf). Or has it? In this combat, only an accidental interruption prevents the reciprocal slaughter of two perfectly matched opponents. Readers brought to consider the earlier battle once again illustrated here might well draw conclusions about the great strength of Amadis' opponent now compared to the two knights whom he easily defeated in the earlier encounter. The case for this hypothesis is strengthened by the reuse of this image in Book VII, again to mark the almost fatally equal combat between members of the same family. This time the joust is between Amadis de Grece and his grandfather, Esplandian, who, like Amadis and Galaor earlier, do not recognize each other.[7] The readers who absorb the message of the picture alternately fear and hope – knowing the combatants are lethally well matched, and knowing as well as the happy outcome of the earlier contest. Both reactions are justified by events here. The same block reappears thematically in books II, III, IV, and V of *Amadis* a total of six times. The catalogue of reappearances could be continued, but the range of thematic and commemorative utility of this scene should by now be clear.[8]

Here we have another woodcut that is reused in multiple ways, a single scene illustrating (*Amadis*, I.12) the knighting of Amadis' younger brother,

Figure 3.

Galaor, by Amadis himself. At the end of the ceremony, a sword that has until now been invisibly hanging from the tree will be presented to Galaor. On the tip of a branch of the same tree (upper-right foreground) the illustrator has also shown the spur to be placed on the right heel of a newly dubbed knight. In the lower-right foreground Galaor's foster father, the giant Gandalaz, rightful lord of the Roche de Galtares, is hiding amidst some rocks, perhaps to remind us of his title. Later, by evoking Galaor's valor (II.7) the commemorative reuse of this block may render it reassuring or tragic at the point where twelve mysterious women take the unconscious Galaor away after a battle. In Book IV the thematic focus changes: here the dubbing of a knight reasserts itself, as that ceremony is performed for two squires, Gandalin and Lasinde. It is again used for this purpose, for example (VI.43) when Olorius of Spain asks Amadis to make him a knight. Plantin's Antwerp edition of *Amadis* also chooses to associate it with knighting a young prince (Norendel) (III.3). Although I have spoken of the reuse of woodblocks, this is sometimes a figure of speech:

Plantin's block was presumably a copy made from the Paris editions, common practice in the period.

The same image is reused to good effect in a different novel, *Palmerin d'Olive* (D3v), when Palmerin is knighted by Florendos, his biological father, with whom he will be knowingly united only later. The giant in the foreground must be overlooked, but otherwise, the situations have a good deal in common. Readers linking the image to its original use may well approximate Florendos to the grandeur of Amadis and cloak Palmerin, early in the novel, with some of the glory of Galaor.[9] In *Dom Flores* (E1r) the image reappears (ch. 58), in the chapter which tells how "le chevalier des Cignes mit à mort le fort géant Madrasian" (title of chapter 58). The following chapter tells readers that in doing so, he is preserving the honor of Galaor's sons, who would otherwise have been defeated by the Giant Madrasian, seeking to avenge the defeat of the Giant's father years before, thousands of pages earlier, by Galaor as his first act of valor which restored the Roche de Galtares to its rightful lord, also a giant.[10] When the print is read commemoratively, evoking its capacity as illustration, it joins past triumphs to the victory recorded here and further reminds us how heroic the family of Amadis remains over the generations.

In the world of *Amadis*, valor and love are closely tied. The first tryst of Perion and Elisene, Amadis' parents, is illustrated in a print containing three successive moments: 1. on the left, we see the maid leading Elisene to Perion;

Figure 4.

2. then the lover's first embrace in the center; 3. while in the background, the maid leaves discreetly with the sword on which Perion swore to be forever faithful to Elisene. This block reappears later in Book I at the retrospective tale of the conception of Amadis' half-brother Florestan. The commemorative function here again acts as a kind of shorthand to assure the reader of Florestan's quality as a true brother, to be considered the quasi-equal of Amadis. The

image recurs (IV.5) when Oriane sends a message to her beloved Amadis. Here, a failure to read the image commemoratively renders it disjunctive. For readers who recall its content as an illustration, the image announces things to come: these lovers will soon be reunited just as Perion and Elisene were. The same woodcut is again used commemoratively, imbuing the characters with the power and achievement of their ancestors (VIII.44), after the wedding of Amadis' grandson, Lisuart, and Onolorie, when she finally tells Lisuart of the birth and the kidnapping of their firstborn son. Readers would no doubt recall that because Elisene and Perion were separated almost immediately after the scene illustrated here, Elisene sent the newborn Amadis out to sea, keeping the incident secret from Perion for many years. Again the illustration remembered promises the happy ending that soon follows.

Readers of other novels were presumed to be readers of *Amadis*, so we find this block in a number of novels printed in the next decade or so. When *Dom Flores*, in the more restrained climate of 1551, uses the same image with obvious thematic relevance at the first kiss of Enone and Flores (04v), it marks the couple's engagement. Another aspect of the theme is evoked there when the wife of Guilian le pensif recalls the happiness of her marriage (Z2v). In *Palmerin* it marks Polinarde's agreeing to meet Palmerin alone (02r) with predictable consequences. In the *Histoire Palladienne* (E6v) it is similarly a good augury accompanying the reunion of lovers. All are occasions worthy to be placed under the auspices of the happy result of the union of Perion and Elisene. In *Primaleon* (Clv), it appears at the reminder of the conception of Palmendos, conceived while the Emperor Palmerin was under a spell cast by the Queen of Tarse, so that she might bear a hero's son (an episode actually recounted in *Palmerin* and only alluded to here). The message now is about the great things to be expected from the sons of great men: the greatness of Amadis, whose conception is implied by the picture, is well known; for the savvy reader the picture now guarantees the valor of Palmendos.

The reuse of intricately encoded images in these novels permits them to perform multiple tasks: they may add to the emotional content of a scene or function prophetically or act as a guide to help readers evaluate events and classify characters. The commemorative functions of woodcuts second textual patterns which call upon the readers' active, combinatory recall of previous episodes.[11] The visual element complements – and mirrors – the verbal. Both are dependent on the active intervention of memory in the creation, the synthesis within the reader's mind, of the completed text, a text which includes the messages of its images.[12]

Paul Klee's *Composition with Windows:* An Homage and an Elegy

K. Porter Aichele

In December, 1918 Paul Klee signed off on the personal diaries he had kept for a number of years. He seems to have been conscious of making a break with the past, for in the future his practice of recapitulating the steps in his development as an artist would take the form of paintings rather than diary entries. One such recapitulation was a painting of 1919 to which Klee himself gave two titles: *Composition with Windows* and *Composition with B'* (fig. 1). Placed in its historical context, this work can be read as the last word and image in an exchange of ideas among Klee, the painter Robert Delaunay and the poet Guillaume Apollinaire. The following essay will propose that the signifying structure of Klee's *Composition with Windows* owes as much to the poetry of Apollinaire as it does to the painting of Delaunay.

Klee was first exposed to Delaunay's works in December, 1911 at the Blue Rider exhibition in Munich and was eager to see more. Before traveling to Paris the following spring, he secured a letter of introduction to Delaunay from Wassily Kandinsky, a mutual acquaintance. Exactly what transpired when Klee visited Delaunay's studio on the morning of April 11, 1912 can only be imagined. The one claim that can be made with any certainty is that Klee saw an early version of the "Window" series on which Delaunay was then working. Three months later at the Moderner Bund exhibition in Zurich, Klee again had the opportunity to examine Delaunay's new work. In a review of the exhibition, Klee singled out *Windows on the City (First Part, Second Motif)*, dated April, 1912 (fig. 2), which he had very likely seen in Paris. He described it as an "autonomous picture", divested of motifs from nature and therefore embodying a "completely abstract form-life" ("Ausstellung", 60). This comment and statements made by Delaunay at the same time hint at one topic of conversation during the April visit.

In Delaunay's "La Lumière", which he wrote in the summer of 1912 and later asked Klee to translate into German, he observed that "as long as art remains attached to the object, it will be descriptive ... literary ... slavishly imitative" ("La Lumière" 147). Paraphrases of this assertion are quoted in Apollinaire's "Réalité, Peinture pure", an article documenting his conversations with Delaunay during the month of August, 1912. Apollinaire's title echoes Delaunay's words, but at the time the article was written, Delaunay's

Figure 1. Paul Klee, *Composition with Windows (Composition with B')*, 1919. Paul Klee-Stiftung, Kunstmuseum Bern. © 1995 Artists Rights Society (ARS), New York/VG Bild-Kunst, Bonn.

"pure painting" was not, in Apollinaire's view, "as abstract as it would like to be" (*Les Peintres Cubistes* 14). Similarly, the painter August Macke, who visited Delaunay's studio in October, 1912, observed that the "Window" paintings were "not abstract at all" (Cited in Vriesen 50). In Delaunay's *Windows on the City (First Part, Second Motif)* Apollinaire and Macke would have recognized fragments of the Eiffel Tower and partial views of Parisian façades, all seen

Figure 2. Robert Delaunay, *Windows on the City (First Part, Second Motif),* 1912. Formerly in the collection of Sonia Delaunay, Paris. ©1995 Artists Rights Society (ARS), New York/ADAGP, Paris.

through pale, transparent reflections in a paned window. Since Klee, like Apollinaire and Macke, could not have failed to see the architectural motifs in Delaunay's paintings, it can be assumed that his reference to "an autonomous picture ... without motifs from nature" was an attempt to come to terms with unfamiliar and inherently vague language picked up in conversations with Delaunay.

It is also true that Klee had never seen a painting that marked a more radical break with mimetic resemblance than Delaunay's *Windows on the City (First Part, Second Motif)*. Like the perceptible but intangible reflections on the window pane, the recognizable objects seen through the window are depicted as patterns of refracted, prismatically colored light that Klee perceived as having "a completely abstract form-life". Along the left and lower borders of Delaunay's painting the geometric light patterns spill over onto the painted illusion of a casement window frame. This internal frame and the abstract patterns it both circumscribes and incorporates call into question the Renaissance tradition that compared a painting to a window onto the external world. Klee understood this, and from 1913 to 1919 consistently referred to Delaunay's "Window" paintings as models for using color to represent light independently of the objects that light renders perceptible. To the extent that Klee's *Composition with Windows* appropriates Delaunay's colored equivalents of natural light and retains schematized vestiges of Delaunay's window motif, it is incontestably indebted to Delaunay's example.[1] There is nevertheless ample evidence in this and other paintings to support the conjecture that Klee's ideas were concurrently and significantly influenced by Apollinaire.

*

* *

In November, 1912 Apollinaire temporarily moved into Delaunay's apartment to recover from an attack of neurasthenia brought on by a year of upheaval in his personal relations. No doubt to reciprocate for the artist's solicitude and hospitality, the poet agreed to write a preface to the catalogue of an exhibition that would feature Delaunay's "Window" paintings. In lieu of a conventional preface, Apollinaire produced "Les Fenêtres", a poem that was first published in a deluxe album of photographs produced to coincide with Delaunay's exhibition at the Sturm Gallery in Berlin in January, 1913. Like the journal of the same name, the Sturm Gallery was directed by Herwarth Walden, the writer, stage director and entrepreneur whom Klee called the "heroic Walden" because of his staunch support of modern art (see *Diaries* 276). A master publicist, Walden kept Delaunay's name in "Der Sturm" for the duration of the exhibition, first publishing Apollinaire's "Réalité, Peinture pure" in German, then Klee's translation of Delaunay's "La Lumière". On the occasion of Delaunay's opening at the Sturm Gallery, Apollinaire delivered a lecture reiterating his recent pronouncements on contemporary painting; this too subsequently appeared in Walden's periodical under the title "Die Moderne Malerei".

In his article on modern painting, Apollinaire predicted that the innovations of French Cubism would lead to a "poetic kind of painting that stands outside the world of observation" ("La Peinture Moderne" *Oeuvres Complètes,*

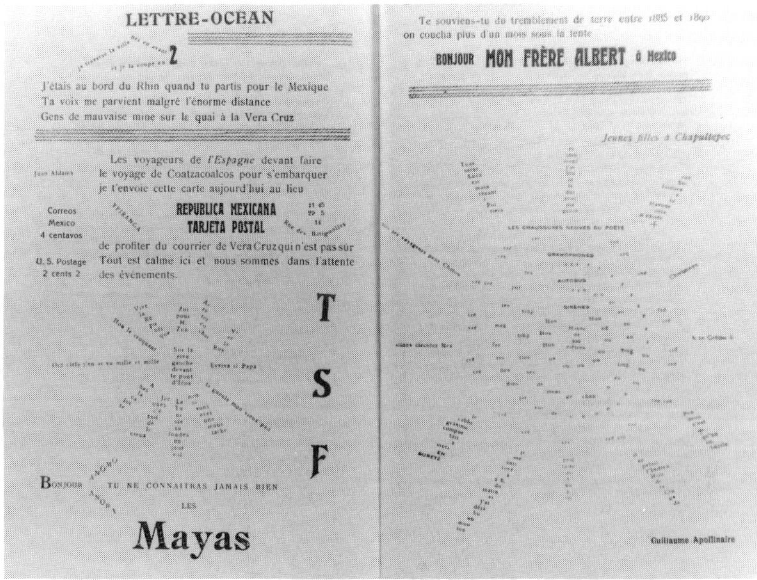

LETTRE-OCEAN

J'étais au bord du Rhin quand tu partis pour le Mexique
Ta voix me parvient malgré l'énorme distance
Gens de mauvaise mine sur le quai à la Vera Cruz

Les voyageurs de *l'Espagne* devant faire
le voyage de Coatzacoalcos pour s'embarquer
je t'envoie cette carte aujourd'hui au lieu

Correos
Mexico
4 centavos

REPUBLICA MEXICANA
TARJETA POSTAL

de profiter du courrier de Vera Cruz qui n'est pas sûr
Tout est calme ici et nous sommes dans l'attente
des événements.

U. S. Postage
2 cents 2

T
S
F

Bonjour
TU NE CONNAITRAS JAMAIS BIEN
LES
Mayas

Te souviens-tu du tremblement de terre entre 1885 et 1890
on coucha plus d'un mois sous la tente

BONJOUR MON FRÈRE ALBERT à Mexico

Jeunes filles à Chapultepec

Guillaume Apollinaire

Figure 3. Guillaume Apollinaire, "Lettre-Océan", *Les Soirées de Paris*, 15 juin, 1914.

IV 282). Apollinaire here used "poetic" as a synonym of "pure" and "abstract", intentionally choosing a term charged with the same ambiguity of meaning as the word fragments in Cubist painting. Following the Cubists' example, Klee experimented with using the arbitrary symbols that constitute the language of poetry as abstract pictorial forms. Beginning in 1913, he excerpted the letter "X" from the latticed scaffolding of the Eiffel Tower in Delaunay's "Window" paintings and isolated it, first as a repetitive decorative motif, then as a structural form. An example is "Inner Architecture" of 1914 with no fewer than ten variations on the letter "X", all of which suggest but do not describe architectural supports.[2] Removed from a specific linguistic context, the randomly placed letters become integral parts of a structural grid that forges what Klee had previously characterized as a "conciliatory relationship" between the objects depicted and the painting as an independent pictorial construct (*Die Alpen* 61).

While Klee was exploring alternatives to the mimetic tradition in painting, Apollinaire was challenging conventional verse forms and poetic syntax. In June, 1914 he published "Lettre-Océan", his first calligram (fig. 3). The letter to which the title refers is registered as a spatial void demarcated by circular and radiating lines of text, all read from an aerial perspective corresponding to the top of the Eiffel Tower. Klee adopted Apollinaire's centrifugal

Figure 4. Paul Klee, *'E' fragmentarisches Aquarell,* 1918. Private collection, Switzerland. ©1995 Artists Rights Society (ARS), New York/VG Bild-Kunst, Bern.

structure in *"E" fragmentarisches Aquarell* (1918, fig. 4), substituting the stencilled initial "E" for Apollinaire's visually present if typographically absent letter "O". In the context of Klee's title, the letter "E" can be identified as an abbreviation of the indefinite article "ein". The imagery framing the centralized initial suggests another reading. Klee's "E" occupies the same focal position in relation to schematically rendered windows, architectural motifs and a Ferris wheel as the Eiffel Tower does in two versions of Delaunay's "Window" paintings. Moreover, it dominates the pictorial images surrounding it, just as the structural lines of the Eiffel Tower dominate the printed text of "Lettre-Océan". It seems likely, therefore, that Klee incorporated the first letter of the name "Eiffel" as a linguistic substitute for visual images of the Eiffel Tower in Delaunay's paintings and Apollinaire's shaped text. In composing a hybrid that inverts the semantic relationship between linguistic and pictorial symbols in Apollinaire's calligram, Klee must have been conscious of creating another example of the "typographic artifices" cited by Apollinaire in a 1917 lecture on new forms of "visual lyricism" ("Esprit nouveau et les poètes", *Oeuvres complètes,* III, 901). When Klee began *"E" fragmentarisches Aquarell* in 1918, he almost certainly knew Apollinaire's "Lettre-Océan", although he probably did not yet know Apollinaire's lecture, which was published posthumously in the *Mercure de France* on December 1, 1918.

*
* *

Apollinaire died in November, 1918 of complications from war wounds. Klee fared better during the war years. He was not called to active duty until March, 1916, at the same time Apollinaire was wounded on the front. Klee's mostly administrative duties did not prevent him from painting or even attending exhibition openings. He had his first one-person exhibition at the Sturm Gallery in 1916, followed by two in 1917 and one in January, 1919, just before he was demobilized and returned to civilian life as a professional artist. It was in his Munich studio later in the year that he painted *Composition with Windows.* Like *"E" fragmentarisches Aquarell,* this work combines symbols from two different language systems and incorporates allusions to the poetry of Apollinaire as well as the painting of Delaunay.

The palette of Klee's *Composition with Windows* combines in a single visual image the scattered verbal notations of complementary contrasts in Apollinaire's "Les Fenêtres" ("Du rouge au vert tout le jaune se meurt"... "insondables violets"), which in turn refer to different color schemes in Delaunay's "Window" series (*Oeuvres complètes,* III, 160-61). Superimposed on Klee's layers of transparent color washes and glazes are non-pictorial symbols, specifically the Greek delta with a period beneath it, the Roman letter B, an apostrophe, and the mathematical "equal" sign. This odd assortment of symbols can be construed in as many ways as the collection of fragmented non-sequiturs that constitute Apollinaire's "Les Fenêtres". Read sequentially from the top down and from left to right, the letters and other symbols compose the German sentence fragment "D(u) bist". Or, if the letter "B" is read as the first letter of a noun, then the non-pictorial symbols might refer to the picture itself ("Das Bild ist ...") or to the act of looking ("Der Blick ist ...").[3]

Isolated, the letter "B" in Klee's painting and subtitle can be identified as an initial denoting a specific place, as initials often do in Klee's paintings – in this case his native Bern or more likely Berlin, the city that is depicted and named in Plate VI of Klee's illustrations to Curt Corrinth's "Potsdamer Platz".[4] The illustration dates from the same year as the painting, and the typefaces of the "B's" are similar, the one difference being the placement of the decorative serif, which in *Composition with Windows* has migrated to the right, becoming the apostrophe. Assuming that on one level Klee's "B" is an abbreviation of the name Berlin, it can be read as an addendum to the series of place names strung together in Apollinaire's poem ("Paris Vancouver Hyères Maintenon New-York et les Antilles"). Klee's addition of Berlin to Apollinaire's list would anticipate Delaunay's pairing of Paris and Berlin in a 1922 drawing and would give closure to Klee's prolonged encounter with French modernism. Klee's concerted efforts to come to terms with contemporary French art had begun with his trip to Paris and continued throughout his association with the Sturm Gallery in Berlin. The end of his professional relationship with Walden's Sturm Gallery in 1918 marked a turning point in Klee's artistic development. *Composition with Windows,* painted at this juncture, is a summary statement of what Klee had assimilated from French modernism. It also anticipates Klee's unique contribution to the concept of simultaneity, which was a recurring theme in Delaunay's writings and in Apollinaire's accounts of his conversations with Delaunay.

For Delaunay simultaneity encompassed both a perceptual and a psychological dimension. From a technical perspective, his "Window" series experiments with the visual phenomenon of simultaneously registered contrasts that affect the perception of color. To the extent that the "Window" paintings represent multiple memory images that converge in a Bergsonian state of consciousness, they also reflect the artist's psychological experience.[5] Other painters, including Klee, focused on analogies between pictorial simultaneity and contrapuntal or polyphonic music. As early as 1912 both Klee and Franz Marc had made comparisons between Delaunay's "Window" series and the fugue,[6] a contrapuntal form in which a single theme is stated concurrently by two or more musical "voices". In 1917 Klee again compared Delaunay's painting to a fugue and went so far as to claim that "the notion of simultaneity stands out even more richly" in what he conceived as "polyphonic painting" than in music because the time element is visually communicated in spatial terms (*Diaries* 374). This and numerous other references to simultaneity in the *Diaries* led Andrew Kagen to observe that by 1919 Klee had a clear theoretical idea of just what constituted simultaneity in "polyphonic painting" (Kagen 78), although little practical experience in giving the idea visual form. The title of Klee's "Fugue in Red" confirms that in 1921 he returned to his earlier musical analogy, attempting to establish coloristic equivalents of musical voices and spatial relationships approximating simultaneity of sounds in music.[7] Like *Fugue in Red, Composition with Windows* implicitly equates transparent color layers in depth with "voices" sounding simultaneously. There are, however, readily apparent differences between these two works, one being the character of the repetitive rhythms, which are more regular and obviously imitative in *Fugue in Red.* The repetitive patterns of descriptive imagery in *Composition with Windows* points to a structural model other than music.

Visual evidence in addition to the color scheme and linguistic symbols suggests that Klee intended *Composition with Windows* to be an extension of the metaphor invoked by Apollinaire to characterize "Les Fenêtres". Challenged by his discussions with Delaunay, Apollinaire was determined to find a literary counterpart of pictorial simultaneity. With the discovery of the calligram, he introduced spatial and other visual elements, thus overcoming some of the limitations imposed by inherited poetic convention. "Les Fenêtres", which predates the calligrams, comes as close to incorporating aspects of simultaneity as the necessity of a temporal reading of free verse will allow. In characterizing "Les Fenêtres" as a "conversation poem", Apollinaire was not simply acknowledging the importance of his dialogues with Delaunay; he was also describing a poetic syntax based on conversational discourse. A comparative analysis of Apollinaire's poem and Klee's painting reveals that both embody certain stylistic devices and structural properties of conversation.[8]

Among the most striking stylistic features of "Les Fenêtres" are the absence of punctuation marks, which are not visible in spoken exchanges, and the elimination of all discursive connectors, both of which make Apollinaire's verbal images collide, in much the same way that voices interrupt one another in conversation. Similarly, the transparent color planes in Klee's painting function like the different voices in a conversation: they abruptly interrupt or, in visual terms, intersect, and they often overlap, like voices speaking at the same time. Klee's colors vary in hue, value and intensity, just as voices vary in timbre, pitch and volume. Clustered together, the squared and rectangular units of color form abstract patterns that are as irregular as patterns of conversational speech or the metric patterns of Apollinaire's conversation poem. At the lower border of Klee's painting the abstract patterns of color coalesce in the distinctive shape of an arrow. With its emphatic downward thrust, the arrow can be read simultaneously as a sign of direction and a symbol of creative energy.

The multiplicity of meaning inherent in Klee's visual and verbal symbols parallels the simultaneous perceptions and trains of thought that are often operative in conversation and that Apollinaire attempted to capture in his verbal collage of names and images. In creating his conversational collage, Apollinaire simulated an overheard conversation by juxtaposing disjointed fragments of conversation with abrupt shifts of time, place and points of view ("Tu soulèveras le rideau / Et maintenant voilà que s'ouvre la fenêtre / Araignées quand les mains tissaient la lumière"). Klee's *Composition with Windows* is likewise characterized by disjunctive semantic units and shifts in perspective that imply simultaneity of space and time. One example is the juxtaposition of the arrow to three sketchily defined windows, each placed at different angles to the picture surface and in different spatial planes. As in conversational discourse, these seemingly unrelated semantic units acquire coherency in the context of shared meanings understood by the participants. Like the reader of Apollinaire's poem, the viewer of Klee's picture actively participates in the making of meaning, and repetition plays an important role in this process.

In "Les Fenêtres" Apollinaire consciously adapted the repetitive rhythms that are fundamental to the coherent organization of conversational speech.

Despite his use of irregular metric patterns, he established internal unity through the rhythmic repetition of sounds (the double vowel 'ou'), words (fenêtre) and lines ("Du rouge au vert tout le jaune se meurt"). While retaining the poetic convention of sequential lines of text, Apollinaire grouped words into repetitive patterns that are vertically as well as horizontally aligned ("Puits / Puits.../ Puits"). These vertical repetitions plot a path of visual movement that competes with the expectation that words be read in linear, sequential order. Similarly, the surface pattern of the grid imposed on Klee's *Composition with Windows* challenges the conventions of reading a painting that conforms to the mimetic tradition. The grid of Klee's painting is defined by black lines that reinforce intersecting planes of color and by a superimposed network of skeletal white lines that delineate what Joseph Koerner has called "transparent *signs*" of windows (74) – not traditionally placed architectural motifs or openings through which the viewer can see recognizable objects, but clusters of multivalent signs in which structure and symbol are inextricably linked. Recent research in the field of discourse analysis indicates that repetitive patterns of visual imagery are primary carriers of meaning in conversational exchanges (Tannen, *Talking Voices* 2-3, 135). The same is true of the repetitive window imagery in Apollinaire's "Les Fenêtres" and Klee's *Composition with Windows.*

Like the linguistic symbols with which they are grouped, Klee's windows are open to multiple levels of connotative meaning. They call forth the analogy between the window and a work of art and the metaphor of the eye as a window onto the artist's soul, both of which originated with Leonardo da Vinci and were echoed by Delaunay in his paintings and writings.[9] Klee's windows are also memory images of prior representations of windows, among them Delaunay's window series and Apollinaire's conversation poem. In addition to the windows and the arrow, Klee's constellation of signs includes plant forms in bulbous states of beginning. Just as Apollinaire's seemingly unconnected verbal images collectively relate to the concept of creation,[10] so too do Klee's pictorial images. In combination with the linguistic symbols in *Composition with Windows,* they relate more specifically to the creation of a pictorial vocabulary and syntax that owed as much to new forms of poetry as to innovations in painting.

Visual and verbal modes of representation and comprehension function simultaneously in Klee's new pictorial language. This complex relationship was one outcome of the extended exchange of ideas and images that is condensed in *Composition with Windows.* As a reinvention of Delaunay's window theme, the painting is an homage to the contemporary painter whose works prompted Klee to explore his own alternatives to the conventional codes of representation that assume iconic connections between pictorial signs and their external referents. Completed in the year after Apollinaire's death, the painting can also be read as an elegy to the critic who championed Delaunay's art and the poet who unwittingly provided Klee with a linguistic model for "a poetic kind of painting".

Notes

1 For comprehensive studies of Klee's debt to Delaunay, see Jordan 45-63 and 171 as well as Kagan 54-80.

2 For a color reproduction of *Inner Architecture*, see *Paul Klee, Das Frühwerk* 410.

3 I extend thanks to the scholars attending the Third International Congress of Word and Image, Ottawa, August, 1993, who participated in the interpretation of Klee's linguistic symbols.

4 Klee's drawing for Plate VI corresponds to the line "Berlin dagegen unsere Hochburg buchte jähe Verzehnfachung seiner Bürger". It is reproduced in Glaesemer 270.

5 See Antliff 341-49. The concept of simultaneity is placed in a broader context in Kern, *The Culture of Time and Space.*

6 For Marc's comparison, see Lankheit, 19; for Klee's more oblique analogy, see review in *Die Alpen*, quoted in Jordan, *Klee and Cubism,* 60.

7 For a color reproduction of *Fugue in Red*, see *Klee et la musique* 103.

8 The comparative analysis makes use of research by Deborah Tannen; see *Conversational Style* and *Talking Voices.*

9 See Leonardo da Vinci, *Traité de la Peinture* and Delaunay's notes on this edition in *Du Cubisme à l'art abstrait,* 174-75.

10 See the commentary on "Les Fenêtres" by eds. Anne Greet and S.I. Lockerbie in Guillaume Apollinaire, *Calligrammes,* 349-55.

References

Antliff, Mark. "Bergson and Cubism: A Reassessment". *Art Journal,* 47 (1988): 341-49.

Apollinaire, Guillaume. "La Peinture Moderne", in *Oeuvres complètes de Guillaume Apollinaire,* IV, ed. M Décaudin (Paris: André Balland et Jacques Lecat, 1965-66) 282.

-----. *Les Peintres Cubistes.* Paris: Eugène Figuière & Cie, 1913.

Delaunay, Robert. "La Lumière", in *Du Cubisme à l'art abstrait,* ed. Pierre Francastel. Paris: S.E.V.P.E.N, 1957.

Glaesemer, Jürgen. *Paul Klee, Handzeichnungen, I.* Bern: Kunstmuseum, 1973.

Greet, Anne and S.I. Lockerbie. Guillaume Apollinaire, *Calligrammes, Poems of War and Peace, 1913-16* . Los Angeles: University of California Press, 1980.

Jordan, Jim. *Paul Klee and Cubism.* Princeton: Princeton University Press, 1984.

Kagen, Andrew. *Paul Klee / Art and Music.* Ithaca: Cornell University Press, 1983. 54-80.

Kern, Stephen. *The Culture of Time and Space, 1880-1918.* Cambridge: Harvard University Press, 1983.

Klee, Paul. *Das Frühwerk, 1883-1922.* München: Städtische Galerie im Lenbachhaus, 1979.

-----. "Die Ausstellung des Modernen Bundes im Kunsthaus Zürich", *Die Alpen* VII (August, 1912), translated in Jim Jordan, *Paul Klee and Cubism.* Princeton: Princeton University Press, 1984.

-----. *The Diaries of Paul Klee, 1898-1918,* ed. Felix Klee. Berkeley: University of California Press, 1964.

-----. *Klee et la musique.* Paris: Musée national d'art moderne, 1985.

Koerner, Joseph Leo. "Paul Klee and the Image of the Book", in *Paul Klee, Legends of the Sign.* New York: Columbia University Press, 1991.

Leonardo da Vinci, *Traité de la Peinture.* Paris: Librarie Ch. Delagrave, 1910.

Lankheit, Klaus. *Unteilbares Sein, Aquarelle und Zeichnungen von Franz Marc.* Köln: M. DuMont Schauberg, 1959.

Tannen, Deborah. *Conversational Style: Analyzing Talk among Friends.* Norwood, NJ: Ablex Publishing Corporation, 1984.

-----. *Talking Voices: Repetition, Dialogue, and Imagery in Conversational Discourse.* Cambridge: Cambridge University Press, 1984.

Vriesen, Gustav and Max Imdahl. *Robert Delaunay: Light and Color,* trans. Maria Pelikan. New York: H. N. Abrams, 1967.

Semiotics, Painting, and Poetry

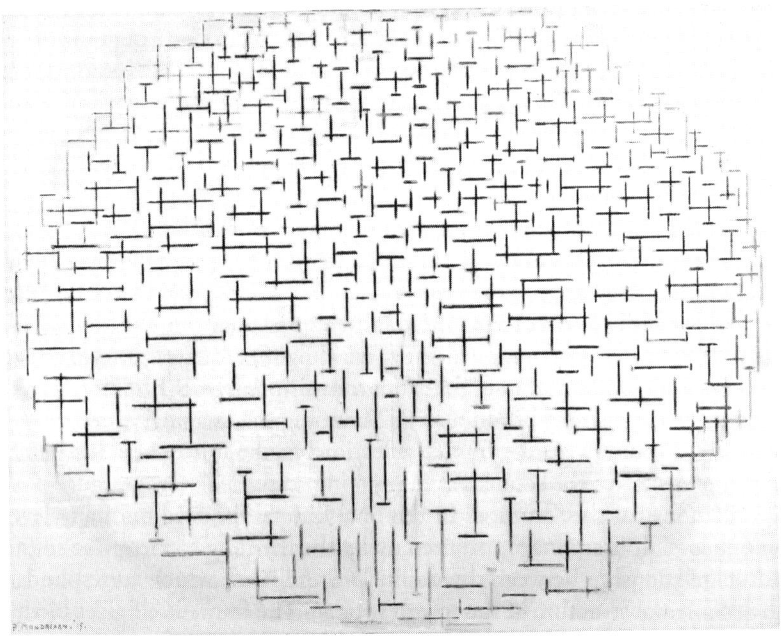

Figure 2. Piet Mondrian (1872-1944), *Compositie no. 10 (Pier and Ocean).* 1915. 85 x 108 cm, Otterlo, Holland: Stichting Kröller-Müller Museum.

textual and imaginary. The image of the "septuor" embodies firstness insofar as it is a pure quality emanating from the words of the sonnet, which cannot be separated from them in the reader's consciousness. However, it also involves secondness in that there is an existential connection between this image and the real, individual characteristics of the words in the sonnet. It embodies thirdness since it is part of the linguistic code, and presupposes a reader with knowledge of this code.[4]

I shall now turn to a painting by Mondrian, *Composition 10 (Pier and Ocean),* 1915 (fig. 2). This is a Mondrian which hovers between figuration and abstraction and which problematizes description of its content in terms of familiar "objects". There are no resemblances between the pictorial sign and its objects in terms of imitation of colour, texture, volume etc. We cannot look at the picture and actually "see" a picture of a pier surrounded by sea. As in the Mallarmé sonnet, the only colours we perceive are black on white. However, our attention is focussed, not on the individual lines, but rather on the relationships between them, which themselves construct the imaginary "objects".

In the lower part of the painting, long vertical lines dominate in the centre, whereas to the sides, there are more horizontal lines and they are more spread out. This gives a sense of pressure emanating from the vertical lines and dispersing the lines to the sides. As one's gaze moves upwards to the middle of the picture and just beyond, the horizontal elements predominate, halting the vertical upward movement and creating a sense of stasis. Beyond this again, the balance between horizontal and vertical evens out, producing a sense of equilibrium. Moreover, the lines here are much shorter and more compact than they are at the bottom, and the oval contour formed by the configuration of lines is cut off far more obviously at the top. This creates a sense that the image is moving both upwards and into the distance, beyond the space enclosed by the frame. The harmonious equilibrium of vertical and horizontal itself recedes into the distance, emphasizing its intangibility and suggesting also its location in a future time and space.

In comparison with a figurative painting, there is relatively less emphasis here on firstness in terms of similarity to a known object. Although the subtitle, "Pier and Ocean", provides a cue and a clue to recognizable objects, the content of the picture can be derived only through direct visual experience of the relations between the pictorial elements as presented in this particular painting. Here, as in the Mallarmé sonnet, content is constituted by the receiver's imaginative engagement with the "forms of relation" embodied in the medium itself. This engagement brings into play elements of firstness, secondness and thirdness. Again, the merging of sign and imaginary object in the consciousness of the receiver involves firstness; the dependence of the object on specific, irreducible characteristics of the pictorial signs constitutes secondness, and the indispensable role of the receiver in discovering the rules or principles of interpretation introduces an element of thirdness. Moreover, although the mode of apprehension is visual, the content evoked by these relations itself exceeds the purely visual, such as the suggestion of invisible space beyond the frame, future time, and rhythm.

Because the objects of diagrams, which are predominantly iconic, are embodied in their form, we can learn from studying this form, which is not the case with symbols. Peirce values the capacity of icons to "reveal unexpected truth" (2.279). However, diagrammatic signs can suggest general, intangible properties, such as dynamism and infinity, which, like symbols, invite the receiver to "create abstractions" (4.531). The objects constructed by the receiver from diagrams, which are pure possibilities, introduce new elements not contained in the data.

For Peirce, who does not believe in an unintelligible Kantian "thing in itself", there is no conflict between beauty and logic, and the objects of icons must be logically possible (4.532). For Kant, however, aesthetical ideas surpass logical concepts and definitions. He admires poetic forms of expression which do not simply refer to a concept, but which "express the consequences bound up with it and its relationship to other concepts" and which "stimulate the

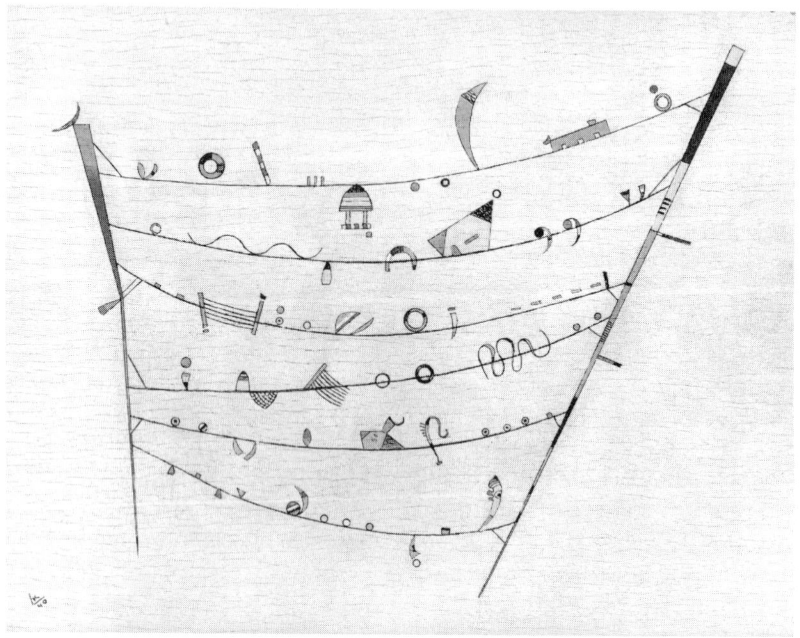

Figure 3. Wassily Kandinsky (1866-1944), *Study for "Petits accents"*. 1940. Ink on paper, 15.9 x 21.7 cm. New York, Solomon R. Guggenheim Museum. © ADAGP, Paris and DACS, London 1997. Photograph: Robert E. Mates.

imagination, so that it thinks more by their aid ... than could be comprehended in a concept and therefore in a definite form of words" (section 49, 159). Like the Peircean diagram, the crux of the Kantian aesthetical idea is its innovatory capacity. According to Kant, it is the function of the highest forms of artistic expression, "whether in speech or painting or statuary" to "disclose a new rule that could not have been inferred from any preceding principles or examples (161).

Like the diagram and the aesthetical idea, the Sartrean "schéma" is situated between image and sign, between imagination and abstract thought. Sartre disapproves of allowing consciousness to identify itself with the spatial schema (220 and 225). Thought must not allow itself to become a "captive" of the "schéma", which could lead it astray by compelling it to think in terms of spatial analogies. However, it is precisely this phenomenon, where "la pensée se constitue elle-même comme chose" (219), which underlies semiotic interactions in painting and poetry, where consciousness identifies closely with the form of the medium itself. This identification stimulates a kind of thinking based on imagination rather than on abstract, conceptual thought.

As pointed out above, a characteristic of indices can be to perform the role

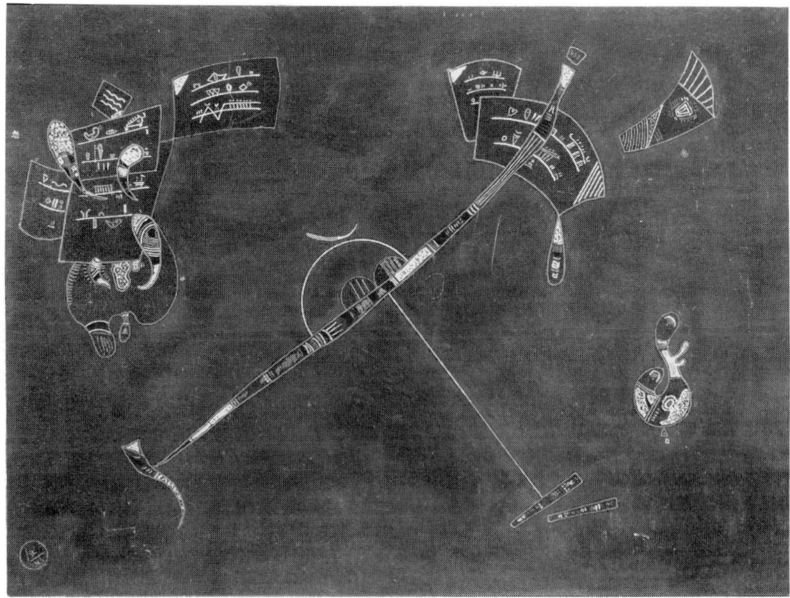

Figure 4. Wassily Kandinsky, *Le milieu sombre.* 1943. Mixed media on cardboard, 42 x 58 cm. Galerie Beyeler, Basel, Switzerland. © ADAGP, Paris and DACS, London 1997.

of strongly compelling the attention of the receiver to the object. Where the object does not have a separate existence from the sign, but consists in the consciousness the receiver has of it (firstness), indexical elements which draw the receiver's attention to this relationship introduce a metadiscursive level which causes imagining activity itself to become reflexive. The receiver's awareness of the "otherness" of the sign, its exteriority to consciousness, involves an element of secondness, but also thirdness in that imagination here becomes reflexive and represents itself to itself in the sign.[5] Reflexivity, then, itself contributes to the semiotic/ontological complexity of the sign, and the consciousness of the receiver is an indispensable element of this process.

In painting, the question arises here of the dependence of the visual image on verbal language in constructing a metapictorial level. Early abstract painters who aimed to increase the autonomy of pictorial language often found that they became dependent on words in formulating interpretative "codes". Kandinsky ultimately decided that it was impossible to construct pictorial "rules" equivalent to grammar.[6] I am not the first to point out (cf. Thürlemann 17-18) that apparently "figurative" elements in Kandinsky's late painting can perform the function of "commentaries" within the pictures themselves. These elements, which induce in the spectator reflexive awareness of the picture as its own object, perform an "indexical" function. In his late work, Kandinsky is sufficiently confident of the autonomy of his pictorial "language" to return to using what might be thought of as "figurative" elements, involving both anthropomorphic and biomorphic "figures", as in *Accord réciproque,* 1942 (see Roethel and Benjamin, 1125). These pseudo-figures are frequently involved in activities of see-sawing, balancing, perching etc. (See, for instance, study for *Petits accents,* 1940 [fig. 3], *Parties diverses,* 1940 [Roethel and Benjamin, 1110], and *Balancement,* 1942 [Roethel and Benjamin, 1124]). The fact that they have strongly organic characteristics and appear to be pictorial "beings" living their own mysterious lives, which involve various kinds of movement, draws the spectator's attention to the function of imagination itself in animating and dynamizing the pictorial elements. In several cases, they resemble hieroglyphs (e.g. *Le milieu sombre,* 1943, fig. 4), pointing to their own function of providing metapictorial "commentaries", while at the same time parodying the concept of decipherable codes and indicating the untranslatability of the pictorial "language".

In conclusion, then, poetry and painting can maximise their semiotic potential without imitating another form, by combining different modes of signifying within their own medium. This combination can usefully be conceptualized in terms of "diagrammatic" interaction between the Peircean icon, index and symbol, involving the categories of firstness, secondness and thirdness.

Notes

1 The work of A. J. Greimas, for instance, has inspired analyses of both words and images which aspire to a quasi-scientific objectivity. For an example of this approach applied to Kandinsky's painting, see J.-M. Floch.

2 Peirce distinguishes between the dynamical object, which is "really efficient but not immediately present", and the immediate object, which is "the object as the sign represents it" (C. S. Peirce, vol. 8, section 343). Hereafter references to this text will give volume number followed by section number. (Peirce makes extensive use of upper case letters, which I have changed throughout to lower case.)

3 Peirce does distinguish between these categories, and creates further subdivisions of signs based on them. See 2.250 ff. and 8.335 ff.

4 This is not of course intended to be an exhaustive account of the ways in which this sonnet involves Peircean categories: I am merely pointing to the most salient features.

5 Peirce describes "pure self-consciousness" (which, unlike the present example, would comprise no exterior element) as a "degenerate thirdness", where "we conceive a mere quality of feeling, or firstness, to represent itself to itself as representation" (5.71).

6 In 1943, he wrote that he still believed in the existence of laws underlying "l'exactitude de la forme réalisatrice du contenu pictural", but that "nous ne les connaissons pas et, je crois, nous ne les connaîtrons jamais". Cited in Derouet, 97.

References

Apollinaire, Guillaume. "Paysage". *Calligrammes. Poèmes de la paix et de la guerre (1913-1916).* Paris: Gallimard, 1925. 27.

Floch, Jean-Marie. "Kandinsky: sémiotique d'un discours plastique non figuratif". *Communications* 34 (1981): 135-57.

Kant, Immanuel. *Critique of Judgment.* Trans. J. H. Bernard. London: Collier Macmillan, 1951.

Mallarmé, Stéphane. "Ses purs ongles". *Œuvres complètes,* eds. Henri Mondor and G. Jean-Aubry. Bibliothèque de la Pléiade. Paris: Gallimard, 1945. 68-9.

Peirce, C.S. *Collected Papers of Charles Sanders Peirce.* 8 vols. Ed. C. Hartshorne and P. Weiss, vols. 1-6; A.W. Burks, vols. 7-8. Cambridge, MA: Harvard University Press, 1931-1958.

Sartre, Jean-Paul. *L'imaginaire.* Paris: Gallimard, 1940.

Derouet, Christian. "Notes et documents sur les dernières années du peintre Vassily Kandinsky". *Paris-Paris 1937-1957.* Special number. *Cahiers Musée National d'Art Moderne* (1982): 84-107.

Roethel, Hans K., and Jean K. Benjamin. *Kandinsky: Catalogue Raisonné of the Oil Paintings. Vol. II, 1916-1944.* London: Sotheby, 1984.

Thürlemann, Felix. "Le figuratif au service de l'abstrait". *Collection les grandes expositions, Vassily Kandinsky.* Paris: Beaux Arts Magazine, 1985. 17-18.

Visual Literature and Semiotic Conventions

Eric Vos

INTERMEDIALITY AND REPRESENTATION

The use of visual means of representation in a literary context is of course not restricted to 20th century avant garde literature, as the age old traditions of the *carmen figuratum* and other "poems in the shape of things" demonstrate (Ernst, *Carmen Figuratum,* Higgins, *Pattern Poetry*).[1] Still, it is safe to say that contemporary experimental writing has produced an unprecedented wealth of types and subtypes of such word/image hybrids, or "visual literature".[2] I can only give a few examples here. Visual poetry (Byrum & Hill) and its various regional offsprings aim at synthesizing a multiplicity of sign structures (verbal and visual ones) into a symbiotic whole.[3] Brazilian poet Philadelpho Menezes, for instance, composes a multi-symbolic statement out of a chewing gum logo, a typographically disguised ideological icon, and anagrammatic puns (fig. 1).

Figure 1. Philadelpho Menezes, [untitled], from Menezes, *Poetics and Visuality,* 183.

In concrete poetry (Vos, McCullough), for instance Heinz Gappmayr's poem discussed *infra,* as well as in visual prose (Ernst, "Typen"), typography is often used to create a field of spatial relationships that supplements or replaces conventional morphologic, syntactic, or narrative structures. In other cases, texts are presented as three-dimensional objects (cf. figure 2) or as environments in which we can enter, whether physically or, in our age of cyberspace, virtually (Weiss, Kac). Semiotic poems (Menezes 63 ff.) are usually series of combina-

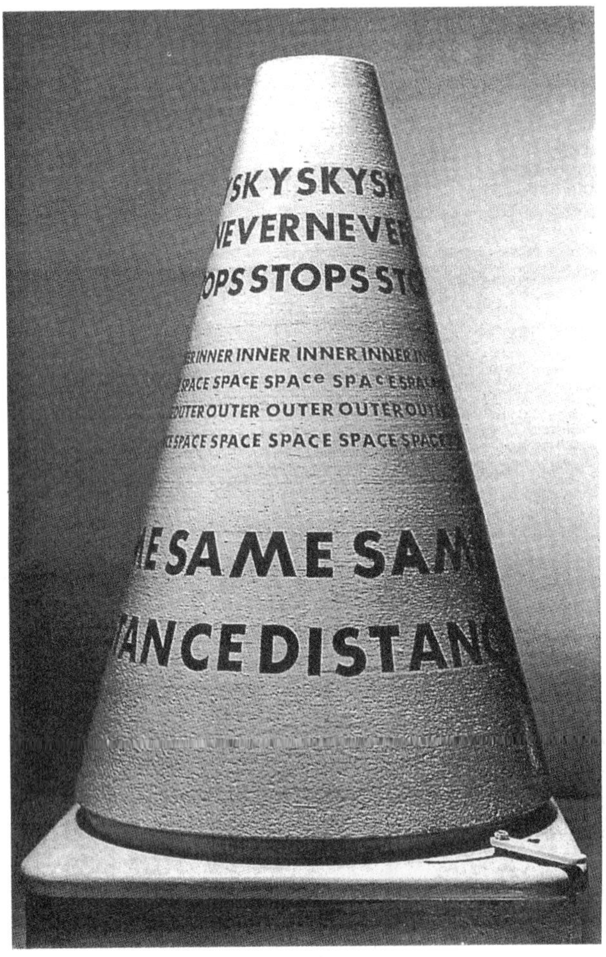

Figure 2. Liliane Lijn, "Poem Kon", from Expo/Internacional de Novísima Poesia/69, [n. p.].

tions and permutations of random graphic symbols, which are semantically charged through their assignment to a "lexical key". In found poetry, like Bern Porter's (cf. *infra*), any piece of "ready-made" communicative material can be employed. Many literary artists' books explore possibilities of using physical aspects of the book, for instance various printing and binding techniques, as text-structural means (Smith, Lyons). And so on.

All these types of works share one important characteristic. Their aesthetic status and function in some way or another rests upon a *fusion* of semiotic features and procedures that, according to habit, belong to separate sign systems or art forms. In particular, this fusion challenges fundamental conventions of both literature and the visual arts, as it questions their established status as distinct, even mutually exclusive media. That is why visual literature is commonly considered to be an *intermedial* art form, something "in between" literature and the visual arts or at least transgressing (purported) boundaries between the two.[4]

Although meanwhile quite established, this intermedial approach to visual literature is not without pitfalls. Anyone who claims that visual literature overcomes or erases borderlines between literature and the visual arts uses the notions of "literature" and "the visual arts" (and possibly also associated concepts such as "text" and "picture") in the habitual manner, and of course we cannot have it both ways. That is to say, we cannot hope to successfully define and analyse visual literature in terms of aesthetic and medial categories that are based on precisely those semiotic conventions that visual literature is simultaneously supposed to challenge or even overrule. We have yet to ascertain to what extent accepted views on aesthetic and medial types can be upheld with regard to the peculiarities of visual literature and used to chart the latter's domain. This will remain an open question as long as the intermedial perspective on visual literature is not supplemented with a thorough discussion of its own semiotic presuppositions. Especially if the interrelation between the verbal and the visual in visual literature is to be regarded as a matter of semiotic integration rather than mere juxtaposition (and this is the commonly accepted opinion, often based on Dick Higgins's meanwhile classic distinction between intermedia and mixed media), it is crucial to ask what semiotic considerations may support such a notion of integration.[5]

The obvious starting point in answering that question is the shared representational status of verbal and visual signs. This, on first sight, may already appear to provide us with a basis to discuss the integration of the verbal and the visual in visual literature. Let me briefly summarize a familiar course of such a discussion. Regarding both verbal and visual representation as primarily a matter of unilateral reference from sign to referent, that is: denotation, the most salient and distinctive feature of visual representation *vis à vis* its verbal counterpart is usually thought to be its reliance on properties self-instantiated by the denoting sign and in some way or another shared with the denoted referent. Visual literature would then be the result of implementing this so-called "iconic" quality of visual representation in a verbal, literary context. All sorts of procedures could be involved here, ranging from simple typographic manipulations to complex, high tech means of verbal-visual communication, including video, holography, and hypermedia (Kac, Lanham). But specifying these procedures is not my present concern. What counts is the thesis that through them, visual literature integrates a self-motivated, hence

before our eyes, so to speak. Gappmayr's work requires the willingness of the recipient to *reconstruct* an inscription of the verbal symbol "licht", that is: to reconstruct language. If the recipient decides to do so, (s)he has procured the means to make sense of the typographic peculiarities of the work. For instance, the individual fragments can now be conceived as particles of "licht" – not the thing, but the word. This notion of "particle" can be easily linked with the *denotatum* of the work's verbal content. I will return later to the question of what semiotic procedures are involved here. At this point, I want to stress two issues that seem particularly important to me. First, I do not believe that there is any sound basis for the claim that the individual marks of Gappmayr's work are visual icons of light particles (the latter now taken as *realia*). They are simply letter fragments; integral parts of the medium of printed texts. We are dealing here with a semiotic and, in extension thereof, aesthetic *functionalization* of a practice to which we are totally accustomed and hence usually disregard in our dealing with that medium, namely the composition of letters out of component parts. Second, at no point does this functionalization lead us out of the verbal framework. On the contrary, it directs our attention *towards* the basics of verbal symbolization, in this case the composition of a lexeme. I submit that this orientation towards the principles, procedures, practices, and conventions of what we habitually consider to be verbal, literary communication is a fundamental feature of visual literature.

Of course there is a difference between the verbal and the literary. Commenting on Goodman's opinions, Claus Clüver (60) has stressed that we should not overlook the difference in semiotic level between a first order system such as a natural language and a second order system such as literature.[9] In Gappmayr's case, the orientation seems to be mainly towards the first order level. In other cases, visual literature is targeted at both first and second order conventions, or even foremost at second order ones. Bern Porter's work (see figure 4 for a specimen) provides a good example of the latter.

Contrary to Gappmayr's text, Porter's visual book *Sweet End* (1989) confronts us with a variety of symbol systems. We recognize unequivocally verbal and numerical inscriptions, but also unequivocally pictorial, pictographic, diagrammatic and ornamental ones. The pages of the book are filled with collages of all sorts of "printed matter", which is just about the only overall classification in terms of media that seems to fit. But of course, this does not explain in which way, if at all, a semiotic integration of all those various signs is accomplished.

Sweet End centres around the theme of death. Many pages of the book are filled with obituaries and death notices, condolence cards, even suicide notes, or fragments of texts on war and military equipment, the dangers of nuclear power and nuclear warfare, starvation, epidemics, cancer, and so on. On other pages we find pictures of and advertisements for hand guns, jet and helicopter fighters, bullets, missiles, funeral homes; we see combat scenes, target graphs, death masks, etcetera. Are all these icons of death? On yet other pages, some of Porter's familiar materials return. For instance fragments from catalogues, whereby some catalogued products can be easily linked with the theme of death (for example guns or tombstones), others not (for example women's garments, hardware, and print supplies). Or we find lists, endless lists of all sorts of listable things; again, some clearly related to death (for example a list of "deceased members" and a list of "safari licences"), others not (for example random fragments from telephone directories and yellow pages or book indices). And we find a large quantity of forms – letter templates, questionnaires, registration and application forms, receipts, announcements, bulk mail. Once more, some of these can be easily connected with the theme of death, particularly questionnaires concerning life insurance. The many tax forms in the book could be linked with military budget and government spending on the war industry (rather than education and health care). But the majority of these forms seems disconnected from the overall theme of death: order forms from bookstores and printers, dozens of sweepstake announcements and reply forms, bank coupons, entry forms and standardized rejection letters from art foundations, and so on. How are we to make sense of this collection of printed matter?

The first step towards an answer to this question lies in recognizing the importance of the arrangement of the book. A careful reading of the book reveals – or, if one prefers, suggests – a pattern. The various elements of the book are presented in series of repetition, and it is only through their place in these series that *all* the individual signs acquire a shared semiotic function. This function amounts to highlighting the patterns of parallelism that constitute the arrangement of the book and that, following all theories of poetic parallelism grounded in Jakobson's pivotal account, create semantic relationships between the elements with which they are filled.[10] It is this typically literary, prosodic, second order convention to which Porter's work first directs our attention and which then serves as a basis for further interpretation.

Notwithstanding all obvious differences between Gappmayr's and Porter's work, this indicates that in both cases one and the same semiotic procedure underlies the integration of the verbal and the visual. In both cases, that is, we are dealing not with a unilateral referential relationship from sign to referent that we could call iconicity, but with a bi- or even trilateral relationship from the sign to some concept that in turn both refers back to a characteristic of the sign in question and leads us toward contemplating conventions of verbal and literary communication. As said earlier, the latter is in my opinion the quintessence of visual *literature.*

Nelson Goodman offers the term "exemplification" to describe the semiotic procedure at stake here. Three crucial points must now be stressed. First,

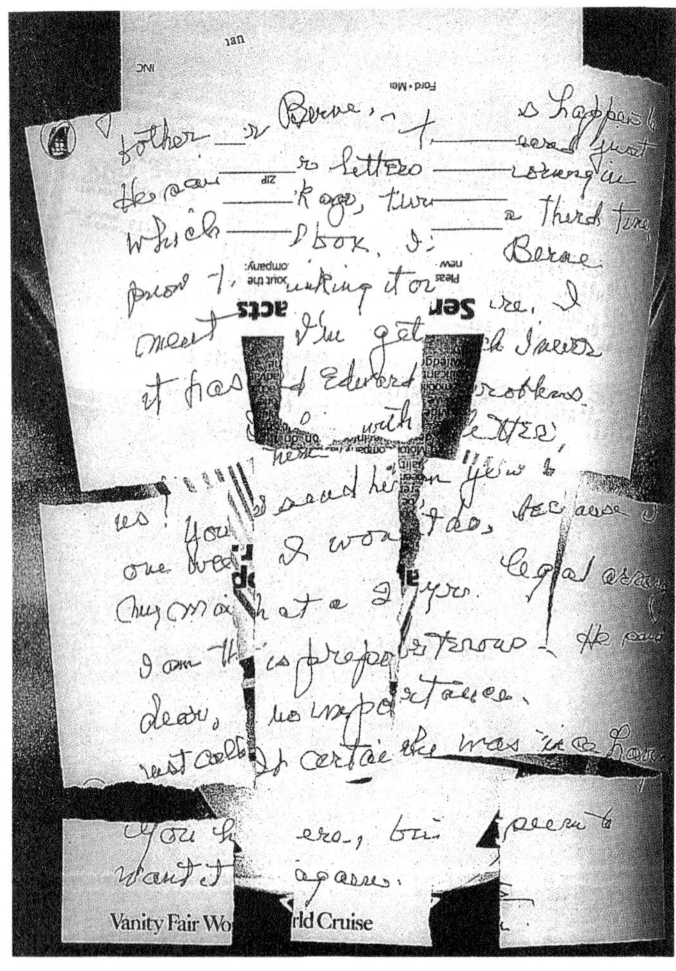

Figure 4a. Bern Porter, "Sweet End" [Fragment], from Porter, *Sweet End* [n. p.].

Figure 4b. Bern Porter, "Sweet End" [Fragment], from Porter, *Sweet End* [n. p.].

acquiring an exemplificative function does not in the least imply that a symbol would lose its ordinary denotative function, which is based on its classification as a symbol of a particular kind. Rather, these two are combined in a pattern of complex reference, without resulting in any semiotic contradiction. In the case of Gappmayr's concrete poem, for instance, it might very well be our knowledge of the denotative value of the word "licht" that gives rise to our exemplificative interpretation of the visual shape of the work in terms of "particles", which can in turn be reconnected with the *denotatum* of "licht" as well as with lexical graphematics and morphology. Second, the exemplificative elements of this referential complex are the prime factors of the work's aesthetic status and function. Evidently, every printed text instantiates some visual, typographic shape. In Gappmayr's case, it is the exemplificative employment of this typographic shape that results in *visual* literature; not the instantiation of any pictorial signs, which the work does not contain at all. Third, exemplification and complex reference are totally unconcerned with boundaries between media and art forms. As exemplifying symbols, verbal and visual signs function in exactly the same way. This and only this is what allows us to speak of semiotic integration of the verbal and the visual in the case of Porter's *Sweet End*. We no longer need to envisage this integration as some mysterious transformation of verbal and visual signs into either each other or some third, lying "in between" them. Hence we can evade the logical contradiction of synthesizing the articulate and the dense. As denotative symbols, iconic or not, the signs out of which this work is composed remain classified in different symbol systems. Their semiotic integration rests upon their shared exemplificative function, their shared stress on the prosodic pattern that they create. The complex of these denotative and exemplificative functions, highlighting "death" as well as "parallelism", may then, for instance, bring to mind notions like "litany" and "elegy", which in turn would provide for a point of view from which militarization and administrative control can be linked with fashion, mass communication, sweepstakes, and even the art institutes.

Let me, in conclusion, summarize the three main points I have tried to make:

1. The habitual argument concerning visual literature, starting off with the iconic properties that the works appear to adopt from the realm of the visual arts, should be rethought. It is not the mere instantiation of visual features or properties that counts in visual literature. As the Gappmayr example shows, such features need not even differentiate visual literature from other printed texts. What counts in visual literature is how these features acquire a *semiotic function*. If visual literature generates a relationship between media and art forms at all, it is because of this functionalization, not because of some transfer of properties.

2. This functionalization involves a referential complex in which specific exemplificative functions interact with ordinary semiotic classifications and denotative functions. The *orientation* of this referential complex is most important. It directs our attention towards the principles and procedures of verbal and literary communication. The impetus to reconsider such principles and procedures may well be the most important *literary* function of visual literature.

3. Exemplification and complex reference are semiotic procedures which are as common to literature as they are to the visual arts, and in fact as common to ordinary language as they are to non-artistic visual symbol systems. This means that we no longer need to adhere to a notion of "transgressing boundaries between arts or media" in order to explain semiotic peculiarities of visual literature – and good riddance to it, since that notion is totally unclear.

Notes

1 Far from pretending to give a complete overview, the references in this paragraph are solely intended as aids in finding a few recent documentations of the mentioned genres; further references can be found there.

2 See Richard Kostelanetz and Peter Mayer for discussions of "visual literature" as a critical term. In German, "visuelle Dichtung" is often used to cover not just visual poetry but also visual prose and/or mixed forms; e.g. by Dieter Kessler (195 f.) and Siegfried J. Schmidt (99). Ferdinand Kriwet uses "visual literature" as an English translation of his term *Seh-Texte*, which is also employed in the comprehensive sense outlined here by Christina Weiss.

3 See Harry Polkinhorn for a recent documentation of specific regional tendencies of visual poetry in various Latin American and South European Countries.

4 Dick Higgins (*Horizons*) develops his account of intermedial art forms, including visual literature, on the basis of Hans-Georg Gadamer's theory of "horizons of expectations" and the fusion thereof. Higgins claims that the latter is required in the case of intermedia precisely *because of* their departure from established conventions.

5 See Higgins (*Horizons*, 24 and *passim*) for elaborations of the distinction between intermedial fusion and mixed medial juxtaposition. Opinions similar to Higgins' are expressed by, e. g., Weiss (8 and *passim*), and A. Kibedi Varga (37f.).

6 See Nelson Goodman (*Languages of Art, Ways of Worldmaking*). For a summary of Goodman's views, and an account of their implications for a theory of concrete poetry, see Eric Vos.

7 To refute this crucially important theorem would not only be at odds with all non-essentialist philosophies of our times (which is a position I, for one, would not care to adopt), but also with a bulk of semiotic evidence. See for that evidence Goodman (*Languages*, 225-231 and *Ways*, 125-137), and also, for instance, Jonathan Culler (40 ff.), Umberto Eco (14 ff.), and John Deely (33-49).

8 This is what characterizes a non-essentialist semiotics. Many theories of visual literature, on the contrary, implicitly adhere to an essentialistic notion of "given properties", as they usually hypostatize the existence and presence of iconic qualities of the works in question and proceed their account of the semiotic function of visual literature on the basis thereof.

9 In fact, Goodman's confrontation of the verbal and the pictorial could be interpreted as a case of overlooking this difference. As a symbol system, painting includes conventions that are far more like the second order ones of literature than the first order ones of language (for instance regarding dramatic composition, pictorial narrative, *clair-obscur*, etc.). According to Clüver, one of the major differences between painting and literature is that the pictorial means of painting (colour, shape) do not constitute a symbol system by themselves, whereas the verbal means of literature (natural languages) do.

10 See Bradford (esp. 42-73) for the most recent and extensive survey of Jakobson's work on parallelism and the poetic function.

References

Bradford, Richard. *Roman Jakobson. Life, Language, Art.* London: Routledge, 1994.

Byrum, John & Crag Hill, eds. *CORE. A Symposium on Contemporary Visual Poetry.* Mentor/OH & Mill Valley/CA: Generatorscore Press, 1993.

Clüver, Claus. "On Intersemiotic Transposition". *Poetics Today* 10 (1989): 55-90.

Culler, Jonathan. *The Pursuit of Signs.* London & Henley: Routledge & Kegan Paul, 1981.

Deely, John. *Basics of Semiotics.* Bloomington: Indiana University Press, 1990.

Eco, Umberto. *Semiotics and the Philosophy of Language.* Bloomington: Indiana University Press, 1984.

Ernst, Ulrich. *Carmen Figuratum. Geschichte des Figurengedichts von den antiken Ursprüngen bis zum Anfang des Mittelalters.* Köln etc.: Böhlau Verlag, 1991.

-----. "Typen des experimentellen Romans in der europäischen und amerikanischen Gegenwartsliteratur". *Arcadia. Zeitschrift für vergleichende Literaturwissenschaft* 27 (1992): 225-320.

Expo/Internacional de Novísima Poesia/69. Buenos Aires: Centro de Artes Visuales/Instituto Torcuato Di Tella, 1969.

Gappmayr, Heinz. *texte.* München: Ottenhausen Verlag, 1978.

Goodman, Nelson. *Languages of Art.* Indianapolis: Hackett, 1976.

-----. *Ways of Worldmaking.* Indianapolis: Hackett, 1978.

Higgins, Dick. *Horizons. The Poetics and Theory of the Intermedia.* Carbondale and Edwardsville: Southern Illinois University Press, 1984.

-----. *Pattern Poetry. Guide to an Unknown Literature.* Albany/NY: State University of New York Press, 1987.

Kac, Eduardo. *Holopoetry. Essays, Manifestoes, Critical and Theoretical Writings.* Lexington/KY: New Media Editions, 1995.

Kessler, Dieter. *Untersuchungen zur konkreten Dichtung.* Meisenheim am Glan: Hain, 1974.

Kostelanetz, Richard, ed. *Visual Literature Criticism. A New Collection.* Carbondale and Edwardsville: Southern Illinois University Press, 1979.

Kriwet, Ferdinand. *Decomposition of the Literary Unit.* Richmond: Nova Broadcast, 1971.

Lanham, Richard. *The Electronic Word. Democracy, Technology, and the Arts.* Chicago: University of Chicago Press, 1993.

Lyons, Joan, ed. *Artists' Book. A Critical Anthology and Sourcebook.* Rochester/NY: Visual Studies Workshop Press [1985], 1993.

Mayer, Peter. "Some Remarks Concerning the Classification of the Visual in Literature". *Dada/Surrealism* 12 (1983): 5-13.

McCullough, Kathleen. *Concrete Poetry. An Annotated International Bibliography with an Index of Poets and Poems.* Troy/NY: Whitston Publishing, 1989.

Menezes, Philadelpho. *Poetics and Visuality. A Trajectory of Contemporary Brazilian Poetry.* San Diego: San Diego State University Press, 1995.

Polkinhorn, Harry, ed. "Visual Poetry. An International Anthology". *Visible Language* 27 (1993) [special issue].

Porter, Bern. *Sweet End.* Brunswick/ME: The Dog Ear Press, 1989.

Schmidt, Siegfried J. *Elemente einer Textpoetik.* München: BSV, 1974.

Smith, Keith A. *The Structure of the Visual Book.* Rochester/NY: K. Smith Books [1984], 1994.

Varga, A. Kibedi. "Criteria for Describing Word-and-Image Relations". *Poetics Today* 10 (1989): 31-53.

Vos, Eric. *Concrete Poetry as a Test Case for a Nominalistic Semiotics of Verbal Art.* Diss. University of Amsterdam, 1992.

Weiss, Christina. *Seh-Texte. Zur Erweiterung des Textbegriffes in konkreten und nach-konkreten visuellen Texten.* Zirndorf: Verlag für moderne Kunst, 1984.

L'espace-temps dans la poésie sémiotique

Francis Edeline

1. Origine et histoire

Parmi les nombreuses formes inventées par les poètes concrets, dans cette période extraordinairement créative où l'impulsion était donnée par des artistes brésiliens dans la revue *Invenção*, il faut faire une place spéciale au *poème sémiotique*. Celui-ci fut introduit et défini par L.-A. Pinto et D. Pignatari dans un texte-manifeste de décembre 1964, suivi de sept exemples proposés par les mêmes ainsi que par R. Azeredo.

On ne peut pas dire que ce genre ait fait fureur ailleurs qu'au Brésil : on ne peut guère en recueillir qu'une poignée dans le domaine anglophone et, ailleurs, il semble purement et simplement ignoré. Il pose néanmoins des problèmes théoriques délicats et intéressants, et a peu été étudié jusqu'ici.

A part des citations du manifeste dans diverses anthologies, on trouvera un excellent paragraphe d'analyse dans Beiman (1974), une douzaine de lignes chez Clüver (1982), ainsi qu'un chapitre dans *Poesia de Vanguarda no Brazil* de Mendonça (1970).

Mentionnons également l'important ouvrage, réédité, de Wlademir Dias-Pino (1973), à la fois anthologie et manifeste, qui présente et systématise le *poème-processus* (PP), héritier direct du *poème sémiotique* (PS), ainsi que d'autres formes dérivées telles le poème-matrice, le poème-animation, le poème signalétique ....

La présente étude s'intéresse aux deux formes, qui ont beaucoup en commun et traduisent une évolution logique. Le corpus des PS doit s'élever à quelques dizaines d'oeuvres alors que celui des PP en compte plusieurs centaines. Toute étude sérieuse doit en effet envisager aussi la deuxième vague, ainsi que les productions non brésiliennes, et non juger un peu vite, comme Clüver, que la pratique du PS fut "soon abandoned".

De même le PS et le PP ne sortent pas de rien. Il existait déjà, au sein de la poésie concrète, des poèmes-processus, montrant les phases successives d'une transformation mais avec des moyens exclusivement linguistiques (fig. 1)

Hiršal les nommait "developers" et les consacrait au passage progressif d'un mot à sa traduction dans une autre langue, par exemple LASKA-LIEBE

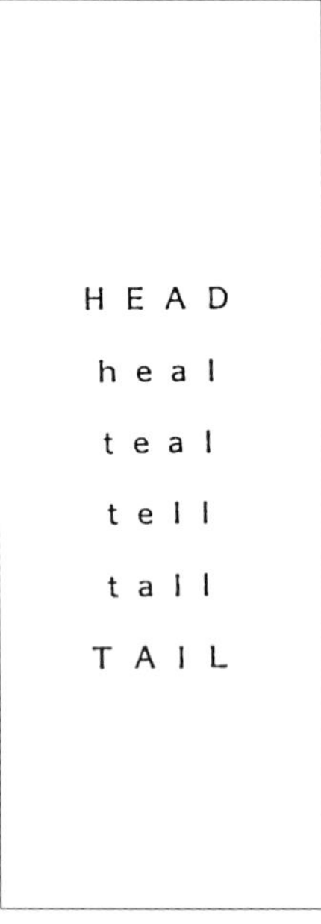

Figure 1a. Lewis Carroll (1879).

w o m b

f o a m

w a r m

d o m e

r o o m

h o m e

d o o m

l o a m

t o m b

Figure 1b. Andrew Belsey.

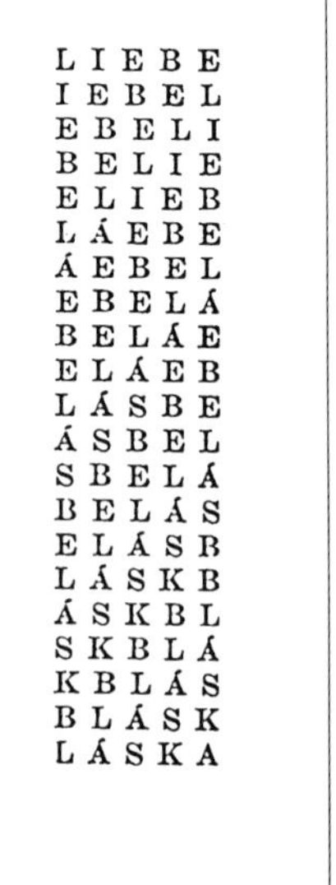

L I E B E
I E B E L
E B E L I
B E L I E
E L I E B
L Á E B E
Á E B E L
E B E L Á
B E L Á E
E L Á E B
L Á S B E
Á S B E L
S B E L Á
B E L Á S
E L Á S B
L Á S K B
Á S K B L
S K B L Á
K B L Á S
B L Á S K
L Á S K A

Figure 1c. Josef Hiršal et Bohumila Grögerová.

SENSE SOUND
SONSE SEUND
SOUSE SENND
SOUNE SENSD
SOUND SENSE

Figure 1d. Emmett Williams (1954-55).

(Amour) ou SVOBODA-FREEDOM (Liberté). Le caractère arbitraire de la transformation, sur le plan du signifié, rendait ces textes peu convaincants. Emmett Williams obtenait un résultat plus intéressant en permutant par paires les lettres de SENSE et de SOUND.

Remontant plus haut encore on trouve le jeu des Doublets proposé par L. Carroll en 1879. Il s'agissait toujours de passer d'un mot à un autre (et le jeu était plus piquant s'il s'agissait de contraires) en changeant une lettre à la fois, en utilisant exclusivement des mots du dictionnaire, et en un nombre minimum d'étapes.

Arbitraires, immotivées, artificielles, ces transitions n'en effectuent pas moins ce que fait toute poésie: réaliser au plan du signifiant une médiation impossible au plan du signifié.

2. Definition

Le manifeste de Pinto et Pignatari débute par un exposé des linéaments de la théorie des signes selon Peirce et Morris. On sait que Pignatari enseigne ces matières, et fut en fréquents rapports avec le théoricien de Stuttgart, Max Bense, lui-même Peircien inconditionnel.

Il retient de ces théories qu'il est possible de concevoir des signes qui seraient partiellement arbitraires et partiellement analogiques (c'est-à-dire ressemblant à la chose à laquelle ils renvoient). De même un système de signes (par exemple le langage) est caractérisé par des relations syntaxiques (entre signes), sémantiques (entre signe et référent) et pragmatiques (entre les signes et leur utilisateur).

Tout système de signes est conçu dès le départ, et souvent évolue par la suite, en vue de rendre aisé un type déterminé de communication. Les systèmes sont donc plus ou moins spécialisés, et aucun d'eux n'est général au point de donner entière satisfaction dans tous les domaines.

Les deux auteurs déclarent que les poètes sont depuis toujours des inventeurs de langages, et suggèrent de rendre plus radicale encore cette fonction en leur proposant de forger de nouveaux ensembles de signes (visuels, auditifs, ...) ainsi que de nouvelles règles syntaxiques et sémantiques s'y appliquant. En particulier, il s'agit de spatialiser l'écriture poétique et de se débarrasser entièrement du caractère linéaire du langage parlé et écrit. La poésie concrète avait déjà fait un pas important dans cette direction en se rendant consciente de "l'espace graphique" mais s'était trouvée aussitôt fort limitée dans les possibilités de "superposition" et d'"interprétation" des signes.

Le poème sémiotique cherche à reculer ces limites en créant un petit répertoire ou dictionnaire de deux ou trois signes (rarement davantage), et en construisant une séquence d'agencements entre ces signes. Les inventeurs invoquent une parenté marquée avec les idéogrammes chinois où subsiste généralement en effet une liaison non-arbitraire ou non-phonique entre le signe et son référent. De même la formation de signes complexes à partir d'idéogrammes élémentaires y est bien connue et manifeste une sorte de syntaxe ou de morphologie analogique. Dans les poèmes sémiotiques le dictionnaire est toujours donné, sous forme de "chave léxica", mais les règles de syntaxe demeurent implicites.

Les auteurs du manifeste précisent bien que les signes employés sont "partiellement arbitraires et partiellement analogiques", ce qui sera confirmé plus loin; c'est donc erronément que Clüver les décrit comme des "formes visuelles auxquelles on donne une charge sémantique arbitraire à l'aide d'une clé lexicale". Pour Clüver, c'est cette nécessité d'une constante traduction intersémiotique qui s'est révélée un obstacle et une limitation de nature à entraîner l'abandon du PS. Pourtant, pendant près de dix ans ont continué au Brésil expositions et parutions manifestant l'évolution lente du PS vers le PP.

Le poème-processus pour sa part se présente de façon identique au PS sinon que la clé lexicale est absente. Généralement le PP a un titre alors que le PS n'en a pas. Les auteurs fournissent volontiers par ailleurs un petit commentaire explicatif qui accompagne leurs oeuvres.

Cette description en termes généraux fait penser d'abord au lettrisme et au calligramme. Or il s'agit de tout autre chose, comme le tableau I le montre, ainsi que la figure 2 où on donne un exemple de chaque catégorie. Le lecteur pourra revenir au tableau I en fin de lecture, et vérifier l'exactitude des distinctions présentées.

3. Analyse

3.1. La clé lexicale

Le PS se présente comme un texte composite à deux zones. L'une est une "chave léxica" ou "lexical key" qui est une sorte de glossaire très réduit où deux ou plusieurs petites figures graphiques sont disposées en colonne, avec en vis-à-vis leur équivalent linguistique tel que décidé par l'auteur. C'est la seule zone linguistique de l'oeuvre, celle-ci n'ayant, sauf rares exceptions, pas de titre autre que "Poème sémiotique".

La seconde zone, qui constitue l'oeuvre proprement dite, ne met plus en oeuvre que les graphismes, toujours très simples et géométriques, à base de lignes, de carrés, de triangles et de cercles le plus souvent. Ce n'est que dans des oeuvres plus tardives qu'on trouve des graphismes figuratifs (comme le coeur) ou des symboles connus par ailleurs (comme les signes ♂ et ♀).

Figure 2a. Poème lettriste
(Roland Sabatier, 1966).

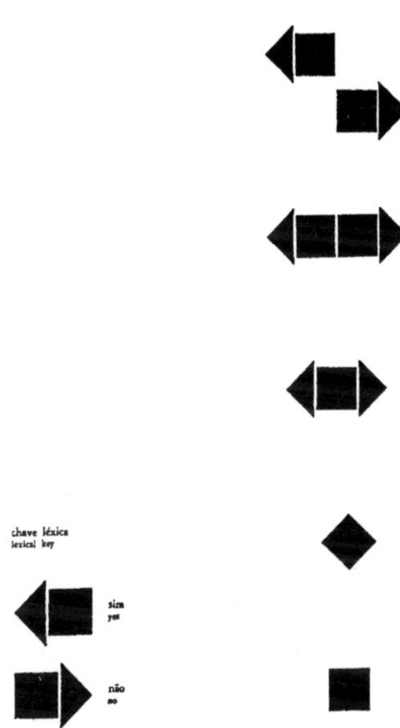

Figure 2c. Poème sémiotique
(Luiz Angelo Pinto).

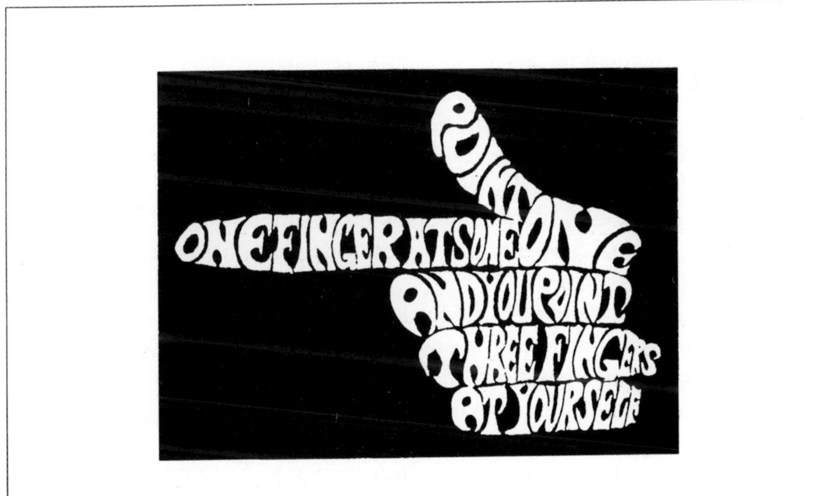

Figure 2b. Calligramme du type "compact" (Peter Mayer, 1968).

Dans leur version la plus simple, les clés lexicales se composent d'un seul couple d'opposés, par exemple oui/non, sommeil/veille, terre/mer, etc.

La clé lexicale constitue un code élémentaire, dont on nous donne le répertoire complet, et qui permet de passer conventionnellement du mode linguistique (concepts sémantiques) au mode graphique. L'opération constitutive du processus que présente le poème s'exécute exclusivement par des transformations graphiques, et le texte s'arrête là. Néanmoins il est implicite que la transposition inverse est possible et que l'opération démontrée graphiquement est censée être possible aussi sémantiquement.

De même on peut dire que la clé lexicale a imprégné les formes graphiques d'un sens conventionnel, et que cette interaction entre les deux codes reste active dans toute l'oeuvre, dont le parcours de lecture est transformé par l'imprégnation et est tout autre chose que l'observation de graphismes vides se transformant ou se combinant.

Par ailleurs l'homologation des figures aux concepts est facile à accepter car les figures sont en quelque sorte "motivées". Ainsi les oppositions polaires comme oui/non ou sommeil/veille sont mises en correspondance respectivement avec deux flèches opposées, et avec la paire carré noir/carré blanc. La clé lexicale permet une resémantisation immédiate, et le lecteur ne ressent généralement pas les figures comme arbitraires. Dans l'exemple précédent le carré noir est accepté comme représentation de la nuit, donc par métonymie du sommeil, et inversement pour le carré blanc. Dans le poème amusant de Furnival un triangle pointé en haut représente un gars, un cercle représente une fille, et une série de lignes verticales serrées un champ de seigle. Sans la clé lexicale, l'équivalence ne peut être découverte, mais une fois la clé donnée elle est acceptée sans difficulté (fig. 3).

Linguistiquement les clés lexicales sont des paradigmes, mais leur brièveté fait apparaître, presque violemment, le système d'oppositions qui est constitutif de toute sémantique. On peut dresser une statistique des clés lexicales, relever celles qui comportent une opposition à deux termes, à trois termes, ou des structures plus complexes. La moitié est franchement binaire, et dans cette moitié encore plus de 50 % sont basées sur une négation (par exemple rationnel/irrationnel). Le reste présente des oppositions plus ou moins polaires (par exemple terre/mer).

La synthèse de ces opposés "irréductibles" est difficile à opérer par les moyens de la rhétorique linguistique. L'opérateur de négation est sans doute celui qui résiste le mieux aux pressions de la *coïncidentia oppositorum*. La poésie sémiotique mise explicitement sur l'absence de négation dans l'image pour tenter visuellement des synthèses difficiles. On pourrait dire que sous ce rapport, la poésie sémiotique est un continuel oxymore. Si comme le soutient le Groupe μ (1977), le but des manoeuvres rhétoriques en poésie est de suspendre les distinctions et d'amorcer un mouvement régressif vers l'indistinction

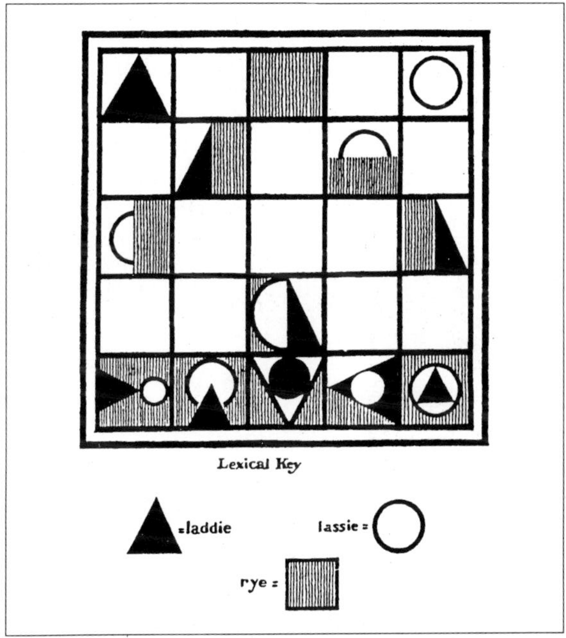

Figure 3. John Furnival, "Semiotic Folk Poem".

générale, alors le PS fournit un moyen particulièrement puissant pour s'attaquer à des oppositions de contenu que les moyens traditionnels (la métaphore particulièrement) étaient contraints de laisser intactes.

Une analyse plus méticuleuse des paires ou des triades de termes montre qu'ils peuvent occuper toutes les positions dans le carré sémiotique, et comportent donc des contraires, des contradictoires et des complémentaires.

Les figures graphiques ne sont pas sans analogie avec des idéogrammes mais, étant décrétés par l'auteur pour la seule durée de l'oeuvre, ce sont des idéogrammes "mous": ils peuvent être déformés, combinés, tronqués selon les besoins, au contraire des signes convenus constituant les alphabets usuels, lesquels sont l'objet de résistances voire de tabous quant à leur mutilation.

Ils représentent également la face signifiante d'un signe dont la face signifiée est donnée (linguistiquement) par un concept. Ce sont au départ des unités purement distinctives, mais nous verrons que le déroulement du processus en fait, via la motivation initiale et la resémantisation mentionnée plus haut, des unités significatives.

3.2. La discrétisation

A très peu d'exceptions près, le PS comme le PP montrent un processus, c'est-à-dire une transformation se déroulant dans le temps. Or l'image est essentiellement statique et ne permet la représentation du temps que par des conventions. La convention ici adoptée est inspirée de la chronosyntaxe du langage écrit, c'est-à-dire la linéarité et ses variantes, la bande dessinée étant une autre référence évidente. En ce sens la prétention de Pignatari et Pinto d'échapper totalement à la linéarité se révèle une illusion.

Le texte possédera donc un point de départ, à partir duquel il se déroulera linéairement. Il peut également être bilinéaire lorsque du point de départ divergent deux séries linéaires. Il peut théoriquement adopter d'autres dispositions telles que la convergence (fig. 4), où deux points de départ distincts mènent à une arrivée commune. Le plus souvent la progression s'effectue de haut en bas (fig. 5).

Pour que la suggestion du temps soit efficace, il faut découper l'action et montrer plusieurs de ses états successifs. Le nombre d'étapes est crucial dans cette discrétisation du temps. Les étapes peuvent correspondre à des pauses logiques, ou être simplement équidistantes.

Si on compte le nombre d'instantanés dans le processus (en incluant le point de départ) on trouve le plus souvent 5 mais la fourchette des valeurs s'étend de 4 à 12 (et même 35). Cinq serait un optimum d'efficacité perceptive : en deçà on court le risque de ne pas faire apparaître clairement le processus, et au-delà on engendre la redondance et l'ennui.

Dans ces oeuvres curieuses on doit constater que l'information n'est pas entièrement contenue dans les images individuelles, mais au moins autant dans la transition entre images. Ces transitions n'étant pas manifestées, le mécanisme implique des comparaisons deux à deux, et la détection des variants et des invariants par le lecteur.

L'accumulation des transitions finit par joindre l'état initial à l'état final qui, s'ils sont comparés directement, semblent généralement incompatibles : le poème-processus en a accompli la médiation par des opérations plastiques qui seront examinées au § 3.4. Une minorité de cas ne discrétise pas son contenu et ne joue pas sur le temps : ce sont des images statiques (fig. 6), des images de structure, ce sont des PS mais non des PP.

3.3. La dimension d'espace

Certaines oeuvres sont bidimensionnelles et ajoutent à la dimension temporelle (généralement verticale et de haut en bas) une dimension spatiale horizontale (fig. 3). Les oeuvres qualifiées ci-dessus de statiques utilisent bien entendu les deux dimensions de la page de façon spatiale.

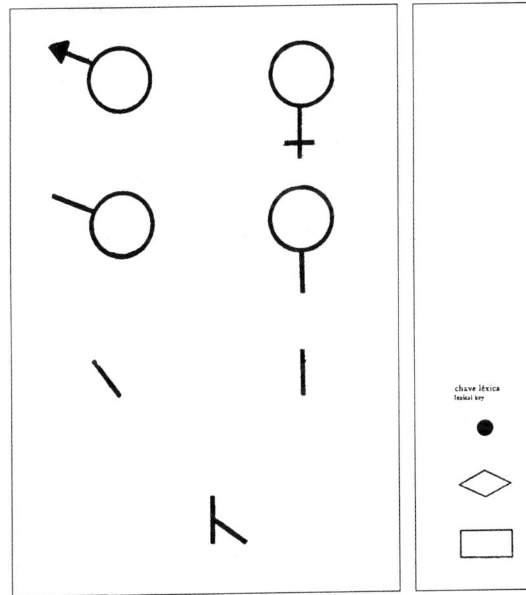

Figure 4. Neide Sà.

Figure 5. Décio Pignatari.

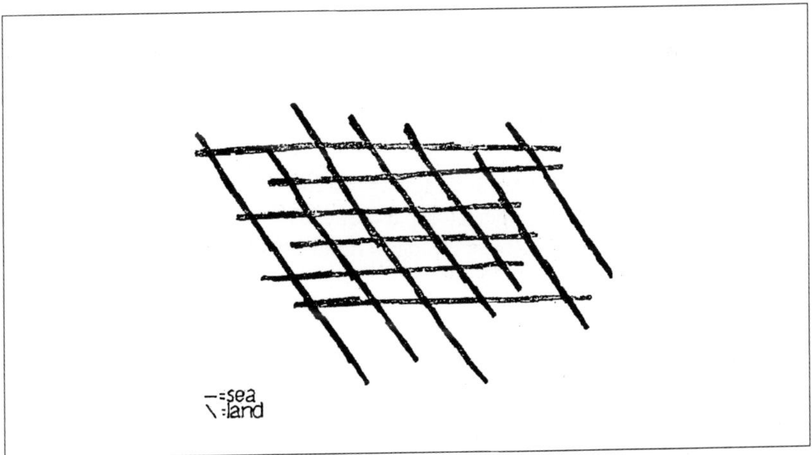

Figure 6. Ian Hamilton Finlay.

Figure 7. Luiz Angelo Pinto.

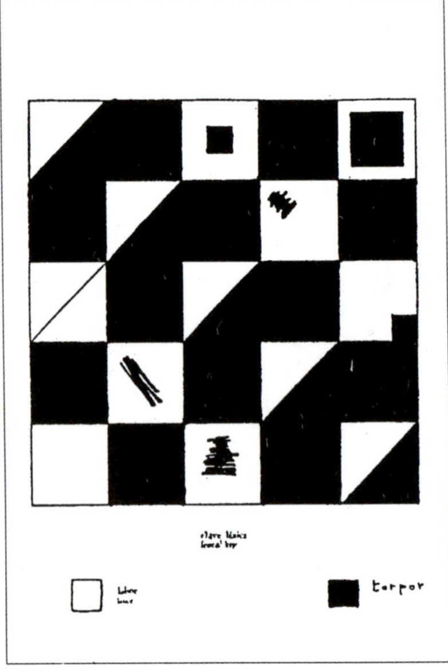

Figure 8. Ronaldo Azeredo.

A y regarder de près les images individuelles sont elles-mêmes spatiales, surtout selon l'horizontale (fig. 7), et alors de façon continue. Le cas extrême (fig. 8) est donné par des oeuvres où même cette dimension spatiale est discrétisée, formant alors une matrice 5 x 5. Apparemment le lecteur découvre lui-même sans difficulté la double convention spatio-temporelle.

3.4. Les opérations formelles

Le passage d'un état du processus au suivant est identifiable à partir des éléments communs invariants et de l'opération par laquelle une caractéristique des entités a été modifiée. L'inventaire en est rapidement fait car elles sont peu nombreuses:

- -rotation angulaire (fig. 9)
- -translation avec tangence ou intersection (fig. 10)
- -permutation (fig. 3)
- -zoom (fig. 11) dans les deux sens
- -superposition (fig. 5)
- -troncature (fig. 4)

La plupart de ces opérations sont continues et doivent donc, lors de la discrétisation, être tronçonnées arbitrairement. La médiation obtenue est du type narratif si l'on se réfère aux distinctions du Groupe μ dans son *Traité du signe visuel* (1992):

-médiation rhétorique (substitution pure et simple)

-médiation narrative (transition séquentielle)

-médiation par synthèse (fusion des caractères)

-médiation topologique (juxtaposition ou concentricité).

Il ne faudrait cependant pas croire qu'il s'agit toujours de démonstrations géométriques rigides et rigoureuses. Elles obéissent souvent à la fantaisie et à l'impulsion, ménageant des surprises de parcours et des intermédiaires inattendus (fig. 5). Néanmoins pour l'essentiel les opérations se sont trouvées programmées dès l'instant que la clé lexicale, par homologation, a transféré les propriétés sémantiques de l'ordre linguistique à l'ordre plastique. Non seulement les entités sont ainsi resémantisées directement, mais toutes leurs relations positionnelles et toutes leurs transformations le sont indirectement.

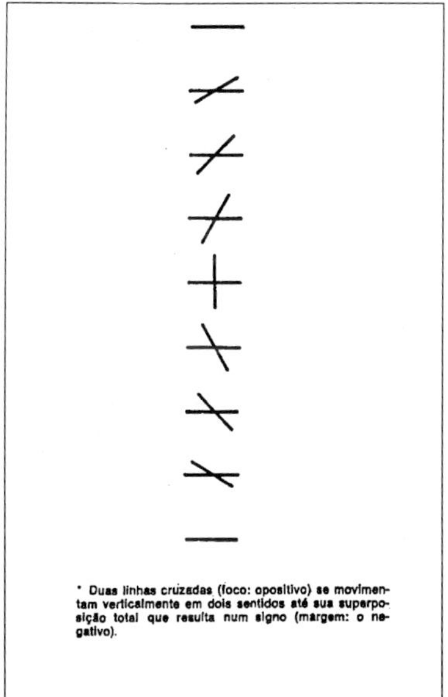

* Duas linhas cruzadas (foco: opositivo) se movimentam verticalmente em dois sentidos até sua superposição total que resulta num signo (margem: o negativo).

Figure 9. Neide Sà.

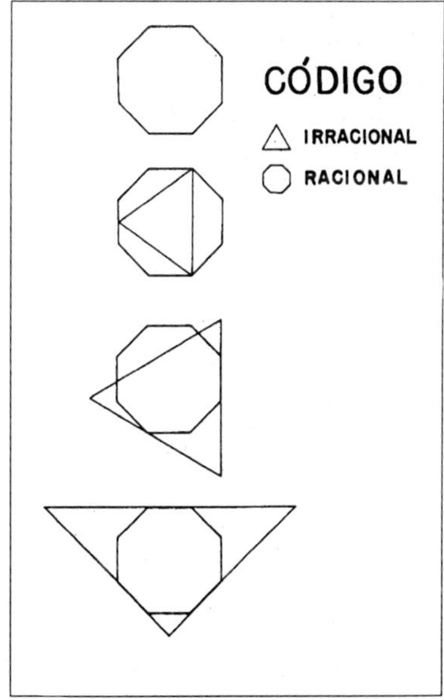

Figure 10. Jurema Brandão.

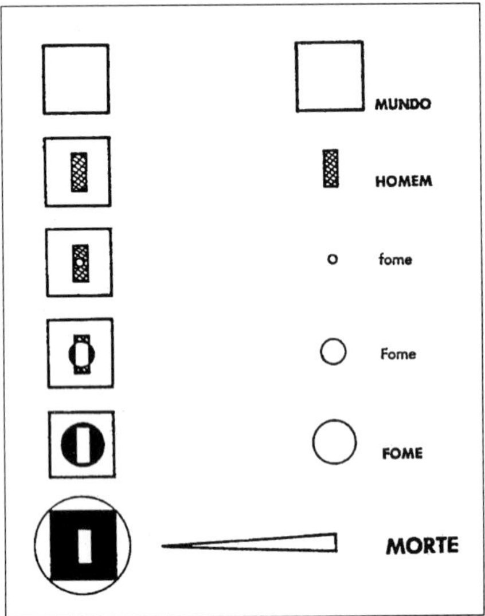

Figure 11. José de Arimathéa.

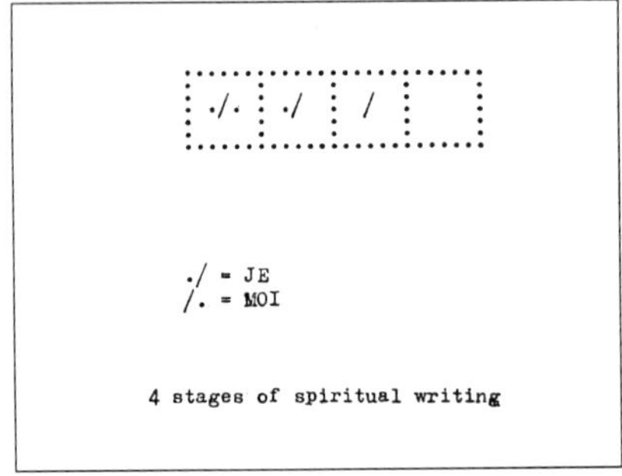

Figure 12. Dom Sylvester Houédard.

3.5. Les thèmes

La formule "médiation plastique d'un couple d'opposés" rend compte de la quasi totalité des PS et des PP, mais les opposés choisis et les implications du processus permettent cependant de spécifier cette formule selon des thèmes plus ou moins généralement fréquentés.

Les thèmes abordés sont étonnamment abstraits :

- logico-philosophiques :	la négation, la contradiction, le rationnel et l'irrationnel, le je et le moi (fig. 12), le positif et le négatif ...
- socio-politiques :	la communication, la faim dans le monde, la civilisation de la TV, ...
- mythico-symboliques :	la table et la croix, la constitution formelle du monde (terre et mer), les 3 règnes, ...
- érotiques :	les sexes, le sommeil et la veille, ...

4. Évolution et postérité

4.1. La couleur, la polysémie

Parmi toutes les oeuvres rassemblées pour notre corpus ne figure qu'un seul exemple en couleurs : c'est sea/land de Ian Hamilton Finlay (fig. 6). Il s'agit d'un PS statique où un réseau de 6 lignes horizontales bleues représente la mer et un réseau de 7 lignes obliques brunes représente la terre. Les traits sont comme hésitants. L'oeuvre fonctionne directement, mais sa signification est renforcée intertextuellement si on se souvient d'un cadran solaire ancien de Finlay où les lignes horaires et les lignes de date sont indexées de la même façon, et si on se rappelle la phrase de son *Table Talk: A Selection* (1981): "Land and Sea are the Warp and Woof of the World".

La couleur offre donc des possibilités quasi inexploitées, surtout si on considère, dans le cas examiné, que la couleur n'est pas encore essentielle à la constitution du sens.

E. M. De Melo E Castro est un poète portugais écrivant dans la foulée des promoteurs du PP. Outre les nombreux PP qu'il a produits lui-même dans *Concepto incerto* (1974), il a suggéré le poème-quasi-infini sous la forme d'un jeu de pièces géométriques colorées.

C'est le lecteur-joueur qui en choisit un assortiment, et attribue à chaque forme et à chaque couleur une signification simple. Il les dispose alors sur la table en construisant toute structure de son choix, après quoi il "lit" le poème ainsi composé, à partir de la clé lexicale qu'il a lui-même établie.

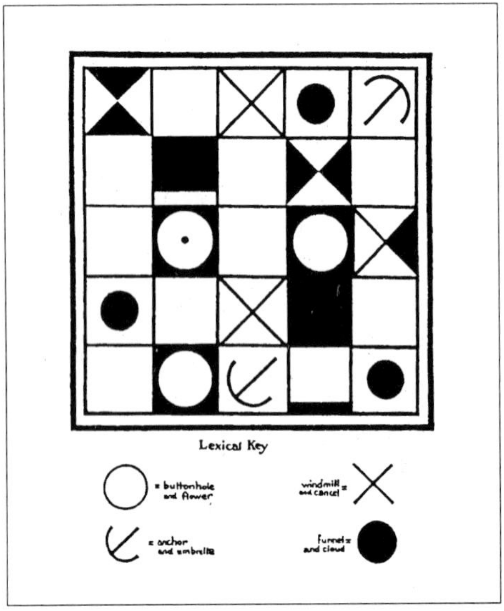

Figure 13. Ian Hamilton Finlay, "Semi-idiotic poem".

Dans un exemple souvent cité et très ironique (fig. 13), le même Finlay dédouble sa clé lexicale et installe la polysémie au coeur même du système. On a 4 signes qui sont des synonymes plastiques : le cercle blanc vaut pour "boutonnière" ou "fleur", la croix vaut pour "moulin" ou "supprimer", un petit dessin formé d'une oblique et d'un demi-cercle vaut pour "ancre" ou "parapluie", un cercle noir vaut pour "cheminée" ou "nuage". Dans un exemple ancien, L.A. Pinto proposait déjà une ambivalence minéral/végétal et végétal/animal.

4.2. Suppression de la clé

L'expansion et le succès de la formule PP montre que la clé lexicale n'est pas (toujours) indispensable. La polysémie des unités graphiques, la participation active et experte du lecteur, l'expérience d'autres codes graphiques (surtout celui de la BD), permettent de s'en passer. Je donnerai deux seuls exemples de ce que peut donner un PP sans clé.

Le premier est dû à José de Arimathéa (fig. 14) et suggère en 6 étapes la progression historique inverse de l'indice et du symbole (au sens peircien), soit de l'empreinte digitale et du code linguistique. Non seulement le réel est désormais saisi de façon médiatisée, mais l'identification de ce réel ne comporte plus aucun contact avec lui (comme dans l'empreinte) et s'effectue au contraire par un système de conventions arbitraires alors que, selon la très belle formule de Bense, "il est dans la nature des indices de ne pas tout garder pour soi-même."

Le second est illustré par n'importe quelle oeuvre du recueil *12 x 9* d'Alvaro de Sà, basé entièrement sur les conventions de la BD. Dans une suite de cases

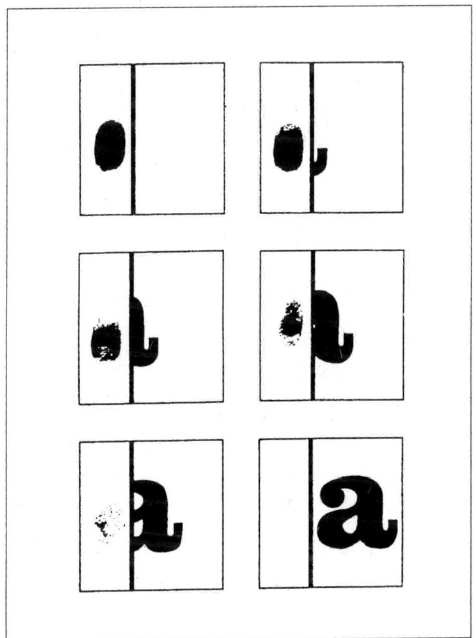

Figure 14. José de Arimathéa.

(dimension temporelle) on fait usage de la convention qui relie le ballon au locuteur par une flèche continue s'il s'agit d'un discours réel, ou interrompue s'il s'agit d'une pensée non exprimée. De nombreuses variations sont proposées sur ce thème, qui fondamentalement établit deux zones tout comme la clé lexicale : une zone d'image et une zone de texte (réel ou mental). Les figures 15 et 16 montrent par exemple un cas de renvois enchâssés locuteurs-discours, et un cas de dialogue symbolique où le discours prononcé s'abrège de 5 à 1 unité, puis est remplacé par un discours mental de plus en plus dense de 1 à 5 unités.

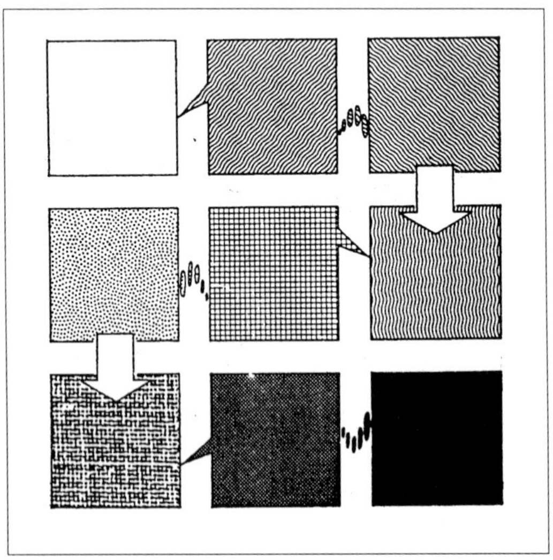

Figure 15. Álvaro de Sà.

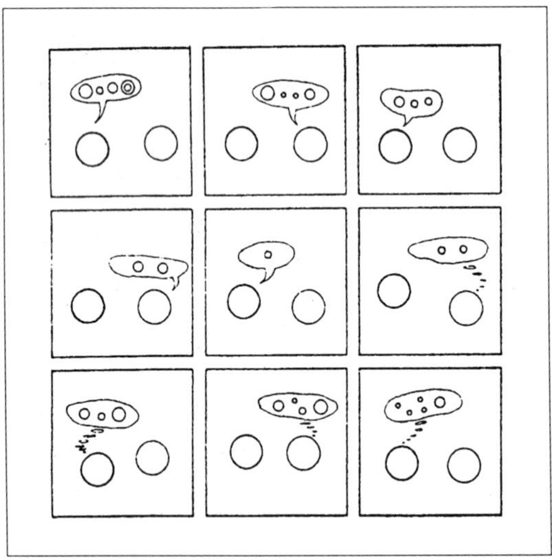

Figure 16. Álvaro de Sà.

5. Conclusions

Leur haut niveau d'abstraction nous indique que PS et PP sont moins des jeux ou des prouesses graphiques qu'une tentative nouvelle de résoudre l'éternel problème des contradictions, abordé par tous les types de poésie, du surréalisme au symbolisme, du Parnasse aux calligrammes et aux poèmes concrets.

Plus encore, la méthode rhétorique employée ici pour apporter une solution à ce problème, insoluble par le moyen d'une fiction régressive, se présente en même temps et avant tout comme une méditation sur la notion de code. Le code, comme possibilité de sauter d'un système à un autre pour exécuter plus facilement certaines opérations (passer des choses aux mots, passer des mots aux images, ... comme on passe des nombres aux logarithmes, ...), est ici employé avec d'importantes conditions restrictives, soulignées tout au long de cette étude :

-répertoire réduit à deux ou trois entités en structure oppositive;

-entités signifiantes "molles", c'est-à-dire déformables;

-manoeuvres plastiques, mais atteignant indirectement le signifié;

-règles syntaxiques et narratives non explicitées.

En fait le processus dont il est question se déroule selon l'imagination visuelle de l'auteur et du lecteur. Nous sommes ici à la racine même de la notion de code, comme le montrait avec force le poème de José de Arimathéa (fig. 14).

Vus sous cet angle général le PS et le PP, son successeur, élaborent une sémantique sauvage fondée sur l'imagination visuelle, douée d'une très grande rigueur locale et *ad hoc,* mais dénuée de la généralité d'un projet scientifique tel celui de Pottier ou de Greimas.

La parenté est cependant frappante entre un *axe sémantique* (voire un carré sémiotique ou même un parcours génératif, selon Greimas, et un poème sémiotique selon Pinto ou Furnival, et force à réexaminer l'intervention du visuel dans une démarche aussi abstraite que celle de Greimas.

Si d'autre part on évalue cette poésie à partir de l'image visuelle plutôt que du texte, on la rattachera tout d'abord à l'art abstrait. Et on s'apercevra qu'elle réussit, grâce au dispositif de codage que constitue la clé lexicale, à resémantiser l'art abstrait.

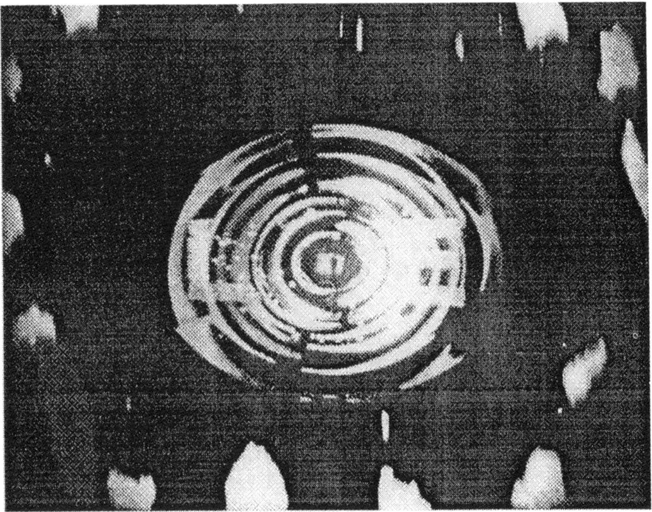

Figure 3. Partial view of *Zephyr.*

shapes and the relative position of the letters in space. As the viewer moves relative to the piece, it oscillates between preserving these oppositions (the affirmative versus the inquiring) and solving them by visually blending the opposite terms.

I used three masters in this piece. The first master contains two letters, L and E, with space between them equivalent to two other letters (I and F, which are absent from this hologram). As the viewer moves relative to the piece, he or she perceives that the letters are made of minute particles, and that these particles fly towards the viewer – as if they had been blown in the air. They crisscross in space and follow a path that – if seen from the top – resembles the letter V. A three-dimensional cloud of particles is formed in space. If the viewer moves in the opposite direction, this cloud flies away from the viewer and reconstructs the letters, as if the viewer had blown them away from him or her with his or her own gaze.

The second master contains the word IF, formed by the two letters extracted from the word LIFE. This word is projected on synthetic water. I perturbed the synthetic liquid surface where the word is projected in order to record visual oscillations of the word. The meaning of doubt raised by the word IF is reinforced by its wavy motion, since the word is perceived as word or abstract pattern depending on the momentary position of the viewer in relation to the holopoem. The letters I and F dissolve into an elliptical form that can be read as the letter O. The word IF is positioned in the perceptual field so as to match the space left in the first master.

Both are integrated into one entity, but they also dissolve into one another. A third master was added, containing stylized images of flames forming a ring around the ripples. Looking at Zephyr, the reader finds buoyant words, as if the particles and the ripples were relying for their movement on the vagaries of air currents and the displacement of small air masses caused by the movement of the viewer himself or herself.

Storms, a Hyperpoem

Looking closely at the cultural dimensions of hypertext, it strikes me that in many ways the discontinuous and metamorphing poetry I've been developing since 1983 with holography shares with hypertext, and with the hyperpoetry created by myself and by others, the same interest for the model of the network, for the readerly interactivity, and for the giving up of absolute textual control on the part of the author. I ask myself, however: if holopoetry promotes a disengagement from the linearity typical of traditional poetry and of the graphic simultaneity of visual poetry, can or should it be considered a kind of hypertext? Holopoetry, which links one letter, 3D graphic fragment, or behavior of a text to myriad others, questions the motionless structure of print-based visual poetry, just as it also questions the authorship and readership created by it.

In 1993 I finished "Storms", my first hyperpoem (fig. 4). It is organized in vocalic and consonantal bifurcations. To navigate through the poem one is invited to click on a letter at any given time. In some instances, navigation can

Figure 4. Screen from *Storms,* 1993.

also take place by clicking outside the word. If the reader does not make a choice, that is, if he or she does not click on a vowel or consonant, or in some instances also on empty space, the reader will remain stationary. The poem does not have an ending. This means that one can continue to explore different textual navigation possibilities or quit at any time by pressing the Command key and the Q key.

After I finished the first draft of this hyperpoem, I noticed that its structure was very similar to the diagram of sefirotic systems typical of the Kabbalah. This made me realize that I could push it further, by borrowing some links I observed in a particular sefirotic system (fig. 5). Kabbalistic writing and mysticism have always had a formal influence in my work, and this influence has resulted in holopoems such as "Abracadabra" (1984/85), "Shema" (1989), and "Multiple" (1989). But the difference is that this time there is a remarkable similarity between the actual structure of my hyperpoem, which promotes the branching from one textual unit to another, and the structure of this metaphysical Tree.

In poetry words are not used, as in ordinary discourse, just to make a point, but to craft a verbal composition. In linear poetry the presence or absence of accent in a word is like the presence or absence of accent in another word. Syllables become units of measurement. Verbal messages are works of

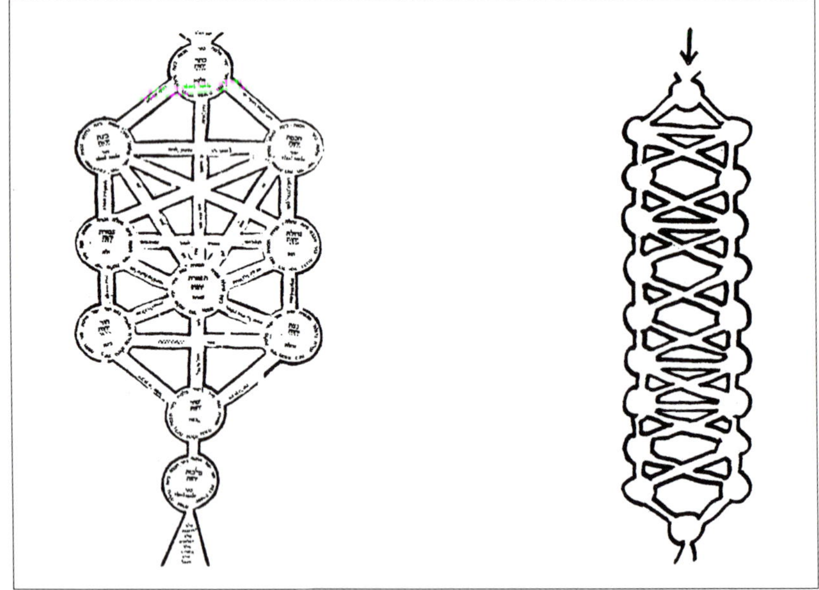

Figure 5. Sefirotic system according to Pa'amon ve-Rimmon, Amsterdam, 1708 (left), and link structure of the hyperpoem *Storms,* 1993 (right).

art because poets of all eras and nations have always carefully selected and arranged words in a particular way, so that their qualities (aural properties, connotative or denotative meanings, graphic form) can resonate within the poet's particular system. As Luis Zukofsky wrote, "condensed speech is most of the method of poetry (as distinguished from the essentially discursive art of prose) (20). While this is still true in hyperpoetry, what seems to be at stake now is a disengagement from the textual distribution characteristic of print. The node – and not the syllable – from which links irradiate is the new unit of measurement. The writer now defines the work as crisscrossing axes of combination. The reader has to make selections in a way that is similar, albeit not identical, to the way the writer has. The reader is now presented not with one narrowed-down selection of words in strings or in graphic layouts, but with an electronic field that is a complex network with no final form. In each node the poet will deploy text or add sound and moving images to it. In "Storms", I decided to work with text alone.

Conclusion

Holopoetry explores actual motion, displacement, and metamorphosis. In my holotexts I employ a syntax of dislocations that continually drive graphemes from their locus. In some poems I use only one word, but in my multiword poems each word is a node or point of intersection. No word is the origin or beginning. Even in the single-word pieces that employ some kind of sequence, this sequence is never hierarchical (i.e., linear) and never assumes a fixed beginning or end. Words are axes which radiate linked words that surround them – but quite often a word loses graphical integrity and becomes temporarily something else, a sign or an abstract pattern with no extra-linguistic or extra-pictorial reality. This textual drift suggests, ultimately, a view of the word and the world as malleable.

In electronic hypertext, one chooses paths but each locus provides stable words on a two-dimensional computer screen, which are scanned by the eye in linear fashion, like in print, from top to bottom, from left to right. In holographic texts the reader can't add to the existing elements, at least not yet, but in addition to choosing paths the readers encounter a space where the graphical substance of the verbal material is under constant disturbance, being transformed, morphed, or disintegrated in a new signifying process.

The writer who works with holography or hypertext must give up the idea of the reader as the ideal decoder of the text and must deal with a reader who makes very personal choices in terms of the direction, speed, distance, order, and angle he or she finds suitable to the readerly experience. The writer must create the text taking into account that these decisions, being personal as they are, will generate multiple and differentiated experiences of the text and - most importantly - that all of these occurrences are equally valid textual encounters. Even those, one must assume, in which the reader finds his or her expectations - built upon the conventions of print - frustrated by the nature of the new experience.

If one is concerned with the development of a new poetry for the digital age, it is important to write visual poetry in a medium different than print, a medium that is fresh and the conventions of which are yet to be invented. To me, holography is such a medium, but I must point out that the use of new media does not constitute, by itself, a standard of quality or of authentic contribution to the repertoire of experimental writing. A rare example of important international digital poetry was shown in the exhibition "p0esle digitale dichtkunst", curated by André Vallias in Germany in 1992.[1]

In western societies we are all used to electronic texts on television performing the most elaborate pirouettes on the screen. A golfer hits a ball and letters announcing a tournament are scattered on the screen. An electric shaver follows a path made of text about the product, "shaving" the text in the process. Logos fly on the screen to sell the visual identity of large corporations, and so on. The dynamic use of language we are used to on television unfortunately promotes redundancy, consumerism, and banalization. The new generation of poets grew up comfortably with television, video, computers, and holography, so it is this generation's challenge to create dynamic electronic texts that recover the conceptual power and the mysterious beauty of language.

Note

1 This group exhibition took place at the Galerie am Markt, in Annaberg-Buchholz, Germany, from September 12 to October 3, 1992. The catalogue can be obtained from: André Vallias, Amtsstr. 69, 22149 Hamburg, Germany.

References

Eliot, T. S. "Burnt Norton". *Collected Poems,* 1909-1935. New York: Harcourt, Brace, 1936. 219.

Kac, Eduardo. "Holopoetry and Fractal Holopoetry: Digital Holography as an Art Medium". *Holography as an Art Medium.* Topical issue, ed. Louis Brill. *Leonardo* 22 (1989): 397-402.

-----. “Recent Experiments in Holopoetry and Computer Holopoetry”. *Proceedings of the International Symposium on Display Holography.* Ed. T. H. Jeong. SPIE (Bellingham, WA) 1600 (1991): 229-36.

Zukofsky, Louis. “A Statement for Poetry”. *Prepositions.* Berkeley and Los Angeles: University of California Press, 1981.

On Monuments

The Rise and Fall of the Literary Monument in Post-Revolutionary France

Michael D. Garval

Introduction

In the *Panthéon Nadar* (1854), the caricaturist and pioneering photographer Nadar depicts a serpentine procession of contemporary literary celebrities, lined up according to their relative prominence (fig. 1). The title "Panthéon", as well as the way in which the "great men" are transformed from caricatures into statues at their death, point to important links between the nineteenth-cen-

Figure 1. Nadar and collaborators, *Panthéon.* 1854. Lithographic Print, 104 x 75 cm. Courtesy John Eastman House.

tury writer and the monument.[1] Moreover, Nadar published the *Panthéon* at a watershed both in his own career and in the history of iconography: he first tried photography as a means of documenting faces for his satirical pantheon and soon abandoned caricature to dedicate himself to the radical new medium.[2] The *Panthéon Nadar* urges us to reflect on the shifting iconographical landscape of nineteenth-century fame imagery, by offering a rare conjunction of caricature, monument, and photography – representational modes which embody the period's divergent visions of literary celebrity itself.

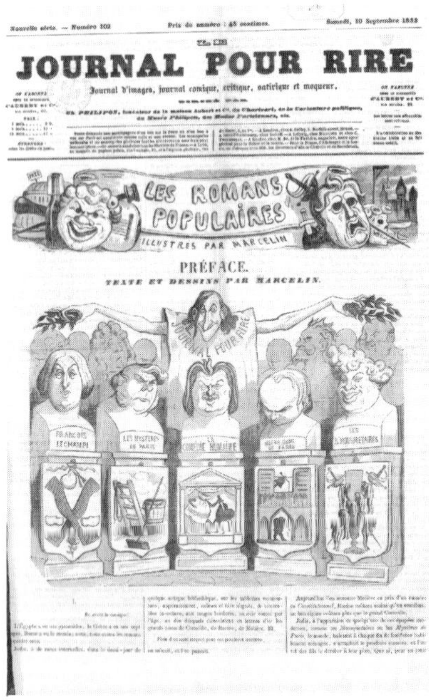

Nouvelle série. — Numéro 102 Prix du numéro : 15 centimes. Samedi, 10 Septembre 1853

JOURNAL POUR RIRE

Journal d'images, journal comique, critique, satirique et moqueur.

PRÉFACE.

TEXTE ET DESSINS PAR MARCELIN.

Figure 2. Marcelin, "Les romans populaires". Early 1850s.

In "Les romans populaires" (1853), the caricaturist Marcelin depicts the novelists George Sand, Eugène Sue, Honoré de Balzac, Victor Hugo, and Alexandre Dumas *père* as marble busts (fig. 2). Above their celebrated heads float the laurel wreaths of fame. On the lower part of each bust we find not the writer's name, but the title of his or her most famous work. On the pedestal, a heraldic shield bears not the author's coat of arms, but a witty emblem of the work in question. In this way, Marcelin's tongue-in-cheek caricature conflates the writer's life, *oeuvre*, and literary afterlife, suggesting vital links not only between the writer and the monument to his (rarely her) glory, but also between the monument and the literary work itself.

Figure 3. Ernest Barrias. *Monument de Victor Hugo.* 1902. Paris: Place Victor-Hugo. (The sculpture was dismantled for scrap metal in 1941; photos are kept in the *Maison Victor Hugo.*)

These two drawings evoke some of the ideological and cultural issues surrounding literary fame and its public visual representation in nineteenth-century France. In order to begin exploring this unfamiliar area in word and image studies, I will focus on two particularly important developments: first, on the rise and fall of the "literary monument", then on the related changes ushered in by the rise of photography.[3]

The Rise of the Literary Monument

What was the "literary monument"? The term will be used here to refer to a work of sculpture designed to perpetuate a writer's fame, a genre beautifully exemplified by Ernest Barrias's *Monument de Victor Hugo* (1902; fig. 3).[4] Of an essentially public and commemorative nature, the literary monument is intended to last.[5] It emerges from a period marked by a new cult of the writer and by a penchant for erecting statues to "great men" – by what Paul Bénichou calls "le sacre de l'écrivain" (title) and by what the nineteenth century already referred to as "la statuomanie" (cf. Agulhon). In a broader sense, the literary monument needs to be understood as part of a whole range of interrelated cultural productions which venerate the writer and his work, and which flourished at the same time as the literary monument itself. These include reveren-

Figure 4a. Figure 4b. Figure 4c.

L'ECLIPSE
AUGUSTE VACQUERIE, PAR GILL
HUGO

Figure 4d.

LES HUGOPHILES
Dimanche 22 Décembre 1907, à 2 h.
78, RUE BONAPARTE (Place Saint-Sulpice)
PRIX : 0 fr. 25
5me FÊTE ANNUELLE DE L'ARBRE DE NOËL
PROGRAMME DU CONCERT

Figure 4e.

Figure 4. Caricatures of Victor Hugo and *Notre-Dame de Paris* (from the archives of the *Maison Victor Hugo*). 4a) M. D., "Hugoth". *La Charge* N° 4, 1833; 4b) Benjamin, "Victor Hugo". *Panthéon Charivarique,* 1844; 4c) H. Meyer, "Victor Hugo"; 4d) André Gill, "Auguste Vacquerie". *L'Éclipse* 3 Nov. 1872; 4e) Fernand Salatte, Program of the annual reunion of the "Société des Hugophiles", 1907.

> sur les larges pieds de ses colonnes géantes; peu à peu, tout ce qui est boue et sable s'en ira, et alors le squelette de marbre du monument apparaîtra encore sur l'horizon, comme le profil immense et déchiqueté d'une ville. Même dans un avenir lointain, si quelque vent terrible, en emportant notre langue et notre civilisation, jetait par terre la carcasse de l'édifice, les décombres feraient sur le sol une telle montagne, qu'aucun peuple ne pourrait passer devant cet amas, sans dire: 'Là dorment les ruines d'un monde' (4-5.)

Like Hugo with Horatian overtones,[10] Zola thus stresses the extraordinary durability of a textual "monument" called *La Comédie humaine.* Furthermore, like Hugo's eulogy, Zola's praise of Balzac is far from selfless. Clearly, each of these authors is also talking about his *own* overriding ambitions, about the monumentality of *his* work, and about *his* literary posterity.

We find much the same conception of the literary work in caricatures from the period. For example, since the publication of *Notre-Dame de Paris* in 1832 the cathedral came to embody both the vastness of Hugo's *oeuvre,* and his immensity as a literary figure (figs. 4 a-e). With their conspicuous pens and giant leather-bound volumes, these drawings highlight the links between the monument and Hugo's own enormous literary production – to the point

Figure 5. André Gill, "Victor Hugo". *L'Éclipse.* 29 August 1875.

of casting Hugo himself in the role of monument-maker, as in the André Gill caricature of Hugo as sculptor, hammering away at busts of Robbespierre, Danton, and Marat, shortly before the publication of his novel *Quatre-vingt-treize* (fig. 5).[11]

Along the same lines, Gill depicts Zola saluting a bust of Balzac, clasping a copy of his own answer to the *Comédie, Les Rougon-Macquart* (fig. 6 a); and, Zola trying in vain to pull Hugo from his pedestal, no doubt in order to take his place: next to him lies the true instrument of his attack, his pen, synecdoche of his own monumental *oeuvre* (fig. 6 b).

Photography and the Fall of the Literary Monument

With the First World War, the frenetic Third Republic craze for monuments subsides. According to art historian June Hargrove,

> la Première Guerre mondiale . . . avait [. . .] donné naissance à une réaction hostile contre une statuomanie qui avait accompagné la genèse de la tragédie. L'incapacité des pouvoirs établis à résoudre une crise internationale sans sacrificier des millions de vies humaines avait jeté le discrédit sur les valeurs traditionelles et terni la gloire des héros révérés . . . . Aux yeux des cyniques de l'après-guerre, les statues des hommes célèbres étaient devenues des anachronismes. ("Statues de Paris", 271)

Hargrove is certainly right to stress the loss of a certain heroic ideal.[12] Yet one must consider other factors as well. First, as Hargrove herself points out (270-71), with the invention of the automobile and the corresponding increase in traffic, public thoroughfares could no longer be clogged with monuments. Agulhon has observed that our modern way of moving through the city does not allow for public statuary to be appreciated properly: "Les anciennes statues de carrefour ou de places publiques ne peuvent plus guère être regardées ni par l'automobiliste qui passe vite, ni même par le piéton qui, pour maintes raisons, n'est plus guère flâneur" (165). Furthermore, unlike the cluttered eclecticism which characterized the nineteenth century's use of space, a sparser style of architecture and urban planning came into favor in the twentieth.[13]

The rise of non-figurative art has, however, led to the installation in public spaces of a new kind of sometimes large-scale sculpture that often has no commemorative or symbolic function whatsoever – short of signaling the aesthetic refinement and enlightened largesse of those funding it. One may even wonder whether in retrospect the nineteenth century's mania for monumental statuary could not be read as a symptom of its own decadence. This was an age

Figure 6a.

Figure 6b.

Figure 6. Caricatures of Émile Zola by André Gill; 6a) Zola saluting Balzac. Wood engraving for *Les Hommes d'aujourd'hui,* 1878; 6b) "Loisirs naturalistes" ("With what M. Zola wastes his time"). *La Petite Lune* N° 44, 1878.

whose political upheavals felled countless statues destined to insure immortality and whose secularizing tendencies subverted the power of Christian statuary. In this context, the period's obsessive commemoration of cultural heroes may well appear like a desperate effort to shift the center of lasting values onto a cultural field already threatened by its own internal revolutions.

The history of the literary monument's decline cannot be told, however, without taking a new phenomenon into account: the role played by photography. In *La chambre claire*, Roland Barthes argues that photography replaces the monument as the locus of cultural memory in the modern world:

> Les anciennes sociétés s'arrangeaient pour que le souvenir, substitut de la vie, fût éternel et qu'au moins la chose qui disait la Mort fût elle-même immortelle: c'était le Monument. Mais en faisant de la Photographie, mortelle, le témoin général et comme naturel de 'ce qui a été', la société moderne a renoncé au Monument. (146)

In nineteenth-century France, before the advent of photography, the two principal modes for publicly depicting celebrity were monument and caricature. While the monumental mode embodied the more traditional vision of celebrity as enduring fame, the caricature expressed a more recent view of celebrity as momentary. Appearing in ephemeral media, the caricature, thriving on contemporary detail, is critical and irreverent where the monument, rendered in durable material such as marble or bronze, is idealizing and reverential. Despite these fundamental oppositions, caricature and monument coexisted peaceably, perhaps even symbiotically, during much of the century. In a sense, within the context of the nineteenth century's iconographical landscape, the monument can be said to have drawn its extraordinary vitality from caricature, which acted as a necessary comic foil to its solemn gravity. At the time, moreover, these modes of visual representation were paralleled by analogous modes of writing: faddish journalistic *prose du jour*, rapidly consumed, easily forgotten, barely outlasting the paper on which it was printed; and, the ponderous literary *oeuvre*, read and reread with reverence, solidly leather-bound in voluminous complete works, clearly intended to outlast the author.

In this connection, a preparatory sketch for Nadar's *Panthéon* proves particularly revealing (fig. 7). Dozens of tiny demons carry flimsy, individual sheets of paper, each bearing the name of a mortal destined for literary immortality. This furious activity, reminiscent of a scene from Hieronymus Bosch, swirls toward the center of the composition, where an allegorical figure of Death records the names in a massive, bound volume (Hambourg 22). Playing a pivotal role in both the preliminary and final versions of the *Panthéon*, death articulates a passage from the ephemeral to the everlasting: from newsprint-like sheets to a monumental *grand livre* in the sketch; and, from caricatures of contemporary writers to statues of deceased literary glories in the completed

Figure 7. Nadar, *Preliminary Study for the Projected Lithograph "Panthéon Nadar,"* 1854, Pencil and charcoal drawing on tan paper. Lucy Dalbiac Luard Fund and Abbott Lawrence Fund, Courtesy Museum of Fine Arts, Boston.

lithograph. Both versions thus foreground the very process of immortalization: in the first, it is depicted as a passage from one *textual* mode to another; in the second, as an analogous passage from one *visual* mode to another.

With the rise of photography, the visual representation of literary fame changed profoundly, as Nadar's emblematic career suggests. When we look at them today, Nadar's photographs of well-known writers, like his wonderfully self-conscious *autoportrait,* still seem remarkably "modern" (fig. 8). Why should this be? Unlike many of his peers, Nadar avoided elaborate costumes, props, and backdrops, which for the modern viewer tend to freeze the image in the past.[14] Instead, he concentrated on making palpable the psychological complexity of the individual pictured; he was aided in this effort by his own intimate knowledge of the Parisian *Bohème* he sought to portray.

Nadar's modernity is underscored by his relationship to the then-popular practice of death-bed portraiture. Casting the photograph in the role of the death mask or the bust in the mausoleum, this retrograde practice attempted to recuperate photography as a form of monumental imagery. Nadar had first-hand experience with the genre, early on in his photographic career: "A partir de 1857, et pour des raisons d'ordre purement commercial, Nadar s'était fait une spécialité des portraits mortuaires" (Heilbrun, 80-82). While he did not

Figure 8. Nadar, Self portrait with chin in hand, ca. 1854-1858, Salt print, 20.5 x 17.0 cm. Collection of the J. Paul Getty Museum, Malibu, California.

hesitate to turn a profit by producing such images of obscure, unremarkable bourgeois clients, Nadar was much more reticent about depicting celebrities in this way. Indeed, although he photographed nearly all the living literary and artistic eminences of his day, he rarely photographed them in death. In 1859, Nadar did a striking death-bed photograph of the poet Marceline Desbordes-Valmore (also the subject of his first documented photograph, in April 1854; Chotard, 150). This was virtually the last of Nadar's death-bed portraits, however, until the mid-1880's, when he made two more, at a time when he had all but abandoned active work as a photographic portraitist. In 1883, Nadar recorded the passing of his old friend Gustave Doré and, two years later, the nineteenth century's most famous photographer was given exclusive rights to shoot a death-bed portrait of its most famous writer, his idol, the incomparably illustrious Victor Hugo. The resulting photo-cum-monument prefigured the poet's imminent, official "petrification": already considered "immortal" in life, Hugo would lie in state beneath the *Arc de Triomphe*, then be enshrined in the temple of the *Panthéon*, truly becoming one with the monument.[15]

Unlike Nadar's monumentalizing death-bed photo of Hugo, the bulk of his innovative photographic *oeuvre* instead urges on the decline of the monument. As Barthes has argued, the new medium of photography supplants the monument in the modern world, providing us with different ways of understanding our relation to time, and to memory. Indeed, with the spread of photography there appeared noticeable signs of such a paradigm shift in the form of a malaise within the other modes of representing celebrity. Specifically, as illustrated by figures 1, 2, and 4-6, more and more statues began to appear in caricatures. This curious phenomenon came to flourish from the early 1850s onward, much like photography itself. With photography blurring the boundaries between the presence and the absence of the subject, between the immediacy and the permanence of his or her image, the old oppositions between caricature and monument, between passing celebrity and enduring fame, began to collapse. From its inception, photography both anticipates and precipitates our own paradoxical conception of renown as fleeting apotheosis – as Andy Warhol's 15-minute fame for all.[16]

Conclusion

In these ways, then, the rise and fall of the literary monument marks a critical transition in a process of cultural formation that leads out of the royal monopolization of renown during the *ancien régime* and into our own amnesiac modernity. Indeed, if anything in contemporary France could be said to function as a modern equivalent of the literary monument it would no doubt be "Bouillon de culture" (formerly "Apostrophes"), Bernard Pivot's video potpourri of the latest cultural luminaries, served up weekly to the hungry but forgetful *téléspectateurs*. Yet, unlike the celebrities in Nadar's *Panthéon*, who still march purposefully toward immortality in our collective memory, Pivot's stars blaze for a brief, brilliant moment, then fade into the oblivion of the electronic night.

Notes

1. At the head of the long line of celebrities there is a small group of statue busts and bas-relief medallions representing deceased male celebrities (Balzac, Chateaubriand, Frédéric Soulié, Paul-Louis Courier, and Charles Nodier), with one exception: George Sand (1804-1876), a woman, who was still very much alive at that time. In the third row there is another cluster of statue busts of women, all still alive. I would argue

that this curious mode of representation embodies women's radical "difference" as celebrities. Nadar's seeming veneration of women in fact excludes them from the all-important *process* in which his male celebrities participate: that of becoming "immortal". Turned to stone, "killed off" before their time, women in Nadar's *Panthéon* are denied the crowning achievement of public success for 19th-century France: the posthumous glory reserved for "great men".

2. While Nadar does not seem to have used photography for documenting his *Panthéon* before 1854, "il est certain qu'en janvier 1854, Nadar a recours à la photographie au moment où il rassemble les portraits de femmes de lettres qui apparaîtront, non caricaturés, dans son *Panthéon*" (Chotard, 81). His brother Adrien, who had been dabbling in the new medium since 1853, was apparently the photographer here. Nadar himself began experimenting with photography between February and April 1854 (Chotard, 82); the *Panthéon* was published in March. One could argue, moreover, that Nadar's experience with the *Panthéon* propelled him toward photography: his obsession with documentary accuracy, as well as the sheer number of effigies crammed into his lithograph, exhaust the possibilities of a certain kind of caricature art, compelling him to explore the representational potential of photography. In short, Nadar the photographer picks up where Nadar the caricaturist left off.

3. The analysis which follows is largely inspired by the recent reflection, in French studies, on republican ideology and, in particular, on the cultural and artistic legacy of the Third Republic. This includes the work of historians such as Maurice Agulhon, or Pierre Nora and his team in the anthology *Les lieux de mémoire*; that of art historians such as Jacques de Caso, June Hargrove, and the late H. W. Janson; and the "revisionist" stance of the *Musée d'Orsay*, as well as of several ground-breaking exhibitions, such as "La gloire de Victor Hugo" at the *Grand Palais* in 1985-86, "La sculpture française au dix-neuvième siècle", also at the *Grand Palais* in 1986, "Rodin et la caricature" at the *Musée Rodin* in 1990, "Nadar, caricatures et photographies" at the *Maison de Balzac* in 1990-1991, and *Nadar, les années créatrices: 1854-1860*, at the *Musée d'Orsay* in 1994.

This project also owes a great deal to the generous help, advice, and encouragement of Claus Clüver, Eric Haskell, Alina Hunt, Ilse Hempel Lipschutz, Jonathan Ribner, and Richard Sieburth. I thank them, and of course take full responsibility for any errors or distortions.

4. For the history of the Barrias monument, from the initial public subscription to its melting down by the Germans in 1941, see Georgel, *La gloire de Victor Hugo*. The catalogue does not, however, address the monument's curious afterlife: in the early 1950's, a committee was formed to re-erect a monument to Hugo on the same site. In a 1952 interview, Picasso reveals his preference for the Barrias over the Rodin monument: "C'est mieux, le Barrias, que le Rodin. Le Rodin ne raconte ni assez de choses, ni assez clairement: les gloires, les trompettes, les palmes ... et les bas-reliefs, la grandmère qui tient son enfant mort, avec deux balles dans la tête, tout cela fait un monument. Le Rodin est une petite chose pour une grande place". If moreover it should prove impossible to put back the Barrias, asserts Picasso, he would rather make a new monument himself than settle for the Rodin.

5. The term "monument" itself is bound up with the idea of memory: as H.W. Janson points out in his seminal essay on the public monument, it derives from the Latin

root *monere*, and means "reminder". Janson also notes that public monuments are "meant to be permanent – as permanent as the means available could make them", (1).

6. "Augustus founded two public libraries, among the earliest in Rome, one connected with the Temple of Apollo on the Palatine Hill (close to his house) and the other on the Campus Martius, perhaps connected with the Temple of Mars the Avenger. Each contained a collection of Greek or Roman authors housed in rooms decorated with busts and medallions of the great writers – the first hall of fame. In the earliest Roman public library, founded by Pollio the historian a few years before, only one living author was so honored, and Horace notes with satisfaction that Augustus had included many" (Braudy, 119).

7. According to Leo Braudy, "the great expansion of the reading and viewing public as well as the means of reaching them which marks the nineteenth century" (476) gave rise to the "modern conception of the marketplace of fame in which all might sell their wares" (342).

8. Writers helped fund monuments through such organizations as the *Société des gens de lettres*, and through committees formed to solicit "subscriptions" for a particular project; the bourgeois public contributed both through private donations and through taxes, which funded the growing government support of the cultural *patrimoine.*

9. "I have erected a monument more durable than bronze". This must of course be understood as part of the broader interpenetration of literature and architecture in the nineteenth century (cf. Hamon).

10. In distinguishing the hexameters of his *saturae* from epic hexameters Horace had claimed that even if a great epic poem had only survived in fragments it would still be possible to recognize these as the scattered limbs of a poet – "disiecti membra poetae" (*Satires i,* 4, 62).

11. *Notre-Dame de Paris* invites us to equate Hugo the writer with *Notre-Dame* the monument, by positing "le livre" as rival – and eventual conqueror – of "l'édifice" ("Ceci tuera cela", 237-254).

    Gill's drawing is by no means an isolated instance of the writer-as-sculptor conceit. In Louis Reybaud's *Jérôme Paturot,* for example, Hugo (called "le Génie") is said to be composing a play, *Les Durs à cuire,* by carving his heroes out of the Pyrenees and making pedestals out of the Alps; the accompanying Grandville illustration, which shows Hugo finishing his sculpture, is sub-titled, "Il avait fendu les Pyrénées pour y sculpter ses héroes" (Paris: J.J. Dubochet, Le Chevalier et Cie, éd., 1846, pp. 260-262).

12. Agulhon makes a similar connection: "[Si] la statuomanie a connu la même courbe d'ascension, épanouissement et déclin, qu'un certain système de valeurs philosophiques, et dans les mêmes temps, c'est peut-être qu'elle lui était apparentée" (152).

13. Picasso explains the modernist rejection of monuments to Great Men by invoking both contemporary "taste" and urban "hygiene": "Il semble qu'aujourd'hui on craigne la représentation des grands hommes dans nos villes. On déguise cette crainte sous des prétextes de goût. Et peut-être d'hygiène, parce que c'est difficile d'enlever la poussière des petits coins ... "

14. As Françoise Heilbrun notes in the catalogue for *Nadar, les années créatrices: 1854-1860,* "l'attention excessive portée aux accessoires . . . retire à l'image cette qualité purement photographique et résolument moderne qui caractérise les meilleurs portraits de Nadar" (91).
15. The idea of Hugo's immortality became a commonplace in the years preceding his death: in a caricature by Cham, for example, a boy attempts to sell passerby Hugo a bullet-proof vest, as an old woman exclaims, "Imbécile, pas à lui, Victor Hugo est immortel!" (reproduced in the 1964 Pléiade *Album Hugo*, p. 289). Hugo himself, with eery prescience, prefigured the itinerary of his own posthumous immortalization: in an 1845 *carte de visite* to Léonie Biard, commemorating their illicit affair, the word SOUVENIR stretches across the Parisian skyline, from the *Arc de Triomphe* ... right to the *Panthéon* ! (drawing at *Maison de Victor Hugo*, Paris).
16. Significantly, this new vision of fame already figures in Hugo's state funeral: Charles Garnier's décor for the *Arc de Triomphe* was, in his words, "[un] monument d'un jour pour cette âme éternelle". The curious impermanence of this "temporary" monument was noted by commentators of the time: as one journalist wrote of Hugo's apotheosis, "ceux qui ne l'ont pas vue, ne la verront jamais, et ceux qui l'ont vue ne la verront plus" (*La gloire de Victor Hugo*, 308-309).

References

Agulhon, Maurice. "La 'statuomanie' et l'histoire". *Ethnologie française* (1978): 145-72.

Barthes, Roland. *La chambre claire.* Paris: Éditions de l'Étoile, Gallimard, Seuil, 1980.

Bénichou, Paul. *Le sacre de l'écrivain, 1750-1830: Essai sur l'avènement d'un pouvoir spirituel laïque dans la France moderne.* Paris: José Corti, 1973.

Baudelaire, Charles. "La beauté". *Les fleurs du mal.* 1857. Paris: Presses Pocket, 1989. 44.

Braudy, Leo. *The Frenzy of Renown.* New York: Oxford University Press, 1986.

Chotard, Loïc. Catalogue, *Nadar: Caricatures et photographies.* Paris: Paris-musées, 1990.

Georgel, Pierre, ed. Catalogue, *La gloire de Victor Hugo.* Paris: Réunion des musées nationaux, 1985.

Hambourg, Maria Morris. "Vers une ressemblance intime: une esquisse biographique de Nadar". In catalogue, *Nadar, les années créatrices: 1854-1860.* Paris: Réunion des musées nationaux, 1994. 6-41.

Hamon, Philippe. *Expositions: littérature et architecture au XIXe siècle.* Paris: José Corti, 1989.

Hargrove, June. "Les statues de Paris". In *Les lieux de mémoire: la Nation.* Ed. Pierre Nora. Paris: Gallimard, 1986. 243-82.

-----. *The Statues of Paris: An Open-air Pantheon.* New York: Vendome Press, 1990.

Heilbrun, Françoise. "L'art du portrait photographique chez Félix Nadar". In catalogue, *Nadar, les années créatrices: 1854-1860.* Paris: Réunion des musées nationaux, 1994. 42-103.

Horace. *The Odes*. Ed. Kenneth Quinn. London: St. Martin's Press, 1980.

-----. *Satires I.* Ed. P. Michael Brown. Warminster (England): Aris & Phillips, 1993.

Hugo, Victor. *Choses vues*. 1887. Paris: Jules Rouff, n.d.

-----. "Funérailles de Balzac". *Actes et paroles: Avant l'exil, 1841-1851*. Paris: Albin Michel, 1937.

-----. *Notre-Dame de Paris*. Paris: Gallimard (Folio), 1974.

Lanfranchi, Jacques. "Les statues de Paris". Ph.D. diss. Paris I, 1979. 250 pp.

Picasso, Pablo. "Picasso propose de faire le monument Hugo". Interview in *Tous les arts*, March 20-27, 1952.

Sand, George [Aurore Dupin]. *Histoire de ma vie*. In *Oeuvres autobiographiques,* vol. I. Paris: Gallimard, 1970.

Zola, Émile. "Balzac". *Les romanciers naturalistes*. 1881. Rpt. Paris: Charpentier, 1906.

Contesting "Meaning" in the Late 19th Century: A Site of American Art, Autobiography, and Ambition

Charles Vandersee

I

"Meaning" is a problematic issue when we assess works of public art; complicating our efforts to establish meaning are attempts by artists and their clients to *control* meaning. They must use language to do this, as must critics and scholars, and W. J. T. Mitchell suggests an abiding vexation:

> The dialectic of word and image seems to be a constant in the fabric of signs that a culture weaves around itself. . . . The history of culture is in part the story of a protracted struggle for dominance between pictorial and linguistic signs, . . . (43)

Few objects on the North American continent reveal so well the complexities of this struggle as an austere bronze figure in Washington, D.C., a city egregiously supplied with conventional heroic bronzes. Often regarded as the masterwork of Augustus Saint-Gaudens, the chief American sculptor of his day, the figure, seated and draped, in the churchyard of Rock Creek Episcopal parish, was commissioned by the historian Henry Adams and erected in 1891. Saint-Gaudens designed or helped design fewer than a dozen funerary monuments (Dryfhout 341); late in life he expressed revulsion against "the monstrosities which dominate in all modern cemeteries" (*Reminiscences* 2: 275).

Immediately on installation his disturbing and unconventional monument gained notoriety, the rector of Rock Creek parish wanting the "unchristian monument out of his churchyard" (Adams, *Letters* 4: 4). The monument quickly became a tourist site, and was destined (as this paper will suggest) to become a *locus classicus* for various hermeneutical ambitions. Not only did contesting interpretations arise, as viewers both thoughtful and impetuous engaged in efforts to render "meaning", but also those individuals positioned to advance a definite meaning chose instead to establish a domain of ambiguity. The figure lent itself to this ambiguity; it did not seem serenely at home either in an American park cemetery or within conventional understandings of form, style, and symbolism.

II

Useful in considering "meaning" and the control of meaning, in both figures and texts, is a frame of reference such as that provided by Mieke Bal and Norman Bryson. They raise the kinds of questions that have concerned recent art historians and theorists who go beyond the principles of iconology and iconography laid out by Erwin Panofsky in the 1930s and after. Bal and Bryson affirm Roland Barthes: Semiotic investigation "'will not teach us what meaning must be definitively attributed to a work; it will not provide or even discover a meaning but will describe the logic according to which meanings are engendered'" (*Critique et verité* [Paris 1966] 63; Bal and Bryson 184). In their own voice they add:

> Since readers and viewers bring to the images their own cultural baggage, there can be no such thing as a fixed, predetermined, or unified meaning. Attempts to fix meaning provide, in fact, the most convincing evidence for this view. The field in which struggles over meaning are fought is a social arena where power is at stake. (207)

But efforts at control are not always lucid and unambiguous, as we see in turning to Henry Adams' *Education.* This book emerged – with calculated diffidence – fifteen years after the monument was erected, being printed by Adams in 1907 for private distribution, in an edition of 100 copies. It appeared in a trade edition only in 1918 (Pulitzer Prize, 1919), and is now regarded as the most important U.S. example of intellectual autobiography. Adams writes of himself in third person; in a long polemical paragraph dealing with the Saint-Gaudens figure, he foregrounds "meaning" (the word occurs four times), but he refuses to commit himself:

> . . . in all that it [the monument] had to say, he [Adams] never once thought of questioning what it meant. He supposed its meaning to be the one commonplace about it – the oldest idea known to human thought. He knew that if he asked an Asiatic its meaning, not a man, woman, or child from Cairo to Kamtchatka would have needed more than a glance to reply. From the Egyptian Sphinx to the Kamakura Daibuts [Great Buddha]; from Prometheus to Christ; from Michael Angelo to Shelley, art had wrought on this eternal figure almost as though it had nothing else to say. The interest of the figure was not in its meaning, but in the response of the observer. As Adams sat there, numbers of people came, for the figure seemed to have become a tourist fashion, and all wanted to know its meaning. Most took it for a portrait-statue, and the remnant were vacant-minded in the absence of a personal guide. . . . [Clergymen] one after another brought companions there, and, apparently fascinated by their own reflection, broke out passionately against the expression they felt in the figure of despair, of atheism, of denial. (329)

Playful, profound, and elusive, Adams seems committed to postmodern tendencies. He distances his reader from the Rock Creek monument by including no illustrations and by overwhelming the reader with these apparent messages:

1. Meaning is contingent upon culture, because the viewer is a cultural construct. If you are a member of a North American culture, or a European one, your gaze will mislead you, while the merest glance by an Asian will be successful.

2. Meaning is a matter of cultural codes. Here, the pertinent codes are Egyptian, Buddhist, Greek, and Christian. They may generate a syncretism, a massive fusion, but they may also constitute an array of conflicting elements.

3. Meaning derives, in part and by default, from the responses that popular culture constructs in citizens. Because popular culture had not coped with this kind of figure, the American tourists are said to be empty-headed. Adams grants that art inevitably mirrors the viewer (whatever else it may do), thus his figure when seen by the vacant-minded viewer will have no accessible meaning.

4. Meaning is implicated in the historical moment. Something happened to the American mind in the late 19th century, suggests Adams. People, especially the clergy, saw themselves in this figure, and what they saw was atheism, despite their Sunday churchgoing.

Two messages were not so plain:

5. Meaning arises from absence, from erasure. The most notorious fact about the *Education* is that Adams excluded his wife, Marian Hooper Adams ("Clover"), whose death by suicide, at age 42, prompted the monument. Furthermore, Adams forbade any inscriptions, dates, or names, over or near the grave, to identify the body or bodies interred there (Samuels 409). Only on the reverse side of Stanford White's granite backing stone does there appear a device of representation: two intersecting wreaths.

6. Meaning includes the status of a work of art as a material object, its position in an economy of buying and selling, and the position of the artist in a professional economy defined by reputation and by body of achievement. The Rock Creek figure is an expensive bronze casting, in a cemetery where stone is the norm. In the paragraph preceding the long passage excerpted above, Adams foregrounds "money" (five times); the typical wealthy American:

> wasted money more recklessly than any one ever did before; he spent more to less purpose than any extravagant court aristocracy; he had no sense of relative values, and knew not what to do with his money when he got it, . . . (328)

Adams thus inscribes in his text one clear meaning that a gaze at the figure-and-site can only vaguely elicit: He himself is a man of distinctive taste and public generosity, a man displaying to the ignorant, mansion-building barons of his generation a more civilized way of deploying publicly one's financial gains.

III

We are now thirsty for gnostic knowledge – what Richard Wollheim calls "cognitive stock" – and we have more than a tourist had in Grover Cleveland's day. Wollheim in an essay on "What the Spectator Sees" insists that "a spectator needs a lot of information about how the painting [let us here say "sculpture"] came to be made. He [sic] needs a substantial cognitive stock" (138). Cognitive stock can be elusive, and instinctively one might reach for a guidebook: "Henry Adams' wife Marian committed suicide by drinking photographic chemicals. Saint-Gaudens' bronze may depict her, but it's commonly called 'Grief' instead: the hooded, cloaked and seated figure seems to remember all human pain" (*Let's Go* 157). Another example of the genre: "In 1890 Saint-Gaudens fashioned the green-bronze figure of a woman shrouded in a hooded cloak for the grave of Mrs. Henry Adams. Her husband, the famous author and diplomat, later was placed beside her" (Robertson 152). Thus, despite lurid details of suicide, and the wrong occupation for Clover's husband (the diplomat was Henry's father), today's inquirers might acquire a plausible *name* for the statue ("Grief") and its *gender* (the figure is a woman). Neither datum arouses suspicion; the alert visitor no less than the impressionable tourist expects a human image to have a name and a gender.

But we typically turn for cognitive stock to more accredited genres, especially primary sources such as letters, diaries, interviews. These varied discourses open a new issue, revealing that an early question about meaning – perhaps indeed the first question – has to do with *who makes* the object. Not client alone, it turns out, and not client and artist in conventional collaboration, but a small group of cultivated men shared the ambition of making and controlling meaning at Rock Creek.

After Marian Adams died, Henry fled to Japan, with an old friend, John La Farge, painter, stained-glass artist. They came back after a few months, Adams musing on serene Buddha figures and La Farge's eye fascinated by the pan-Asian goddess Kwannon, who represents mercy and compassion. Saint-Gaudens, an old friend of both men, was sought out by Adams, who commissioned for Clover's grave (and eventually, of course, his own) a figure expressing "the acceptance, intellectually, of the inevitable" (Kobbe). Saint-Gaudens knew that Henry and Clover were both agnostics. Adams asked Saint-Gaudens to look at photographs of Buddha figures and also of Michelangelo's figures in the Sistine Chapel. Shortly thereafter, La Farge, thinking about Kwannon and painting her, was designated as go-between (La Farge, Jan. 26), since Adams regarded artists as "hideously sensitive" to suggestion (May 1, 1904; 5: 579). Adams in his diary called the project his "Buddha" figure (April 29, Sept. 2, 1888; 3: 112, 137); Saint-Gaudens, for his part, was never able to express his thoughts, said Adams (Apr. 21, 1903; 5: 488) – Adams conveniently availing himself of a romantic convention concerning artists.

The community surrounding the commission soon expanded to include a fourth person, John Hay, an old and close friend, later Secretary of State. Hay, before Adams himself saw the monument, wrote the nearest thing to a canonical statement about its meaning, if by "canonical" we understand the text that the community itself repeatedly fell back on. Hay composed a careful reaction, because Adams had not seen the figure and was worrying – traveling in the South Seas (once again with La Farge):

> The work is indescribably noble and imposing. It is to my mind St.-Gaudens' masterpiece. It is full of poetry and suggestion, infinite wisdom, a past without beginning, and a future without end, a repose after limitless experience, a peace to which nothing matters – all are embodied in this austere and beautiful face and form (March 25, 1891; qtd. in Adams' letter to Saint-Gaudens, June 23, 1891; 3: 496).

The words produced in Adams a "fit of tears" (June 1; 3: 480). In bringing Hay into the community of interpretation, we should note one of the many attractive negotiations that can occur between image and text: Hay is surely doing more than describing what his eye sees. He is also confirming to Adams that the sculptor produced something that Adams will find acceptable – Hay knowing something of what his intimate friend hoped for because Adams, living next door in Washington, would have talked with him about it.

IV

The project for control of meaning was not without comedy. In 1908, a year after Saint-Gaudens' death, the Corcoran Gallery put on a retrospective exhibition. Theodore Roosevelt, then president (also a longtime intimate of the Adams "community"), spoke at the opening, and called the Rock Creek figure a "strange, shrouded, sitting woman", according to the *New York Times.* Adams, his dismay contesting with friendship, wrote to Roosevelt the next morning:

"If you were talking last night as President, I have nothing to say. Whatever the President says goes!" However,

> After March 4 [of 1909, Roosevelt's last day in office], should you allude to my bronze figure, will you try to do St Gaudens the justice to remark that his expression was a little higher than sex can give. As he meant it, he wanted to exclude sex and sink it in the idea of humanity. The figure is sexless (Dec. 16, 1908; 6: 198).

With this striking insistence on androgyny we see a major point of contestation between image and text, since virtually all viewers, in guidebooks, letters, or conversation, intuitively and confidently report the figure as *female.* For Adams, the figure already ambiguous enough in style and form to be called "eternal" must be indeterminate enough in gender to be also *universal.*

Possibly Adams' greatest obstacle to controlling meaning was Michelangelo. Adams, we recall, had asked Saint-Gaudens to consider figures on the Sistine ceiling. During Adams' early consultations with Saint-Gaudens, once they had settled on a human figure, Saint-Gaudens began demonstrating possible poses. One, particularly unsatisfactory, Adams rejected as a "Penseroso" (Kobbe). Adams likely had in mind, probably from his extended visit to Florence in 1872, with Clover, the statue of Lorenzo de' Medici, commonly called "Pensieroso". It vexed him. "I never quite knew what to think of it", he later told his wife's niece (Apr. 21, 1897; 4: 466). When he made a special trip to Florence to study the statue again, he saw the Lorenzo as pondering, "but not seeing either Hope or Consolation or Faith" (May 20, 1899; 4: 727). Michelangelo's Pensieroso, and the Medici tombs generally, were to Adams' mind "his greatest work" (July 13, 1899; 4: 735); in rejecting a "Penseroso", Adams seems to urge Saint-Gaudens not to compete with Michelangelo. To achieve an "eternal" work of his own, Adams needed to avoid the anxiety of some single powerful influence.

Two other passages from Adams' letters display Adams' efforts to maintain the vitality of the figure by resisting specificity and closure – and by pushing eventual readers of these letters closer to his precise degree of indeterminacy. To Richard Watson Gilder, the most influential magazine editor of the day, Adams wrote with unaccustomed candor: "The whole meaning and feeling of the figure is in its universality and anonymity. My own name for it is 'The Peace of God'" (Oct. 14, 1896; 4: 430), probably referring to the familiar liturgical blessing from St. Paul, the Peace of God which was real but beyond comprehension – "which passeth all understanding". Writing to Saint-Gaudens' son some years later, Adams chose not to supply that name:

> Do not allow the world to tag my figure with a name. Every magazine writer wants to label it as some American patent medicine for popular consumption –

> *Grief, Despair, Pear's Soap,* or *Macy's Men's Suits Made to Measure.* Your father meant it to ask a question, not to give an answer; . . (Jan. 24, 1908; 6: 109).

Yet in 1904 the sculptor himself, when pressed, had tagged the figure "The Mystery of the Hereafter" (*Reminiscences* 1: 362), being perhaps not as inarticulate as Adams insisted, yet also, as noted, sensitive to suggestion, according to Adams (May 1, 1904; 5: 579). Was Saint-Gaudens' name for the figure, therefore, something supplied by Adams? Stanford White meanwhile, working on the stone backdrop, had called it "the Nirvana", in a letter to Adams (Adams, *Microfilms,* reel 10, Jan. 6, 1893).

Thus Adams' efforts at control involve some exclusions – no Penseroso, no gender specificity, no grief or despair, no limiting labels. Inscribing Prometheus and Christ into it, he obviously did not exclude narrative: stories of suffering, adversity, and triumph of sorts. We would therefore like his reaction to a narrative very different from these two, a modern narrative, devised by a young woman he met in Washington when he was very old. She was filled with doubts about herself and her capabilities, Eleanor Roosevelt was, as wife of Franklin Delano Roosevelt, secretary of the Navy on the eve of World War I. "Sometimes I'd be very unhappy and sorry for myself", she said. "When I was feeling that way . . . I'd come here [to Rock Creek] alone, and sit and look at that woman. And I'd always come away somehow feeling better. And stronger. I've been here many, many times". She made this revelation to a friend while visiting the monument the day before her husband was inaugurated president in 1933 (Lash 1982, 132). Her narrative imagined "a woman who had transcended pain and hurt to achieve serenity" (132), who had achieved "absolute self-mastery" (Lash 1964, 196).

After visiting the figure frequently for ten years, Adams wrote Saint-Gaudens of an experience he himself had with it:

> Every now and then, in certain lights, I see, or think I see, an expression almost amounting to defiance, in the mouth and nostrils. You did not put it there; nor did I; nor am I sure of it; nor is it intended in the conception; nor am I consciously seeking it, nor can you perhaps see it even when I say it. Is it there? You don't know, and I'm not sure; but I'm curious whether others feel it (Apr. 30, 1902; 5: 382).

This "defiance" is a clue to Adams' reason for inscribing Prometheus in the figure. It is one of Adams' many power plays – efforts to push his monument into an ever larger space in art history, writing letters and a private autobiography (the *Education*), texts that he knew would be published, thus barring many viewers from coming to the figure with a vacant mind or innocent eye.

In returning to the comedy of control, we notice Adams' own rethinking – or possible self-contradiction. In the *Education,* when he firmly inscribes

Buddha into the figure, and privileges the Asiatic gaze, he departs from his own response on seeing the first photographs of the figure: "St Gaudens is not in the least oriental, and is not even familiar with oriental conceptions" (To John Hay, June 21, 1891; 3: 494). A recent historical handbook to Washington adds to the comedy, offering without attribution a tale concerning a Japanese ambassador, of unidentified era, who visited the monument having heard that it "reflected elements of Eastern mysticism". After studying it in silence for some time, the ambassador "stormed off in a rage, proclaiming it a great insult to Japan" (Bergheim 263).

V

A discussion of an orchestrated and prolonged attempt to control the degree of ambiguity of meaning is apt to end with evasion. But we can sum up without closing down. First, Henry Adams and his civilized conspirators compel us to recognize the infinite complexities – even in simple America – that may be involved in contestation, in struggle for domination between the visual and the verbal. At a minimum, there is the naked work itself, the conventions that any particular art form acknowledges, the will of the creator(s) insofar as disclosed (constructed) by the creator(s), the discoveries of scholars, the insights of critics, the innocent absurdities in vulgate texts such as guidebooks.

Second, implicit in the foregoing discussion is the suggestion that if and when a modern work of art becomes a *locus classicus* for exploring "meaning", that classic status is earned by a variety of efforts. It does not just happen. The strongest strategy for bringing it about may be, as in numerous poems by Emily Dickinson (Henry Adams' exact contemporary), a shrewd determination to control *degree of ambiguity* rather than attempt to control by assigning and reiterating a single *specific meaning.*

Third, *meaning* in reference to works of art, in theoretical formulation and in critical practice, depends to some degree on the problems of meaning we encounter in specific works of art. Some works of art supply questions we did not know existed. This is not to say, by default, that "meaning" is finally a gathering, a simple summation, of all the problematic issues. In fact, a prominent contemporary art historian/theorist urges us to fall back upon "pragmatics" in seeking the meaning of any particular work (Bryson 73), since pragmatism urges that we not spend an eternity engaged in a futile attempt at totalizing. A *locus classicus* will not be a field of measurable touchstones but a meadow of questions changing with the seasons and years as grasses and flowers do. The Saint-Gaudens monument of 1891, its early community of construction and interpretation, and the subsequent interventions by clergymen, guidebooks, a president, and a president's wife help us a century later to understand our own hermeneutical projects – our own efforts to make texts and images talk to each other, while we listen, as Adams did. "Naturally every detail interested him; every line . . . every point of relation. . . . he was apt to stop there often to *see* what the figure had to *tell* him that was new; . . " (emphasis mine).

Finally, the Rock Creek monument and its texts suggest that some questions about the production and control of meaning, in both the Panofsky and the postmodern senses, will not be adequately predicted. To become effective interrogators of visual images, we should not necessarily trust the usual combination of resources on which we consciously or unconsciously rely: our eyes, our knowledge of artistic conventions, our understanding of how style and form and symbolism have evolved, our sense of how the prevailing cultural markers operate in a given era. Nor in examining literary texts, whether in well-theorized genres (autobiography) or in genres ill-theorized (personal letters), should we assume awareness of all the struggles going on beneath. Important kinds of power and control may be attempted in texts and portions of texts that seem playful or transient.

References

Adams, Henry. *The Education of Henry Adams.* Boston: Houghton Mifflin, 1918.

-----. *The Letters of Henry Adams.* Eds. J. C. Levenson, Ernest Samuels, Charles Vandersee, Viola Hopkins Winner. 6 vols. Cambridge MA: Harvard University Press, 1982-1988.

-----. *Microfilms of the Henry Adams Papers.* 36 reels. Boston: Massachusetts Historical Society, 1981.

Bal, Mieke, and Norman Bryson. "Semiotics and Art History". *The Art Bulletin* 73 (1991): 174-208.

Bergheim, Laura. *The Washington Historical Atlas: Who Did What When and Where in the Nation's Capital.* Rockville MD: Woodbine House, 1992.

Bryson, Norman. "Semiology and Visual Interpretation". *Visual Theory: Painting and Interpretation.* Eds. Norman Bryson, Michael Ann Holly, Keith Moxey. Cambridge: Polity/Blackwell, 1991. 61-73.

Dryfhout, John. *The Work of Augustus Saint-Gaudens.* Hanover NH: University Press of New England, 1982.

Kobbe, Gustav. "Mystery of Saint Gaudens' Masterpiece Revealed by John La Farge". New York *Herald.* Jan. 16, 1910. Magazine section, part 2. 11.

La Farge, John. "Mr. La Farge Explains". Letter to the editor. New York *Herald.* Jan. 26, 1910. 10.

But exactly what is it that makes Finlay's art so difficult for some and so attractive for others? Which issues are taken up by him, and how? Among the "propaganda" material produced during the "Battle of Little Sparta" is a card which shows, as a white line drawing on black ground, the outlines of a blade with a diagonal cutting edge. The blade bears the inscription "The Medium is the Message", and at the bottom of the card there appears the line "Death to Strathclyde Region" (fig. 1). This repeats the war-cry of the "Battle of Little Sparta" which was in fact fought about the question of just what place art can or should occupy in our lives and societies. A silk-screen print of a similar combination of blade and inscription on red ground reads "Laconic", complemented at the bottom by the explanatory line "Homage to Neo-Classicism" (fig. 2).[9] The calligraphic lettering on both prints in capitals is of a distinctly modern (no seriphs), ascetic, yet classicizing character (U is given as V). Both prints work with a tenuous web of tensions, of paradox, and contradictory messages: the blade stands for the guillotine – yet not only as an instrument of death but as a symbol for ultimate reality and unremitting convictions. The quote from Marshal McLuhan's analysis of a media-dominated society is turned around and radicalized – it now refers to real conflicts of interests, real actions, real pain – in history and today. But it does so as a sign, in a fictitious context. "Death to Strathclyde Region" has the distinct flavour of Tom Sawyer and Huck Finn playing at villains. In the guise of boyish insolence it makes a serious point about the place of art in our society. *Style* is turned into a weapon: "Laconic", Spartan, radical, republican. Style – Neo-Classicism – is presupposed to be a meaningful part of a work of art. Style stands for values rather than being arbitrarily superimposed, it refers to the spirit rather than the surface of a work of art.[10] Again, within the images of both prints, a tension builds between what has come to be thought of as post-modern freedom of choice as to form – anything goes, why not Neo-Classicism? – and the assertion of a still meaningful meaning of this form going back to Roman republican austerity. Form and iconography are fused, a narrative to be reconstructed as a mental image informs the blade prints, which are exemplary of many other of Finlay's works drawing on the emblematic tradition. The use of Nazi imagery in other works proves the artist to be conscious of the historical implications of what he shows us. Ambiguity has a share in this radical position, it is present in the prints and the sculptures in many guises.

The "battle of ideas", however, does not seem to be Finlay's ultimate concern. Neo-Classicism stands for both the pondered, immobile form and for the challenge and overthrow of frozen structures and systems, for revolution. One of his cards, composed of two contrasting quotations, revolves around the classical column as a symbol both of continuity and of the driving force for change: "'In the back of every dying civilisation sticks a bloody Doric column' (Herbert Read, quoted by Charles Jencks) – 'In the foreground of every revolution, invisible, it seems, to the academics, stands a perfect classical column.'"[11] The card unfolds its challenge only in a contemporary context where aesthetic and political concerns have become completely separated. Neo-Classicism in its twentieth century forms could not have been more discredited than by the use it has been put to by the National Socialists in Germany, the Italian fascists, and other totalitarian regimes. The artist knows this and still believes that the risk must be taken.

The Verbal/Visual work in the Garden

One is faced with an *embarras de richesses* trying to survey the artist's work, which consists of about 1000 items issued from his Wild Hawthorn Press ranging from small cards and booklets to catalogues and large prints.[12] There are also works in many other media: stone, neon, textile, bronze, wood, glass, plaster, mosaic, designed by the artist and executed in close collaboration for him by artists who are skilled to handle the different techniques and media.[13] A number of motifs have been varied by the artist and combined in many ways in these different materials, such as ships and fishing boats, tanks and aircraft, flowers and trees, columns and sundials. Among the themes Finlay has turned to again and again, the French Revolution may be the most important; but almost equally prevalent are language and nature, the nature of language, and Classical mythology. Over the years Finlay has created what could be called a visual history of art incorporating quotations of widely differing works by Dürer or Mondrian, Poussin or Anselm Kiefer, to address the history and meaning of landscape painting, the question and problem of the avant-garde, and other issues.[14]

Almost all of Finlay's works use both texts and images, or sometimes texts as images; however, the weight and importance of the image and also the material aspects of the transmission of messages has grown markedly over the years. This has to do, to some extent at least, with the artist's perhaps most acclaimed achievement: his garden Little Sparta in Scotland, near Dunsyre, Lannarkshire, which has been laid out and developed since 1966. It contains a great number of art works on a smaller scale, and several large-scale installations, including architecture.[15]

The garden functions in different ways: it *represents* both *nature* and *culture*, or one working on and with the other – but within the garden, thus understood as a symbolic form, many of the sculptures and inscriptions are referring to the hard, cold, and violent core in both realms, while at the same time retaining the traditions of the elegy and the idyll as their literary inspiration. The garden is a *medium* which enables the artist and the viewer to place contradictory statements and paradoxical arrangements within its microcosm to allow for constellations and variations unrestrained by hierarchies. It is also a *gallery of carefully composed pictures* – very much in the spirit of some of the smaller English landscape gardens of the early 18th century, such as those created by the poets Alexander Pope in Twickenham on the Thames or William Shenstone's The Leasowes.[16]

These images – to be visited and seen in a suggested if not compulsory sequence – fuse their elements: light and shade, "glooms and solitudes" the vibrating shapes of the leaves of carefully chosen plants, the smoothness of weathered wood or highly finished stone, elegiac inscriptions.[17] The garden as an artform is fraught with historical implications, yet is also a simple, down-to-earth reality, shaped in accordance with the limitations of climate, size, and means. All of its elements and different layers of meaning are employed by the artist to spell out – and to provide as a spatial and visual experience – his critique of the state of our culture. The garden also relies on the viewer's curiosity to explore, turn to the artist's commentary in his work, to contemplate the many allusions and follow them up.

Kulturkritik

Finlay's cultural critique may be summarised – with a measure of simplification – in three points. Firstly: the permissive society has become "criminal"; it must therefore be held responsible for its own decay and ultimate demise.[18] Secondly: hypocrisy reigns supreme on all levels of society; true relations of cause and effect, the power structures at the basis of decisions are being glossed over and lied about. Thirdly – we are rapidly giving up our own tradition – and here Finlay refers to Europe and its heritage – but we have nothing to replace it with – intellectually or spiritually. The artist can be seen in a long tradition to voice such warnings and the three points here are by no means all the artist has to say –[19] but they may suffice to sketch out the direction of his criticism, traditionally linked to what seems to be a European obsession: the longing for an earlier, now lost state.[20] He laments the loss of the "sacred" and an "absolute" and his answer as an artist is the call for a "neoclassical rearmament", a return to some kind of norm.[21]

In taking up the French Revolution as a theme, Finlay sums up an historical process which is coming to the end of its possibilities: it would perhaps be fair to say that he unremittingly confronts what we have come to think of as "civil society" with its origins, the price it has to pay, the ideals it originated from. Again, his means are simple and sophisticated at once: historiography, biography, philosophy, literature; the classical orders in architecture; the accumulated knowledge of art history – all are equally used as resources for his own works.[22] The system of clearly defined disciplines and genres in which they have come to us is being ignored by the artist. European thought and history have been used as material for different works of art in different media, displayed, in the non-hierarchical layout of the garden, in a collage-like combination, on the assumption that they all share in one inseparable whole, in one tradition, including its ruptures. The artist's claim seems to be that we are bound up with this tradition inexorably: that we have no choice but to accept the Enlightenment paradox as the backbone of our culture and indeed survival, and that all hope for reconciliation (with nature, with our own nature, with different societal models) is but self-delusion. The insistence on exposing the inescapable price for civilisation – violence, human sacrifice, war – is the scandal that is at the root of this work's provocation. He is called a moralist – respectfully – and the issues raised by him are rarely taken up, sometimes sharply criticised.[23] The artist, however, insists, and does so by radicalizing his statements formally and iconographically, and by shifting towards the image as a tool of intellectual analysis.

Guillotines

Among the often varied and repeated motifs the artist uses, the guillotine belongs to the wider thematic complex of the French Revolution. There can be no question of just how powerful both as a form and a symbol the guillotine was – and still is. It is with a work that uses this image that Ian Hamilton Finlay first became widely known in Germany, the installation "A View to the Temple" during *documenta* 8 (1987).[24] Four oversized guillotines had been axially arranged on an alley leading to a neoclassical garden temple at the far end (fig. 3). Those four guillotines were at once fascinating and repellent in their monumentality and quickly grew to be the emblem of the 1987 *documenta* – albeit an emblem that was neither scrutinised nor read carefully.[25] At least that is what could be concluded from the fact that the inscriptions on the guillotines' bronze blades were not documented or commented on in the catalogue or elsewhere. In cards which Finlay realised with Gary Hincks, these inscriptions are given in red lettering on four blades: "The form of each thing is distinguished by its function or purpose; some are intended to arouse laughter, others terror, and these are their forms" – "Frighten me, if you will, but let the terror which you inspire in me be tempered by some grand moral idea" – "The government of the Revolution is the despotism of liberty against tyranny. Terror is an emanation of virtue" – "Terror is the piety of the Revolu-

Figure 3. "A View to the Temple" (1987) with Keith Brookwell and Nicholas Sloan, wood and bronze, Kassel *documenta* 1987 (left). Blades (1987), with Gary Hincks, cards in folder; texts by Nicholas Poussin, Denis Diderot, Maximilien Robespierre, Ian Hamilton Finlay (right).

tion".[26] The linking by quotation of the neoclassical landscape painter Nicolas Poussin with Denis Diderot, Maximilien Robespierre, and the artist himself was not acknowledged or interpreted in connection with the guillotines as sculptures. Apparently, the subject matter was not only too closely connected with the bloodshed of the *terreur* period of the French Revolution, it also touched upon and linked areas which, for various reasons, one does not like to see so connected. While Finlay's installation was markedly present visually in the media, there was a similarly marked silence on the side of critical analysis. This sheds a specific light on the difficulty of Finlay's concepts. His serious play with the aesthetics of the sublime not only points to politics in a general way, but to its central driving forces: power and violence. A reference, in bronze lettering, to their legitimation by virtue, that is, a normative set of values, constitutes (at least in Germany) a maximum on an otherwise rather limited scale of possible provocations in contemporary art.[27]

What remains of the classical parks in Cassel with their alleys that subjugated the land to their geometric axiality and thus to its sovereign, serves as an appropriate stage for the sculptures: we are compelled to remember the fact that our view of landscapes and nature for a long time has been and continues to be shaped by the formulae of classical landscape art and painting; we are reminded that there is a core of idealistic moralising and of violence at the heart of democratic society; that legitimate power is derived from secularized religious ideas. With an installation of terror we are reminded of the early history of modern art, the humanities, and science. The quotations truly become blades below which our gaze passes towards the little temple of around 1820. "History" is being aestheticized and then brought into contemporary reality. The power of the image arises from this translation of a concept into the concrete.

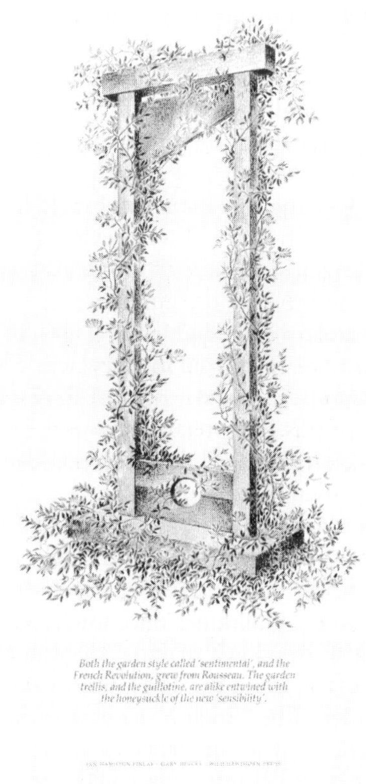

Both the garden style called 'sentimental', and the
French Revolution, grew from Rousseau. The garden
trellis, and the guillotine, are alike entwined with
the honeysuckle of the new 'sensibility'.

Figure 4. "Both the Garden Style ... " (1987), with Gary Hincks, lithographic print.

of the Apollo of Belvedere to have been further transformed into the silhouette of an 18th-century youth in a dancing pose. The artist – who elaborates on this theme in a number of prints –[35] intends us to identify Apollo with St. Just, the revolutionary: ardently, bloodthirsty, amorously pursuing his political aims. Again, there is irony built into the group, the setting, the colouring. One might even find a humorous comment on any desirous pursuit in these two figures, showing us the intended rape as an eternal dance, choreographed two thousand years ago, and as an equally eternal ultimate denial.

Several of Finlay's prints since the early 1970s elaborate on the theme, on Ovid's text, on the violent implications of the legend, on its potential as a parable for what might be called the ultimate disappointment of the redemptive powers of the Western tradition. The artist draws attention to the political implications of the ancient parable: the destructive element inextricably bound up with the driving forces of European culture and politics. His using Bernini's sculpture to do this (and perhaps even Bernini's use of the Apollo of Belvedere) seems to be a suggestion that this knowledge was always present and must only be remembered, recollected.

Wandering further up the garden, we encounter once more the sun-god but now his severed, monumental, glaringly gilded head, firmly planted under a tree, this time sharing his facial features with St. Just, whose portraits

Figure 8. "Apollon Terroriste" (1988), with Alexander Stoddart, resin and gold leaf, Little Sparta.

were, in turn, modeled after the Greek god (fig. 8). Across his brow, the god's head bears an inscription in the manner of Cain's mark: "Apollon Terroriste". Fragmentation, inconsolable beauty, cold classicism, blindness, incongruous setting – all is used by the artist to create a *shock of seeing* that might lead to comprehension, understanding. The god-like young revolutionary paid with his life for an absolute commitment that he had tried to superimpose on an

Figure 9. "The Present Order is the Disorder of the Future Saint Just" (1983), with Nicholas Sloan, stone and inscriptions, Little Sparta.

entire society. His words "The present order is the disorder of the future" are given a monumental, perhaps an eternal form in Finlay's garden (fig. 9). Huge, grey, seemingly unmovable blocks of granite are arranged to form that Heraclitean sentence turned political, offering its author "Saint Just" as a prime example to its truth.[36] One is made to see, to sense even, that only a major natural disaster could ever rearrange these blocks.[37] We are confronted with a monumentalism which, while it is its own parody, insists on monumentality, sublimity, the awe-inspiring quality of the work of art and of "nature" so much discussed in 18th-century philosophy and garden-discourse. From this part of the garden one overlooks the surrounding hills and valleys – the enclosed, secret garden opens up towards the Scottish landscape – art and nature are fused, a quotation, as it were, of earlier such fusions in gardens of the 18th century. Even elusive elements like the appropriating gaze over vast areas, then introduced into landscape art, are incorporated by the artist in his work.

Finlay's garden was created without much funding (just like Shenstone's) in the period of affluence after the Second World War; it remained a solitary undertaking, removed from the mainstream's fashions and movements but not cut off from artistic or intellectual developments of those decades. Its place on the periphery is crucial for its (and, perhaps, the artist's) most important features: aesthetic and intellectual rigour; uncompromising convictions visualised within a non-hierarchical, non-systematic structure; the will to endure and form that difference, to be in opposition whenever necessary. It is hard to think of any other *Gesamtkunstwerk* (garden or otherwise) that puts what we have come to understand as intertextuality into practice in a more visible, concrete, tangible way. The strength of such concreteness grows from the distance the artist endures as the prerequisite of aesthetic and intellectual analysis.

NOTES

1 This paper is the revised version of a lecture given at the University of Hamburg in a series of lectures on garden history and politics during the summer semester in 1993, and a paper presented at the Third International Congress of the International Association of Word and Image Studies in Ottawa, in August 1993. I should like to thank friends and colleagues for their critical remarks and helpful suggestions: Horst Bredekamp, Claus Clüver, Anne Rorimer, Pia Simig, Lauren Weingarden. I am grateful to the artist for letting me work in complete freedom in his garden and archive and answering my questions patiently.

2 The sign of the SS was used for a sculpture containing the word "osso", 1986; several prints, among them a calligraphic metamorphosis of two humanistic long ss to the Germanic runes; objects forming scythes as s-runes; a card with images of such scythes and a quote from Abraham a Santa Clara on "Death is a reaper": s. Abrioux, 283, 291, 298.

3 Hill, 59-61; see also Abrioux, 7-9, for a short account of the events.

4 Gwyn Headley and Wim Meulenkamp, *Follies. A National Trust Guide,* London: The National Trust, 1986; for a forceful reaction to Finlay's "war" waged on the National Trust over this issue, see Meulenkamp, 45-61.

5 "Proposal for a Garden Commemorating the French Revolution and the Rights of Man 1789-1989, Hôtel des Menus Plaisirs, Versailles". Ian Hamilton Finlay, Alexander Chemetov with the participation of Sue Finlay and Nicholas Sloan, *Art and Design* 4 (1988): 34-37; Stephen Bann, "A Revolutionary Garden in Versailles," *Art and Design* 4 (1988): 38f.; Brian Sewell, "Ian Hamilton Finlay: Sculptor or Poet?", *Apollo* 120 (1989): 116; for a short account cf. also Abrioux, 14f.

6 "7000 oaks. City forestation instead of city administration" – the pun, of course, is lost.

7 Adriani et al., 158.

8 For a list of exhibitions see Abrioux, Bibliography compiled by Pia Simig, 317. Not included there numerous exhibitions to which the artist contributed work.

9 For "Laconic" see Abrioux, 32; also about the rôle of Neoclassicism for Finlay is Gintz, 111-116.

10 See Rosenblum for the original 18th-century moralising implication of Neoclassicism; on the "Exemplum virtutis" topic: 50-106.

11 Card (1981) illustrated in Abrioux, 224.

12 See the section misleadingly headed "Bibliography" (compiled by Pia Simig) in Yves Abrioux' monograph, 312-317; see also: *Ian Hamilton Finlay & The Wild Hawthorn Press. A Catalogue Raisonné 1958-1990,* Edinburgh: Graeme Murray Gallery, 1990.

13 This prevalence of the *disegno* over execution as the true contribution of the artist is of course a result of the movement towards conceptualism since the 1960s.

14 For an attempt to situate Finlay in the tradition of modernism and to describe his own contribution as an artist see Carlson, 38-53.

15 Descriptions of the garden by Bann, "Description", 113-144 and "Finlay's Fane", 21-25.

16 Clark, 165-189; 166-177; Riely, 202- 209; von Butlar, "Gedanken", 7-19.

17 "Classic gardens are composed of Glooms and Solitudes and not of plants and trees". See plan for the garden, Little Sparta, which gives some of Finlay's "Detached Sentences on Gardening". From the model of William Shenstone's "Unconnected Thoughts on Gardening" in: *The Works of William Shenstone,* vol.2, 125-147 (rpt. John Dixon Hunt and Peter Willis, *The Genius of the Place. The English Landscape Garden 1620-1820,* London and Cambridge, Mass: MIT Press, 1988 (2nd ed.), 289-297); the move from "unconnected thoughts" to "detached sentences" is characteristically a move to more poignancy, to aphorism: more "Detached Sentences" by Finlay: Abrioux, 40 and Ian Hamilton Finlay, "More Detached Sentences on Gardening in the Manner of Shenstone" in: *PN Review* 42 (1984): 18-20.

18 See Finlay's adaptation of Piranesi's frontispiece to the *Carceri* (with Gary Hincks): "When the World Took to Tolerance it Took to Crime" (1991): Abrioux, 266 and 314, 316.

19 There is a vast body of literature on the subject. There can be no doubt that some of the critics of culture, particularly in Germany but also elsewhere in Europe, writing around the turn of the century, have fed their ideas to the totalitarian regimes that developed later – see Dorowin on Henri Massis, Ramiro de Maeztu and Leopold von Andrian; for Germany cf. Hepp, *Moderne Kunst, Kulturkritik und Reformbewegungen nach der Jahrhundertwende.*

20 For an exploration of the *topos* see Graber, passim.

21 In this Charles Jencks sees Finlay related to Robert Rauschenberg, David Salle, Hans Haacke, Stephen McKenna ("Post-Modern und Spät-Modern", 220). One might also think of recurring tendencies in the 19th century, German *Nazarener,* for example, and the Preraffaelites.

22 This attitude towards the immaterial as material may have been developed by the artist in concrete poetry, which does not regard language "as being a system of references to a reality outside itself, but as being itself a concrete reality: as being, in fact, the raw material out of which the poem is made" (Scobie, 65).

23 Compare the assessments in Abrioux:, 250-255, and Meulenkamp, 45-61.

24 *Documenta* catalogue, Kassel 1987.

25 See Gerould, on Finlay: 305-309; further on the guillotine: Arrasse, *Die Guillotine*, (French: *La Guillotine et l'imaginaire de la terreur*, Paris: Flammarion, 1987, 47-111); for ample illustrative material see: La Ghigliottina del Terrore, exhibition catalogue, curated by Daniel Arrasse and Valérie Rousseau-Lagarde, Florence: Istituto Francese di Firenze, 1986.

26 *4 Blades* (1987) with Gary Hinks, cards in folder; see Abrioux, 272.

27 Finlay is not the first to see such connections. Compare Heinrich Heine's scandalous remark on Kant: "Wenn aber Immanuel Kant, dieser große Zerstörer im Reiche der Gedanken, an Terrorismus den Maximilian Robespierre weit übertraf, so hat er doch mit diesem manche Ähnlichkeit. ... Zunächst finden wir in beiden dieselbe unerbittliche, schneidende, poesielose Ehrlichkeit. Dann finden wir in beiden dasselbe Talent des Mißtrauens, nur daß es der eine gegen Gedanken wendet und Kritik nennt, während der andere es gegen Menschen anwendet und republikanische Tugend betitelt" (*Der Salon,* 518-623, 584).

28 Carol Blum, "Representing the Body Politic: Fictions of the State", in: *Representing the French Revolution. Literature, Historiography, and Art,* ed. James A. W. Heffernan, Hanover and London: University Press of New England, 1993, 123-134.

29 See Abrioux, 148-149, with a photograph of the trellis with an appended plaque "Julie et Saint-Preux" leading to "Julie's Garden" in Little Sparta.

30 Butlar, *Landsitz.*

31 Williams, 73-96; Voght, *Flotbeck in ästhetischer Ansicht*, ; first in: *Die Gartenkunst* 1 (1989): 125-155: "Jenisch-Park und Quellental in Flottbek bei Hamburg".

32 See in Abrioux "Et in Arcadia Ego", 241-247, with numerous renderings of the theme.

33 There are numerous works relating to Apollo in the garden as well as prints varying the theme: see Abrioux, 62, 64, 67, 141, 143, 285.

34 See for a comment by Ian Hamilton Finlay on these matters an interview with Peter Hill: "Spartan defence", 61.

35 Notably: "And even as she fled … " in two versions with John R. Nash, 1987, and "After Bernini" with Gary Hincks, 1987.

36 "The Present Order is the Disorder of the Future Saint Just," with Nicholas Sloan, 1983.

37 There is also a card, "The Present Order …" (1983, with Nicholas Sloan) with the added subscription: "Cut around the outlines. Arrange words in order. Louis-Antoine Saint-Just, 1767-1794", see Abrioux, 256.

REFERENCES

Abrioux, Yves. *Ian Hamilton Finlay. A Visual Primer.* 1985. Introductory notes and commentaries by Stephen Bann. London: Reaktion Books, second rev. and expanded edition 1992.

Adriani, Götz, Konnertz, Winfried and Thomas, Karin. *Joseph Beuys. Leben und Werk.* Köln: DuMont, 1986 (third ed.).

Arrasse, Daniel. *Die Guillotine.* Reinbek: Rowohlt, 1989.

Bann, Stephen. "A Description of Stonypath". *Journal of Garden History* 1 (1981): 113-144.

-----. "Finlay's Fane – Metamorphoses at Stonypath". *PN Review* 42 (1984): 21-25.

Butlar, Adrian von. "Gedanken zur Bildproblematik und zum Realitätscharakter des Landschaftsgartens". *Die Gartenkunst* 2 (1990): 7-19.

-----. *Der englische Landsitz 1715-1760. Symbol eines liberalen Weltentwurfs.* Mittenwald: Mäander, 1982.

Carlson, Prudence. "The Garden on the Hill". *Arts Magazine*, 64 (1990): 38-53.

Clark, H. F. "Eighteenth Century Elysiums. The Rôle of 'Association' in the Landscape Movement". *Journal of the Warburg and Courtauld Institutes* 6 (1943): 165-189, 166-177.

Dorowin, Hermann. *Retter des Abendlands. Kulturkritik im Vorfeld des europäischen Faschismus.* Stuttgart: Metzler, 1991.

Gerould, Daniel. *Guillotine. Its Legend and Lore.* New York: Blast Books, 1992.

Gintz, Claude. "Neoclassical Rearmament". *Art in America* 75 (1987): 111-116.

Graber, Klaus. *Der Locus amoenus und der locus terribilis. Bild und Funktion der Natur in der deutschen Schäfer- und Landlebendichtung des 17. Jahrhunderts.* Köln, Wien: Böhlau, 1974.

Heine, Heinrich. *Der Salon I. Zur Geschichte der Religion und Philosophie in Deutschland. Sämtliche Werke in drei Bänden.* Bd. 2. Stuttgart: Weltbild Bücherdienst, n.d., 518-623.

Hepp, Corona. *Moderne Kunst, Kulturkritik und Reformbewegungen nach der Jahrhundertwende.* München: dtv, 1987.

Hill, Peter. "Spartan defence" (interview). *Studio international* 196 (1984): 59-61.

Hunt, John Dixon and Willis, Peter. *The Genius of the Place. The English Landscape Garden 1660-1820.* London and Cambridge, MA: MIT Press, 1988 (2nd ed.)

Jencks, Charles. "Post-Modern und Spät-Modern". *Moderne oder Postmoderne?* Ed. P. Koslowsky, R. Spaemann and R. Löw. Weinheim: acta humaniora, VCH, 1986, 205-235.

Meulenkamp, Wim. "Portfolio/De god van 'Little Sparta': Over Ian Hamilton Finlay, de Follies War en andere onkiese zaken". *Maatstaf* 3 (1988): 45-61.

Riely, John. "Shenstone's Walks: The Genesis of The Leasowes". *Apollo* 110 (1979): 202-209.

Rosenblum, Robert. *Transformations in Late Eighteenth Century Art.* Princeton: Princeton University Press, 1967.

Ross, Stephanie. "Gardens, Earthworks andEnvironmental Art". *Landscape, Natural Beauty and the Arts.* Ed. Salim Kemal and Ivan Gaskell. Cambridge: Cambridge University Press, 1993, 158-182.

Scobie, Stephen. "Metaphor Beyond Language". *The Structurist,* no.12, 1972-73, 63-67.

Shenstone, William. "Unconnected Thoughts on Gardening". *The Works.* Vol.2, 125-147.

Voght, Caspar. *Flotbeck in ästhetischer Ansicht.* Ed. and comment. Charlotte Schoell-Glass. Hamburg: Christians (second ed.), 1991; also in: *Die Gartenkunst* 1 (1989): 125-155.

Williams, Robert. "Rural Economy and the Antique in the English Landscape Garden". *Journal of Garden History* 7 (1987): 73-96.

Cartoons and Caricature

"Faire comprendre au peuple": représentation caricaturale et éloquence démocratique dans la culture politique française de 1848

Mirela Saim

> Avec cette espèce d'argot plastique on était maître de dire et de faire comprendre au peuple tout ce qu'on voulait. *Baudelaire, De l'essence du rire.*

Au XIXe siècle, les pratiques de l'imprimé de presse imposent avec force un *ordre mixte de communication,* où le dicible et le visible, la parole et l'image (graphique), sont étroitement liés, au service d'une stratégie d'intervention active dans le discours de la "démocratie", il s'agit d'une stratégie qui englobe la théorie diffuse des formes, des modèles et des pratiques discursives de visée "populaire".

La chanson, le pamphlet, le vaudeville et la caricature sont considérées comme les formes par excellence, brèves et "accrocheuses", de la communication populaire, formes d'une très grande efficacité dans la formation de l'opinion publique. Particulièrement intéressant est le statut de la caricature politique, discours d'une image graphique non seulement contextualisée mais aussi co-textualisée[1] par l'écrit et diffusée, après 1830, par l'imprimé de presse. Le succès de la caricature, perçue comme "écriture" d'une éloquence démocratique de persuasion immédiate, a d'abord un rapport direct avec une idéologie post-révolutionnaire qui prescrit au *discours pour le peuple* un modèle rhétorique bref, à la fois imagé et railleur.

Dans son *Livre des Orateurs,*[2] "le Quintilien français", L.M. de Cormenin (1788-1866) remarquant que "la passion a sa logique plus serrée, plus entraînante encore que le raisonnement" estime:

> Figures saisissantes, mouvements rapides, entremêlés de repos, voilà l'éloquence qui convient, en tout pays, au peuple. En France, pays moqueur, ajoutez-y un peu d'ironie amère et fine.[3]

Soutenue par cette logique d'une éloquence démocratique à la fois rapide et amusante la caricature politique devient la contre-partie graphique d'une oralité d'espace public, qui engage avec le pamphlet et la chanson une rhétorisation spécifique du "populaire", registre qui doit obéir au classique *docere e movere* par une expression claire, directe et rapide. Altaroche (1811-1884) explique, ainsi, que pour "enseigner et émouvoir les classes populaires", classes d'"une intelligence sûre, mais moins exercée", l'idée doit s'exprimer "par une formule vive et concise, ou d'une manière piquante et dramatique".[4]

Comme telle, la caricature intègre et étaye une énorme force de persuasion, le couple image (graphique)-parole (imprimée) articulant ensemble un *discours* d'intense rhétorisation, porteur d'une argumentation opaque, mais non moins chargée de partis-pris idéologiques et axiologiques. L'adhésion aux valeurs communiquées par le discours caricatural, emportée par une distanciation ironique d'avec la fiction oratoire, engage la participation totale du récepteur, car rire, c'est toujours prendre position. "Révolution crayonnée" selon Champfleury, "argot plastique" populaire d'après Baudelaire, la force immédiate de communiquer de la caricature en fait un outil de choix dans le combat politique: une bonne caricature peut être tout aussi efficace que le pamphlet, genre critique bref avec lequel elle partage plusieurs traits – dans la pensée même de l'époque.[5]

La Révolution de 1848 en France offre à la réflexion un objet d'étude privilégié. Fidèle aux idées libérales républicaines, déjà affirmées en 1830, le gouvernement provisoire institue, dès les dernières journées de février, dans le pays entier un immense espace de délibération publique, laissant libre carrière à la liberté d'expression. Pour citer les paroles de Louis Garnier-Pagès, ministre dans le Gouvernement provisoire: "La Révolution avait ouvert toutes les issues à l'esprit humain; le gouvernement provisoire n'en avait fermé aucune".[6]

Cette volonté d'ouverture communicationnelle s'est manifestée par l'articulation plurielle de l'espace libéral de l'opinion populaire, légitimation des voies offertes à la pratique sociale de la parole: ainsi, le droit d'association permet l'essor des clubs, domaine de riche discursivité orale, et de même, les lois sur la liberté de la presse provoquent une véritable explosion médiatique (journaux, placards, affiches, etc.). La presse est particulièrement encouragée, par l'abolition de la censure et par le soulagement fiscal: "A chacun était accordé la liberté illimitée de répandre ses pensées dans un journal. Plus de timbre, plus de cautionnement!"[7]

Depuis le début, le nouvel espace de publicité est envisagé comme territoire de propagande politique, ce qui revient à le saisir comme lieu d'une intersubjectivité orientée par l'effort réfléchi de construction civique. La transparence de la chose publique est ainsi posée en principe de gouvernement et considérée, dans les milieux politiques du libéralisme républicain, comme ayant la capacité de régler directement l'action révolutionnaire et d'instaurer la démocratie;[8] ensuite, l'élection du corps représentatif sera investie du pouvoir de constituer aussi un mécanisme de communication sociale[9] et de consacrer la condition démocratique de l'action politique.

La communication est donc considérée lien social fondamental et investie du pouvoir de guider les actions politiques du gouvernement démocratique. Or, c'est à l'intérieur de cette idéologie de l'aide et du contrôle du politique par la publicité que la caricature reçoit un rôle précis, justifié d'ailleurs par son statut critique – confirmé par une tradition polémique déjà bien établie pendant les années 1830-1835. "En politique, la Caricature est de bonne guerre" – écrivait Charles Blanc, pour ajouter:

> La Caricature est le plus puissant moyen de discréditer, dans l'esprit du peuple, le mauvais gouvernement./ . . . / Un gouvernement fort et populaire, résumant en lui toute la dignité d'une nation et faisant de grandes choses, n'aurait pas à s'inquiéter des sarcasmes de la Caricature.[10]

Dans ce qui suit, je voudrais examiner la manière dont l'invention caricaturale engage un mécanisme interdiscursif complexe qui, partant d'une affiliation doxique libérale à l'idéologie de la communication, se définit néanmoins par la mise en discours d'une hétérogénéité fondamentale: entre le préjugé et le paradoxe, la caricature politique du temps de la révolution saura produire une critique *efficace* de la dérive démagogique du discours politique du social. Deux images caricaturales parues dans *Le Pamphlet,*[11] journal de tendance républicaine modérée, serviront de base à mes remarques.

La première de ces images prend pour sujet la question même de la lecture populaire: "*L'homme ne vit pas seulement de pain*" (fig. 1) de Lorentz[12] fait voir avec intensité combien la figuration de l'imaginaire social articule un discours complexe, soutenu par une procédure de *réduction litotique,* qui vise le contrôle des rapports interdiscursifs.

Figure 1. *L'homme ne vit pas seulement de pain.*

Par son sujet, par son style, clair et précis, mais aussi assez plat, l'image graphique place au centre la corporalité sociale du rapport parole-image, rapport qui identifie l'"écriture"/lecture de l'imprimé de presse avec une typologie sociale indexicale. La scène montre la lecture des journaux en pleine rue, dans un climat de "fête populaire": les trois personnages lisent chacun son journal avec une attention si profonde qu'ils négligent le vin et le pain, notamment mentionnés dans la légende et présents au premier plan – détail souligné aussi par la réaction des deux bêtes. Illustrant la multiplicité polytopique de l'objet imprimé, l'image rend visible le "marché de l'opinion" comme *spectacle typologique* de la place publique.

La dimension typologique, de référence universelle et populaire, est aussi renforcée par la forme proverbiale de la légende, qui, tout en recouvrant l'adage biblique, renvoie à l'idée si rebattue à l'époque selon laquelle les besoins "spirituels", voire communicationnels, du peuple sont plus importants que ses besoins matériels.[13] Entre la sentence de la légende, formant un argument d'autorité par son renvoi à une sagesse commune, de crédibilité universelle, et l'image juxtaposée qui veut offrir une illustration réaliste, réinterprétation "actuelle" de l'énoncé biblique, le couple image/légende engage une relation synecdochique, d'explicitation réciproque, sur l'axe sémantique *nourriture "spirituelle" (journaux) / nourriture "corporelle" (pain, vin, eau).*

À première vue, ce rapport légende/image implique une relation d'amplification substitutive où l'image serait à voir comme périphrase d'illustration: la forme négative du texte-légende implique une *réticence élocutive* intégrant – par une opération de suppression sémique préliminaire – un "vide de signifié",[14] vide qui, à son tour, ouvre l'énoncé à la possibilité d'une expansion interprétative presque illimitée. Et c'est par l'*image juxtaposée* que le sens de l'interprétation est sélecté, figé, élucidé par son ancrage dans la référence à la communication: tout ce qui n'est pas du "pain" est restreint aux seuls journaux.

Pourtant, à bien regarder, le rapport de cohérence qui lie l'image à la parole prend aussi une signification seconde: l'intrusion de l'imprimé dans la caricature implique en fait un deuxième système d'intercodage texte/image, système engagé par l'*écrit intratextuel* montré dans l'image et formant un paradigme citationnel. Le plan de la parole est ainsi dédoublé selon sa position, intérieure ou extérieure, à l'image graphique.

Le paradigme citationnel formé par les trois titres, *La Presse*, *La Vraie République* et *Le Canard*, se construit comme rapport spatial et corporel de valeur trans-idéologique identifiant un secteur précis du discours social, de signification allégorique par rapport à la question de la communication politique en général. Les trois journaux déploient un dispositif pluriel de représentation de la presse d'opinion "démocratique": *La Vraie République*[15] du socialiste Théophile Thoré, *Le Canard*,[16] légitimiste, mais "railleur"[17] et *La Presse* d'Emile de Girardin, journal d'opinion républicaine "populiste", osant une ouverture publicistique "sans rivages".[18]

Mais voilà qu'une dimension purement ironique, ambiguisant l'espace discursif de la caricature, est introduite par l'axe chronologique implicite: à la date où la caricature est publiée dans *Le Pamphlet* (13 juillet) les trois journaux de citation intra-graphique n'existent plus. *La Presse* et *La Vraie République* sont suspendus depuis le 27 juin par "arrêté du chef du pouvoir exécutif",[19] tandis que *Le Canard* a cessé sa parution dès le 25 juin.[20] Ainsi, l'axe paradigmatique formé par les titres des journaux construit une figure de l'*absence*: la parole citationnelle est celle du renvoi à un signifié disparu, vidé. L'intérieur de l'image graphique apparaît clairement comme lieu de l'irréel et, finalement, comme image visible de la presse populaire censurée.

L'espace graphique recouvre une dimension paradoxale, car le vide de signifié, déjà posé dans la tournure des paroles en légende, est ressaisi désormais comme néant, image visible d'une suppression. Ainsi, le silence textuel de la légende et l'absence suggérée par le paradigme citationnel intragraphique coïncident et tout converge vers la mise-en-faux de la présence montrée par l'image. Le rapport entre la parole dédoublée et l'image est ainsi établi comme distance de valeur ironique variable et inscrit, au-delà d'un marquage axiologique objectivé, une attitude de résistance critique. Dans ce sens, la caricature se lit comme énonciation d'un non-dit indiciel pour l'état de fait en juillet ("la presse populaire est morte, tuée par l'état !"), dénonciation d'une "trahison" majeure dans l'ordre politique du républicanisme démocratique, et comme telle, subversion de l'ordre libéral de la révolution.

Or, si la caricature de Lorentz procède par une substitution réductive de la relation interprétative texte-image, jouant sur les non-dits d'une réalité qui contredit, justement, les principes fondant l'idéologie dominante, voilà maintenant deux images caricaturales qui révèlent une stratégie polémique différente.

Dans "*Les Souvenirs du Champ-de-Mars*", il s'agit d'une mise à point *paralogique* de l'usage conventionnel des concepts-valeurs mal appréhendés du discours politique. Prenant leur référence de la Fête de la Concorde du 21 mai et illustrée dans un style conventionnel, presque académique, par le dessin de Cham de 24 mai (fig. 2), les deux images caricaturales publiées par *Le Pamphlet* deux jour plus tard, le 26 mai, sous la légende commune de "*Souvenirs du Champ-de-Mars*"[21] (fig. 3), ont une évidente valeur satirique, de visée polémique.

D'abord, elles réinscrivent la fête nationale dans la sphère de l'équivoque, vu que les "souvenirs" de la légende peuvent se lire comme renvoi double à la tradition révolutionnaire: la fête révolutionnaire de la Fédération, en 1790 et, également, le "massacre de Champ-de-Mars", de 1791.[22] Mais si le registre verbal est ainsi mis en place par une énonciation allusive d'accrochage référentiel

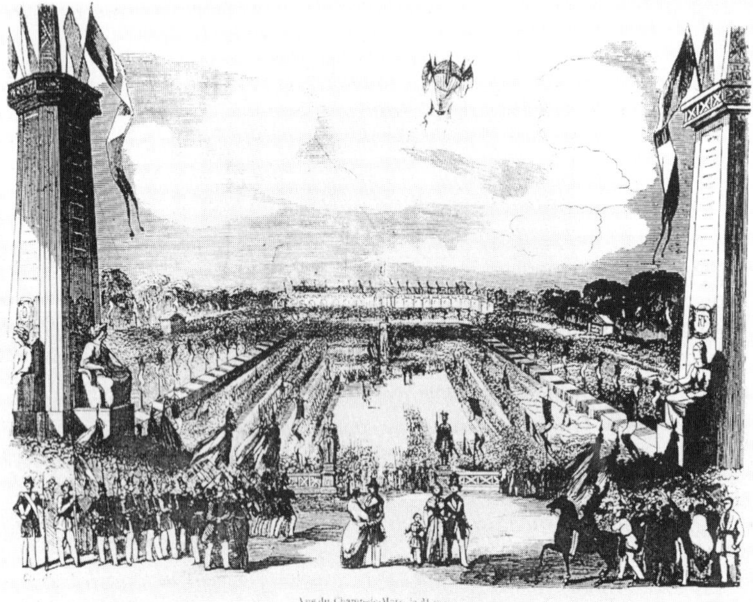
Vue du Champ-de-Mars, le 21

Figure 2. *Souvenirs du Champ-de-Mars.*

Figure 3. *Souvenirs du Champ-de-Mars.*

Gigi
Gigi
Statue de l'*Abondance*, destinée à inculquer aux populations l'amour de la faim.
Statue de la *Liberté*, ainsi faite pour indiquer que la République doit avoir le bras long.

ambigu, les légendes particularisant les deux images vont beaucoup plus loin dans leur volonté de montrer le vide de contenu caché par les notions représentées. Car, en effet, les deux caricatures révèlent avec astuce l'érosion générale du discours républicain.

Ainsi, la construction paradoxale des deux légendes, nommant les figures de la "Liberté" et de l'"Abondance" par une formulation antiphrastique,[23] mimant la définition, sert à souligner le contradictoire et à orienter la resémantisation du concept par un renversement global, entamé néanmoins par un détail incongru qui devient attribut d'identification.[24] Dans le dessin de la *Liberté*, le détail incongru, de rapport synecdochique – le bras trop long, symbole de répression – accueille un déchiffrage herméneutique, de transfert métaphorique restrictif qui compromet radicalement le concept. De même, la représentation allégorique de l'*Abondance* serait, à son tour, "destinée à inculquer aux populations l'amour de la faim".

Textualisé dans la légende, le détail incongru est montré dans l'image et renforce, par son non-sens évident, un discours de l'incompatibilité logique. L'effet de non-sens est encore souligné par un graphisme dépouillé qui sait exploiter les effets de déformation et de parodie: ainsi, le code du vêtement romain, consacré par les représentations sublimes de la figuration révolutionnaire, est ici trivialisé et, en fait, contribue à l'irréductible laideur des figures déformées.

L'expression corporelle que la personnification graphique attribue aux concepts est ainsi en concordance avec l'énonciation paradoxale des légendes, mais en totale discordance avec le statut lexical des concepts représentés: la corporalité concrète attribuée à la personnification du concept est ainsi constituée comme aberration et devient un argument polémique qui transmet la non-recevabilité de l'abstraction. Représentations malaisées des "passions politiques" du temps, les deux figures de Fabritzius consacrent avec intensité le vide conceptuel et le glissement de significations caché par un discours politique déjà compromis: le corps revêtu qui "remplit" *de visu* le concept personnifié fait mieux percevoir la réalité "nue" des attentes populaires trahies. De la sorte, la caricature jouant sur la représentation de l'imprésentable,[25] signale la polysémie infinie d'un concept imprécis pour exposer la dimension démagogique de tout discours qui s'en sert.

Ainsi, la reconcrétisation du concept par renvoi au quotidien est d'habitude en mesure d'arrêter la dérive des significations et de combler d'une manière efficace cette "boîte à double fond" qui est l'abstraction et dont l'abus serait, d'après une fameuse remarque de Tocqueville, la tentation majeure d'une éloquence démocratique en mal de stabilité.[26]

Mais ici, dans les caricatures de Fabritzius, cette reconcrétisation de l'abstrait se fait aussi d'une manière plurielle, vu que la resémantisation du concept par la parole *et* par l'image comporte des projections multiples: à la double mémoire discursive de la révolution, à la réalité quotidienne, à une intuition désabusée du politique. D'où l'intensité de sa force polémique.

La fonction argumentative des figures caricaturales de "Gigi" est confirmée et sensiblement renforcée par leur réutilisation, dans une pagination différente, dans le *Pamphlet* du 20-23 juillet (fig. 4), donc après les journée d'insurrection ouvrière de juin, suivies d'une répression impitoyable. La gravité symbolique des lieux topiques du *sublime civique* est maintenant effacée pour faire place à une axiologie *anti-pathétique claire,* qui engage une remoralisation cynique

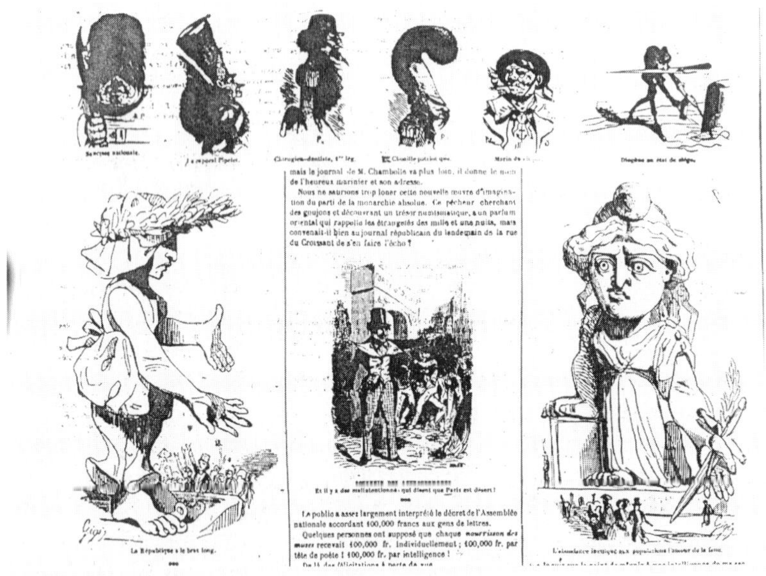

Chirurgien-dentiste, 1re lég.

La République a le bras long.

mais le journal de M. Chambolle va plus loin, il donne le nom de l'heureux marinier et son adresse.

Nous ne saurions trop louer cette nouvelle œuvre d'imagination du parti de la monarchie absolue. Ce pêcheur cherchant des goujons et découvrant un trésor numismatique, a un parfum oriental qui rappelle les étrangetés des mille et une nuits, mais convenait-il bien au journal républicain du lendemain de la rue du Croissant de s'en faire l'écho ?

Et il y a des malintentionnés qui disent que Paris est désert !

Le public a assez largement interprété le décret de l'Assemblée nationale accordant 100,000 francs aux gens de lettres.

Quelques personnes ont supposé que chaque *nourrisson des muses* recevait 100,000 fr. individuellement ; 100,000 fr. par tête de poète ! 100,000 fr. par intelligence !

Figure 4. *Le Pamphlet* du 20-23 juillet.

globale du discours politique dominant.

Porté en faux par les pratiques répressives arbitraire du Pouvoir le discours ainsi mis en cause par les caricatures au niveau de la crise de désignation est montré comme incohérent, irrationnel, disqualifié par la mauvaise foi de ses tenants. En tant que *topoi* emblématiques pour la critique de la rationalité discursive du libéralisme républicain, les deux concepts mis en images prosopographiques, *la liberté* et *l'abondance,* résument en fait les deux enjeux de la phénoménologie révolutionnaire en 1848, le politique et l'économique: pour cette raison, la républication des caricatures selon une co-textualisation qui annule le lien narratif à la tradition festive, leur confère une autonomie symbolique qui ne fait qu'intensifier leur force critique.

Figures emblématiques du faux-parler, les "portraits" de Fabritzius, comme la caricature de Lorentz examinée plus haut, engagent une critique habile, de l'intérieur, des arguments centraux de la culture politique, par confrontation avec leur usage. Il s'agit d'une critique du discours social fondée en raison, mobilisant, même au niveau de l'image, des procédés de réduction à l'absurde et engageant une stratégie soutenue de recours au réel. "Les fait, les vérités et les présomptions" (Perelman) cachées par les mots sont sans cesse dévoilées, les creux du discours politique sont exposés avec humour et finesse; c'est à ce titre que, pendant l'année révolutionnaire 1848, le discours caricatural poursuit une action de "nettoyage", de salutaire recouvrement du sens, de la raison et de la franchisse dans la sphère publique.

Notes

1 Terme proposé par Claude Duchet au cours d'une discussion (Montréal, mai 1994) sur le statut signifiant de la pagination de l'imprimé au XIXe siècle. Il indique un rapport de simple coexistence matérielle, beaucoup plus libre que la contextualisation, articulant, néanmoins, un *effet de sémantisation* perceptible à la lecture.

2 Cormenin-"Timon", *Études sur les Orateurs Parlementaires,* Paris, Pagnerre, 1838.

3 *op.cit.*, 292.

4 À l'article "Chants civiques", du *Dictionnaire politique* de Garnier-Pagès (Paris, Pagnerre, 1842, 213-214), véritable encyclopédie de la *doxa* libérale du temps.

5 Dont une force directe et immédiate de convaincre par l'appel à la logique et au sens commun: "Si le Pamphlet est à la portée de tout le monde, c'est qu'il parle comme tout le monde" (*Dictionnaire politique* de Garnier-Pagès, article "Pamphlet") explique Timon (Cormenin), reprenant une idée déjà exprimée par P.-L.Courier. Sur les stratégies argumentatives propres au pamphlet en tant que type discursif, voir les analyses de Marc Angenot dans *La Parole pamphlétaire,* Paris, Payot, 1982.

6 Louis Garnier-Pagès, *Histoire de la Révolution de 1848*, Paris, 1861-1867, vol. VI, 338.

7 *Ibidem*, vol VI, 338.

8 "Le mot Publicité est synonyme de liberté, d'égalité. / . . . / . . . les actes d'un peuple libre ne sauraient avoir trop de Publicité."- lit-on dans le *Dictionnaire politique* (*op.cit.*, 791); et encore: "Cette Publicité non moins utile aux gouvernants qu'aux gouvernés" (*ibidem.*)

9 Sur toute la complexité de cette question, ainsi que sur les aspects historiques de l'idéologie moderne du choix électoral, voir l'analyse de Pierre Rosanvallon, dans *Le sacre du citoyen. Histoire du suffrage universel en France. Paris,* Gallimard, 1992.

10 *Dictionnaire politique*, Paris, Pagnerre, 1842, 192-193.

Although *Salomé* has been illustrated by notable twentieth-century artists such as André Derain and Louis Jou, Beardsley's drawings are so universally known that any illustrator of Wilde's text must eventually come to terms with them. Shenton does so by stating that "Beardsley gave *Salomé* an élitism which mine doesn't possess. Mine's a little bit slapstick – it's a funny, comic, book – although the smile is wiped off everybody's faces as they look at the last few pages".[4] With his cartoon-book format, Shenton de-eliticizes *Salomé.* This paperback album is a far cry from other illustrated versions of the text most of which are bibliophile publications, printed on special papers in limited editions, and often signed by the artist. With its dramatic cover image and accessible price, Shenton's edition is designed for mass appeal. Furthermore, he likens this work to "an illustrated rock opera".[5] In no way does it emulate the rarified tradition of the *livre de peintre* which has figured so predominantly in *Salomé's* lineage since the text became fashionable with French illustrators in the twenties and thirties. Shenton's radical departure from this tradition seeks to debunk the notion of a single, conventional format – such as the bibliophile's *édition de luxe* – and to expand the perimeters of how a text can be pictured and packaged to attract a contemporary public.

Shenton's de-eliticization continues past the physical format of the book to affect its linguistic content. Wilde's text is calligraphed in its entirety... almost. This is to say that unlike most cartoon albums that recast the narrative in over simplified, often trivialized manners, Shenton preserves Wilde's original, deleting from it only its stilted constructions. For example, the text's biblical tonalities ("Thou hast", etc.), used no doubt by Wilde for local color in his recasting of a Judea of 30 B.C., are modernized in order to increase the text's accessibility for the contemporary reader. Although hundreds of minor changes are made along these lines, they do little to blemish the rarefied aesthetics and poetic extravagance of Wilde's original. The illustrator's intent is not to deface the literary work. Rather, he seems set on enabling it to reach the widest of readerships possible.

This is the readership of the street, not of the rare book archive, and Shenton modernizes his images as he modernizes Wilde's text, but in a much more daring, flamboyant, often flagrant fashion. Thus, the Princess Salomé chews gum and blows bubbles at inappropriate moments in the textual scenario while her mother, Queen Herodias, eats chocolates. Masses of watermelons and bananas are served at Herod's banquet, and the various ethnic groups in attendance are identified by the sort of signage used to distinguish heads of state at international political round tables. Later, when Salomé prepares for the dance of the seven veils, giraffes serve as her dressers. Because of the outrageous nature of such details, they are the first elements of Shenton's pictorial universe to strike the reader-viewer. All of them stem from a humorous bent, built on anachronism, that is part and parcel of his recasting of *Salomé.*

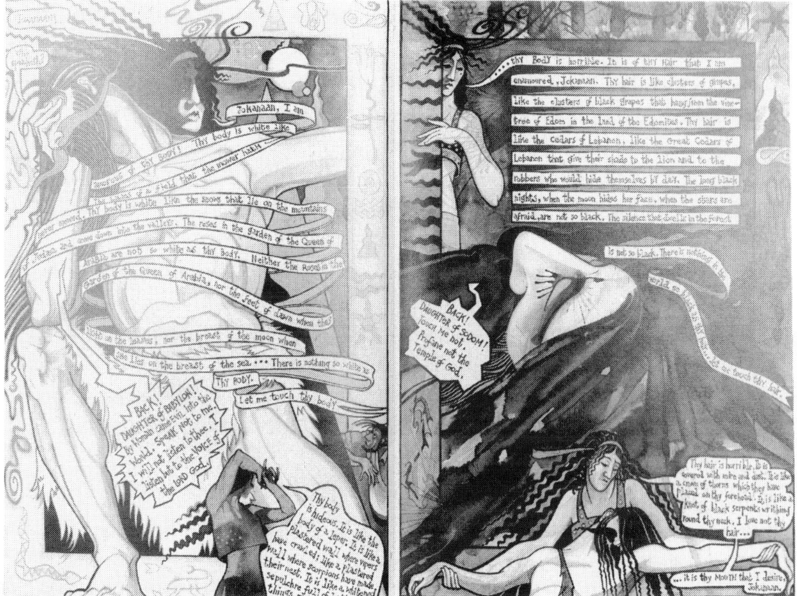

Figure 1. David Shenton, ill. for Wilde's *Salomé* (20-21), 1986, © courtesy of the artist.

If this comic rendering of graphic details seems often out of sync with the Symbolist underpinnings of Wilde's drama, it is nevertheless in line with the artist's intention to de-eliticize the text. And yet, how far can this goal be carried before the imagery degrades textual integrity? Wilde's stage directions do not call for Salomé to chew bubble gum. Nor does Herodias eat chocolates. Has Shenton misread Wilde? If his imagery is not generated by the play and therefore out of line with it, then what is its interpretative value vis-à-vis the text? In other words, at what point does illustration cease to be illumination?

The answers to these questions lie beyond a cursory viewing of Shenton's work which, on its surface, first appeals to us through anachronistic humor, then proceeds to draw us irrevocably into the vortex of Wilde's symbolic network. Shenton's contribution to the evolution of illustrated editions of *Salomé* is due to an adept transfiguration of prominent textual themes and to the originality of technique involved with this process. Thus, the answers to the questions posed above reside at the intersection of thematic articulation and technical prowess so central to Shenton's illustration of *Salomé*.

Let us first examine technique. It is, after all, the artist's most salient innovation. In terms of the cartoon format, the term technique encompasses the multiplicity of ways in which text and image play upon the page. Shenton's treatment of text begins by adhering to the traditional encapsulation of words within textual bubbles. However, as dramatic tension mounts and Salomé begins the series of what one critic has appropriately called her "blazons"[6] of Iokanaan's body, the text bursts from its bubbles to emulate the grandiloquent flow of Wilde's poetics. Inscribed on a serpentine ribbon, the text surrounds and envelopes the very object of its desire: Iokanaan's body (fig. 1). This image is entirely in keeping with our very first visual encounter with the princess who is pictured on page one as a serpent devouring its prey. Later, after the slaying of Iokanaan, Salomé's inability to control her strident verbiage is replicated by the way in which it cuts across the page obscuring image and transgressing the limits of the pictorial frame. Shenton's calligraphic treatment of the text allows for yet another layer of image-text meaning. Straightforward and regular at the outset, it soon reflects the tumultuous tenor of the text. Capitalizations, underscoring, bolding and shifts in caliber allow the calligraphic gesture an illustrative life of it own that bears heavily on how we perceive and then interpret the words and sentences that comprise Wilde's scenario.

Both the breakdown of the textual bubbles and the accentuation of calligraphic gesture evolve hand-in-hand as the passions of the play wax toward the fatal dénouement. Functioning much in the same way as a barometer, Shenton's framing devices follow this trajectory as they serve to shore up its tragic tonalities. Thus, the opening frames are conventional and rectilinear in outline. Soon they break from the standard vertical-horizontal scheme to perform on the diagonal. With imagery taking its cue from the text, order eventually gives way to chaos. On page eighteen (fig. 2), for example, these diagonals function as corridors along which characters race at such breakneck speed that one of them must use the pictorial frame as a balustrade in order to keep apace with the action. Space and depth are thus inscribed within the visual plane through this clever use of framing which allows for bird's-eye views and even voyeuristic perspectives into the action of the play. On the facing page, a technique akin to collage displays the frames in such a way that they echo the disarray of the textual moment which is the passage of the angel of death. Fittingly, the backdrop for these collaged frames is none other than the angel of death's gigantic, skeletal wing.

Elsewhere, the frame moves from rectilinear to curvilinear forms that recall the outline of the textual bubbles. Page 11 exemplifies this intriguing case. In the second register's middle frame, another innovative metamorphosis occurs as text displaces image. This frame, inhabited entirely by Iokanaan's prophetic message, suggests that the Baptist's voice occupies a visual presence in the play and therefore merits representation as a pictorial entity. Indeed, the voice is the driving force behind the drama because it constitutes an incessant prefiguration of the tragic ending. Thus, here again, Shenton demonstrates a keen understanding of Wilde's symbolic structures which he pictures in potent ways. The eventual outcome of the frame precisely follows that of the

Figure 2. David Shenton, ill. for Wilde's *Salomé* (18-19), 1986, © courtesy of the artist.

play. The moral disorder that provokes death is echoed by the physical fragmentation of the frame which, at the close of the drama, finally breaks away from its own verbal scenario and falls listlessly into the void of the final white page (fig. 3).

Our preoccupation with Shenton's frame is crucial in understanding how his rendition of *Salomé* sheds new light on our reading of the text. In book form, the cartoon functions more like a film than like traditional illustration. Let us consider how. The illustrated book's habitual separation of text and image relegates them to distinct planes that can defy interaction. Often, the placement of illustrations within the pages of text is so out of sync with the narrative that it prompts further alienation of verbal-visual correspondences. Even more problematic is the fact that, within the realm of the traditional illustrated book, text dominates image. The artist customarily selects a noteworthy moment from the plot, renarrates it through his graphic gesture and thus elevates it to the state of a pictorial icon which is intended to "re-present" the text. Like a series of signposts, the illustrations reside across the fabric of the text as a summation of its privileged moments, a graphic account of its *très riches heures*. Textual density is echoed but rarely matched on the pictorial plane. This verbal-visual inequity is often the fate of the traditional illustrated book.

Figure 3. David Shenton, ill. for Wilde's *Salomé* (82-83), 1986, © courtesy of the artist.

However, with Shenton's cartoon format, text and image are displayed in equal proportions. Neither upstages the other. The result is a running, image-text scenario which we read much in the same way that we view a film. The frames that compose the cartoon strip are unequivocally linked to the motion-picture frame. The most significant innovation of Shenton's work is the manner in which the reader-viewer assimilates his *Salomé* through frames. Radically different from separate planes for image and text which force us to shift from one to the other then back again in staccato fashion, this assimilation is a progressive activity whose focus is a single plane in which image and text are unified. As they unfold in a gradual sequence that erases the mechanism of shifts, the power of the work to entice and captivate the reader-viewer is substantially increased. In short, Shenton's de-eliticization of *Salomé* is further accelerated by his creative reconfiguration of framing devices inherent in the cartoon format which dissolve the barriers between the viewer and the viewed.

Technique alone cannot account for the merits of Shenton's cartoon version of *Salomé*. The artist's understanding of the author's thematic structures and their symbolic underpinnings is everywhere apparent in his illustrations. Technique goes hand-in-hand with the aesthetic effect of the ensemble. On page two, for example, the Young Syrian is featured within a circular frame which magnifies his facial expression in a close-up view commonly used to signal introspection and the immediacy of an intense textual moment. Later, as the drama disintegrates, Salomé, too, will be the object of a magnified, single frame close-up which accentuates her moral disarray. The grotesque contours of this portrait prefigure those of Iokanaan's soon-to-be severed head and foretell the decomposition of the princess's skull in the final frame of the book. Beside it floats a frameless feather, symbol of the angel of death's passage. Significantly, each of the text's three deaths (19, 48) are marked by the presence of a feather. And to underscore that death is the ultimate reality of Wilde's drama, these feathers are not drawn but rather photographed. Thus, in ways as subtle as this photographic intrusion onto the cartoon strip, Shenton extrapolates upon the text's move from life to death and from order to chaos.

As we have seen, the illustrator does not always follow the author's textual directives. This is evidenced in such humorous additions as Salomé's weakness for bubble gum. However, not all of Shenton's additions are generated by humor nor are they necessarily detrimental to the text. For example, nowhere in Wilde's play is Salomé associated with a serpent. And yet, on page one, Shenton pictures her as a snake devouring its prophet-prey. The serpentine imagery, repeated on page three, is associated just five pages later with the reptile that guards the prophet's underground jail. This assimilation in turn inspires the undulating contours of Herod's palace which are generated by the creature's scaly backbone. Thus, the architectural scheme of the drama's setting serves to personify the grotesque contours of the princess's passion as the sinuous parapets of this Gaudyesque fortress house the very object of her desire.

Sensuality is affiliated with the serpentine presence of Salomé, and Shenton orchestrates his scenario under the sign of carnal craving as it manifests itself through the gaze. Because Wilde's play is essentially about looking and the dangers of excess associated with the lustful gaze, it is fitting that staring is so often exaggerated throughout Shenton's suite. For example, Salomé is mesmerized by Iokanaan's glance which is designed on the diagonal across an intriguing double-page sequence that pictures the poetics of her tirade (22-23). Later, the price of too much looking is paid in the crazed, darting looks exchanged by Herod and Herodias (52-53) or in the horrific gaze of Salomé as she contemplates the severed head of Iokanaan (80-81). Shenton replicates the thematic of staring so prevalent in the play onto his graphic scheme with verve. An excess of looking is, after all, the infernal machine that provokes the deaths of the Young Syrian, Iokanaan, and Salomé. Even Herod's death knell is sounded by the gaze, for his empire is ultimately doomed by the Baptist's beheading.

In a drama based on the dialectics of desire as expressed through staring, the definitive action is the dance of the seven veils. It provides not only the terrain for viewing the unviewable but also the necessary bargaining chip that

Figure 4. David Shenton, ill. for Wilde's *Salomé* (54-55), 1986, © courtesy of the artist.

allows Salomé access to the inaccessible. Shenton's portrayal of the dance is a parody of eroticism. First, a sheet is draped over the cartoon frames to create an impromptu dressing room for the princess (51). Next, the spot light is focussed on the stage curtain in anticipation of the dance (53). Finally, a cringing satyr pulls back the curtain to reveal a tartan-clad Salomé more interested in the dynamics of bondage proposed by her giraffe dresser than in the execution of her steps (fig. 4). On the facing page, Shenton deliberately fragments frames and conjugates the gaze in order to underscore the grave consequences of the choreographic interlude.

In the meantime, Shenton has banished text from image. The dance possesses a language of its own. The following double-page illustrates various moments of a choreography whose inspiration is more Moulin Rouge than mystic. Giraffes serve as *habilleuses* and *deshabilleuses* as the dance becomes a sort of prismatic slap-stick replicating the colors of the rainbow and insinuating its potent seduction of Herod. The culmination is proposed on the following page (fig. 5). Here, on a Vegas-style dance floor inspired by the film *Saturday Night Fever*, Salomé gyrates à la John Travolta. The setting restates Shenton's de-eliticization of the play, and yet the image is cleverly charged with symbolic analogies inherent in the dance of the seven veils. Thus, Salomé poses in seven stances. She is backed by seven giraffes and surrounded by seven flowers. In

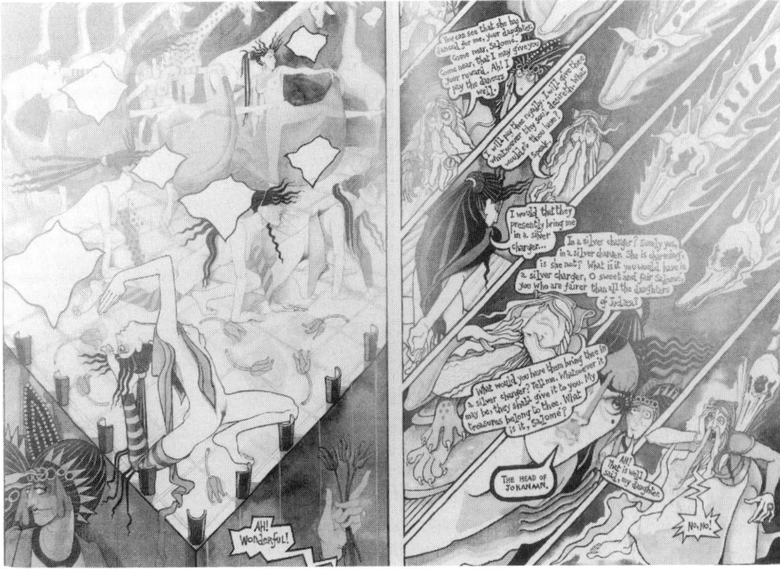

Figure 5. David Shenton, ill. for Wilde's *Salomé* (58-59), 1986, © courtesy of the artist.

this Escher-like configuration, seven veils appropriately float above. These are fittingly textless bubbles whose virginal white is soon to be soiled by Salomé's irrepressible demand for the Baptist's head.

When the text resumes at the bottom of the page marking the end of the dance, the break to diagonal framing insinuates that this is also the beginning of the end. Salomé's request provokes the metamorphosis of the giraffe's head into the beak of the angel of death which then perforates Herod's body as a prefiguration of eminent disaster. In such ways, Shenton demonstrates an intimate understanding of the play by privileging the dance on which pivots the dramatic intensity of the ensemble. And although neither the posturing of giraffes nor the skewering of Herod actually take place in Wilde's scenario, these additions explore and expand the text's graphic potential without betraying it. Clearly, this sort of illustration is nothing short of illumination.

In conclusion, Shenton's work shores up a series of issues related to the picturing of texts and to the textualizing of pictures. In the early stages of his *Salomé,* conventional configurations of word and image draw the reader-viewer into a scheme. Soon, this scheme is forced to break its mold in response to violent shifts in textual tenor. Thus, transfigurations result as complex systems of framing manipulate the eye in unexpected ways to mirror the dynamic tension and grandiloquent theatricality which typify Wilde's play. An inventive graphism which functions as carrier of ideas reactualizes the symbolic networks of the text. This graphism is at once central to our understanding of how meaning is derived from image and critical to our comprehension of how a text can be pictorially reperformed with insight and élan. Finally, Shenton's recasting of Wilde within these diverse contexts helps us not only to re-view *Salomé* in filmic terms of the cartoon format but also to reconsider this format within the larger paradigm of illustration as interpretation.

Notes

1 This particular volume is a "Brilliance Book project" for Quintet Books (London, Melbourne, New York). The illustrations, done in ink and pencil crayon, took the artist fourteen months to complete.

2 Cited on the back cover of the volume indicated above.

3 See author's *L'Interprétation Figurée: Les Illustrateurs de la Salomé de Wilde* (Ann Arbor, Michigan: University Microfilms International, 1980).

4 Michael Griffiths, "Stanley Meets Salome", *Time Out*, January 1987, n.p.

5 Jennie Brookman, "Shenton Lifts His Mask", *Capital Gay* (London), n.p., n.d. (circa Jan. 1987).

6 Jeffrey Wallen, "Illustrating *Salome:* Perverting the Text?", *Word & Image*, vol. 8, no. 2, April-June, 1992, 124.

Word-Image Interactions in Far-Eastern Practices

'The Three Perfections': Isomorphic Structures in Works of Late Chinese Poet-Calligrapher-Painters

Mingfei Shi

Anyone who has even a little experience with Chinese culture will have noticed the fondness that Chinese painters have for inscribing poems in their paintings. In the tradition of Chinese literati painting,[1] the arts of poetry, painting, and calligraphy often find a unitary expression by one and the same hand. This tradition of triple talent – poet-painter-calligrapher –, called *sanjue* or "three perfections" in China, produces multilayered sign structures that are of singular interest to the interarts student.

In this paper I will explore this aesthetic phenomenon from a cultural and semiotic perspective, propose a notion of "isomorphism" to designate its interartistic structuring, and examine how the three arts are made to interact in the work of later Chinese literati painters towards creating an artistic whole. By the word "isomorphism" I refer to a structural reciprocity between the two semiotic systems of calligraphy and painting both in visual and conceptual terms, as well as to the possible semantic significance that this reciprocity carries for the process of signification. I will first focus on a painting by Gao Fenhan (1683-1748), a master from the Yangzhou area during the Qing dynasty (1644-1911),[2] and then briefly examine a series of other examples from the late tradition in order to deal with related cultural issues.

Gao Fenhan's painting, entitled *Flowering Plums*, a hanging scroll dated 1737 (fig. 1, overleaf),[3] is characteristic of the later style of literati painting. Its pictorial image is painted entirely in shades of black ink by a free and rhythmic brush. As an integral part of the visual structure, the massive verbal inscription enriches the design in significant ways. It is divided into two parts. The one filling in the space on the right is composed of a traditional *wujue* or five-character regulated poem, a dedication to a friend for whom the work was done as a gift, the artist's signature, and the month and year of the Chinese lunar calendar. A distinction is made by the different size of the script between the poem and the rest of the inscription. The other in the upper left corner consists of the exact date[4] as well as the phrase "virtues of a recluse" in large characters of the clerical script, which refers to a conventional use of plum trees as a pictorial motif. The poem reads:[5]

> Fragrance comes from tough experience.
> Arising out of bitter cold and layers of snow,
> It pierces through a thousand yards of ice.
> The will, indomitable and unyielding,
> Is as strong as a hundred feet of iron.
> Braving the cold, it will never die.

In looking at the painting, one may have immediately been struck by the manner in which the verbal inscription is integrated into the pictorial image. The words and the image, which belong to two different sign systems according to Western semiotic classifications, show an interesting formal correlation. Compositionally, the poetic inscription seems to be sprouting and growing from the same ground as the plum trees, forming an indispensable part of the spatial balance. Corresponding to the claw-like image of the trees, the verbal text is written cursively both in shape and arrangement; some characters, for instance in the first line on the right, are even deliberately written off the line to enhance the irregularity. In order to ensure a continuity between word and image, the painter has interspersed the verbal text with the tree in the lower right corner. With the last line inscribed between the two trees, interconnected with and finally fading into the ink dots that suggest the vegetation on the ground,[6] the two sign-types are intermingled in such a way that the inscription does not look at all like an embellishment isolated from the image, but rather like sharing the same living space. It is fascinating to note that both the pictorial and the calligraphic signs become smaller and denser from their respective sides toward the center, thus jointly conveying a wonderful sense of recession into the slightly ink-washed, misty background.

Figure 1. Gao Fenhan (1683-1748), *Flowering Plums.* 1737. Hanging scroll, ink on paper, 83.9 x 40.9 cm. Nanjing Museum.

But still more interesting is the way in which the calligraphy semiotically complements the pictorial image. By virtue of using the same ink and brush, the inscription and the image produce a structural affinity and an interplay based on the smallest syntactic unit in the composition: the brushstroke. This unit provides the painting with a unifying means in terms of such visual motifs as the dot, the hook, and the brushline. Both signs are composed of streaky, harsh, yet energetic strokes, some of which are rendered with a dry, bald, or worn-out brush. The cursive script transmits a rhythmic touch similar to that of the pictorial image, for the way of handling the visual motifs of the two is virtually identical. If the brushwork of the image looks similar to that of calligraphy, the idiosyncratic and off-balanced script equally displays a form akin to the graphic and pictorial. While the former bears on a *calligraphic conception of painting,* the latter presents a *painterly form of calligraphy.* As a result of this reciprocity, the same quivering movement pervades the overall design and significantly accentuates the visual continuity as well as the integration between the inscription and the image.

For a better understanding of the two crucial terms I have italicized here, we need to make a cultural and historic detour to understand the particular relationships between writing and painting in Chinese literati culture.

In Western cultures, writing and painting have traditionally been viewed as separate and disparate sign systems. This distinction between script and pictorial representation is connected to the distinction between words and images generally traced back to Plato *(Cratylus),* though it did not necessarily originate with him. According to this way of defining the difference between the two forms of representation, the relation of the verbal sign to the thing is merely a matter of agreement without any particular reasons, and the word is thus an "artificial" or "arbitrary" or "conventional" sign, while an image is motivated by nature and represents the thing by likeness and is therefore a "natural" sign. This distinction extends to verbal texts such as poems and to paintings; as put by the Abbé Du Bos early in the eighteenth century, a poem uses words and is therefore a *signe artificiel,* a painting consists in images and is therefore typically a *signe naturel* (cf. Wimsatt and Brooks 268). The same distinction is retained in many modern theories of semiotics. In French post-Saussurean semiology, the opposing labels are *arbitraire* versus *motivatée* or *non-analogique* versus *analogique* (cf. Barthes 51-52); and in Peircian semiotic classifications, the linguistic sign becomes a "symbol", whose relation to its referent is mostly accidental and thus meaningless without social convention, whereas the representational visual sign is an "icon", which has an inherent relation with the things it depicts by embodying certain formal features of its referent.[7] The visual representation of the verbal text by letters of the alphabet has been customarily linked with the status of the word, and writing has thus been considered a very different activity from painting.

Chinese culture, on the other hand, tends to sustain an affinity between writing and painting by seeing the two as having the same source and sharing the same spirit; as the ninth-century art historian Zhang Yanyuan (815-875) put it, "Writing and painting have different names but a common being".[8]

duced, as a corollary, an increasing sketchiness and abstraction in the painting: under the influence of the verbal sign, the pictorial image inevitably acquired tendencies toward the formulaic, relying on a striking calligraphic conception rather than on pictorial verisimilitude. Practically, these tendencies turned the brushstroke into a tangible syntactic unit, a discrete component that builds a structural correlation between the two arts, as we saw in Gao's work. Historically, the brushstroke not merely played a pivotal role in the unification of structure to attain a visual correspondence between inscription and pictorial image, but further triggered explorations of the isomorphism in composition, style, rhythm, and configuration as well as tonality. Let us look at some instances of these explorations selected from the work of two different literati painters: Ke Jiusi and the well-known Qing painter Dao Ji (also called Shi Tao, 1641-c.1710).

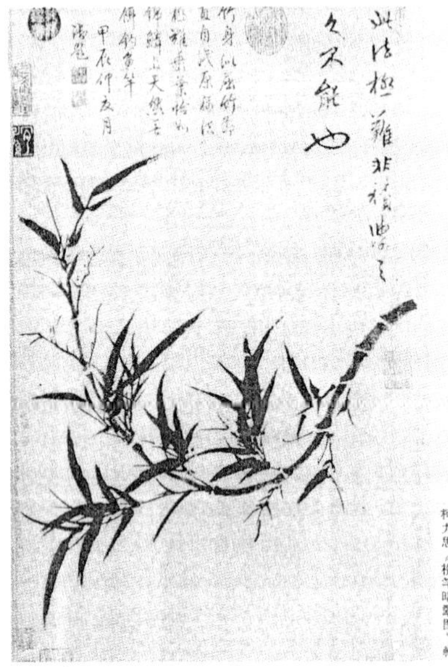

Figure 3. Ke Jiusi (1290-1343), *Bamboo in the Clear and Blue Sky.* Hanging scroll, ink on paper, 50.2 x 29 cm. Collection unknown.

1. Compositional reciprocity: The painting *Bamboo in the Clear and Blue Sky* by Ke Jiusi (fig. 3) contains his own inscription in the upper right of the design.[18] Inspecting the brushstrokes of the painting, a trained reader will readily recognize the calligraphic methods advocated by the artist in the poem cited above. What most interests us, however, is his way of writing the character *ye* ("too, "also"), the last in the second line of the inscription, which wonderfully echoes the graceful curve of the stalks. The innovation created especially for this composition can only be understood when one sees the standard modes of writing the character, either in the running or cursive scripts (fig. 4; from Fan Ren'an, 1:34). Ke's break with these conventional ways in order to create the formal correspondence achieves a striking effect.

2. Stylistic consistency: The *Bamboo and Rock* by the same artist (fig. 5) presents a clearly different style. The image is obviously more simplified: the bamboo leaves are delineated by three or four strokes in a formulaic pattern. It is easy to recognize the artist's attempt to keep a correlation between the image and

Figure 4. The standard modes of writing the character of *ye*. From Fan Ren'an, 1:34.

the inscription by the proper selection of script type and the careful handling of the brushwork. In contrast to the vigorous and strong brushstrokes in the previous painting, the strokes here appear rather soft and plump, displaying an effort to keep the brush-tip moving in the middle, again achieving a stylistic consistency of both image and inscription.

Figure 5. Ke Jiusi, *Bamboo and Rock*. Fan painting mounted as an album leaf, ink on paper. National Palace Museum.

3. Tonal correspondence: *Peonies* by Dao Ji (fig. 6) shows a further step towards isomorphism in terms of controlling tones and using water on the rice paper. Just as the flower is finished in the techniques of *lavis* by adding dark black ink on the wet wash of light color, the inscription is also made up of the two contrasting tones of ink by the same technique. Some characters, such as

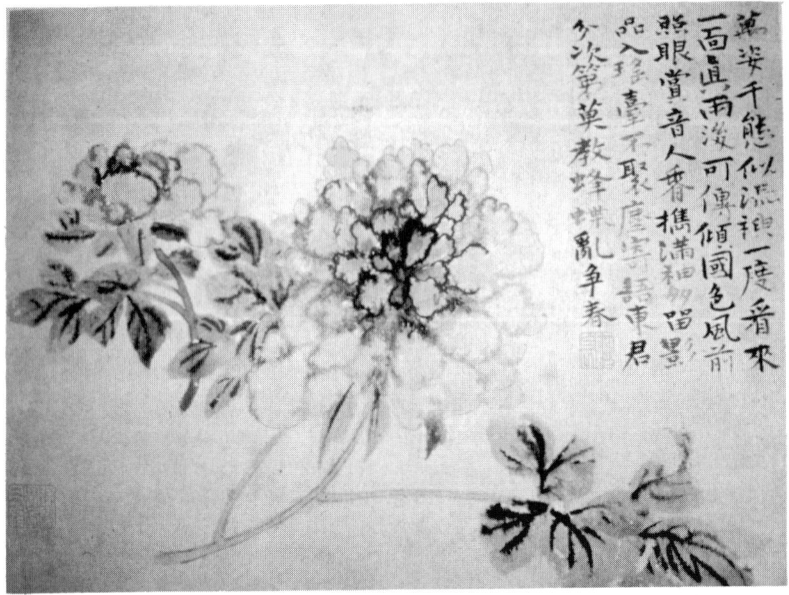

Figure 6. Dao Ji (1641-c.1710), *Peonies.* Ca. 1698. Album leaf, ink and color on paper, 18.9 x 25.6 cm. Art Museum, Princeton University.

the one at the bottom of the third line from the right, were purposely washed out by water when the ink was still wet (a technique traditionally called *pomuo* or "broken ink"); as a result, some parts of the inscription appear dissolved, foggy, tonally corresponding to the image created by the same water techniques.

4. Rhythmical and configurational affinity: In Dao Ji's *Village Among Green Willows* (fig. 7), both the image and the inscription were executed by a dry brush-tip that seems to have been dragged along on the paper surface in a slow tempo; thus both – even including the image of hills – are endowed with an ethereal and massless quality. An affinity of form can be easily found for the design: the repetition of the curved or zigzagged line. Correlative with the configurations of hills and willows, some vertical strokes in characters – for instance, the bottom one in the first line and the top one in the fifth line from the right – are winding and zigzagged as well. The calligraphic inscription

therefore becomes more or less a visual extension of the pictorial image.

Changing the conventional way of writing a character for the purpose of achieving a visual correspondence and employing the inscription as a graphic element responsive to the image makes for what I have called the painterly

Figure 7. Dao Ji, *Village Among Green Willows.* 1682. Album leaf, ink on paper. Dafeng tang Collection.

form of calligraphy. The inscription thus takes on the peculiar qualities of a painter's brush style, and the calligraphic sign amounts to a visual motif as essential as the image for the composition, beautifully exemplified in the album leaf *Chrysanthemum* by Huang Shen (1687-1770; fig. 8, overleaf). In this way, Chinese poet-calligrapher-painters are able to inscribe their verbal texts anywhere they think appropriate for the design and to produce a truly isomorphic structure of poetry and painting via calligraphy.

Returning to our primary example, Gao Fenhan's *Flowering Plums,* we are surely able to perceive in the painting more than before about the sophisticated formal reciprocity we discussed above. But if what is meant by "isomorphism" also includes a possible semantic function carried by this syntactical reciprocity, how does it work for this painting? To answer this question, we have to consider the iconographic meanings of the flower in traditional Chinese culture.

The flowering plum is a pictorial motif that has rich literary associations arising out of the flower's appearance and its situation in nature. Since it is the earliest to blossom in spring, often appearing in late winter before the last snow has disappeared from the bleak landscape, it is traditionally viewed as the harbinger of spring and greeted with wide-ranging metaphors. Sprouting its buds alone in a still cold and desolate scene before all other flowering plants, the plum presents a solitary picture that is metaphorically associated with the situation of neglect or noble withdrawal, thus becoming a symbol of a recluse. Seen against the layers of snow and the icy blasts in wintery scenes, different aspects of its delicate, fragrant white blossoms have inspired different poetic feelings. To cite Maggie Bickford's study of the flower's iconographic meanings, the plum "prompted some poets to pity their vulnerability and sure destruction, some to marvel at the flower's courage and fortitude, some to grieve over the fleeting beauty of the blossoms, and some to celebrate the endurance of the rugged ancient tree" (18).[19]

Figure 8. Huang Shen (1687-1770), *Chrysanthemum.* Album leaf, ink on paper. Collection unknown.

As his inscriptions indicate, Gao Fenhan here has chosen the traditional motifs of fortitude and endurance as the theme of his painting, for the inscribed poem clearly draws an analogy between the fortitude of the flower in harsh winter and the unyielding human will in adverse conditions. Yet, by the pictorial image he has also added a motif of rejuvenation to the traditional repertoire.[20] In the painting, young branches with clusters of exquisite flowers are depicted shooting up from an aged, seemingly dead stump and its twisted, gnarled roots. The stump seems to have been battered by a hundred winters, yet it still has the vitality to burst forth into new life every year. The whole painting is permeated with great intensity by the streaky, harsh, and vigorous strokes that constitute both the inscription and the image. If the heavy and rugged brushwork is able to reveal a toughness that expresses the endurance of the plum trees, the energetic and brisk brushstrokes significantly enhance the feeling of rejuvenation with a shivering rhythm that suggests a subtle yet undeniable excitement for the renewal of life. Thus, the form of Gao's painting becomes part of the very content that the image signifies: there is no clear-cut division between the two. The poet-calligrapher-painter has achieved a unified isomorphic sign structure syntactically and semantically alike, in a masterly demonstration of the art of "three perfections".

NOTES

1. The term "literati" refers to a long-standing Chinese institution that made qualification for government office dependent on scholarship and poetic skills. Many of these learned officials, or "literati", would also paint; literati paintings are characterized by the inscription of verbal texts, mostly poems, in the pictorial field. For a general discussion of the term, see Bush 1-2.
2. Many masters in the Qing dynasty (1644-1911) were associated with the Yangzhou area. The area is especially well-known for a group of painters called "The Eight Eccentric Masters of Yangzhou", whose exact membership is still controversial among Chinese art historians. Gao was occasionally numbered among the eight masters, along with fourteen other painters connected to the area. He was born in Shandong province and came to live in Yangzhou about 1736. He had served as a magistrate in Anhui province and as an associate inspector of the salt department in an area close to Yangzhou before he was wrongly accused of a crime and dismissed. Having suffered from severe physical torture in prison, he lost the use of his right arm through rheumatism and began to write and paint with his left, which made his painting freer, more expressive and individualistic. The painting we are going to examine is one of Gao's later works done with his left hand. See Wang Buoming 606-21; Cahill 188; Capon and Pang 152; and *Nanjinh bowu changhua* 74.
3. The painting (ink on paper; 83.9 x 40.9 cm) is now in the Nanjing Museum, People's Republic of China. See *Nanjing bowu changhua* 74.
4. The first inscription tells us that the painting was done for a friend in winter, the 12th lunar month of 1737; the second contains the precise dating of the work: the first of the 12th lunar month.
5. Translations are mine unless otherwise noted.
6. It may be necessary to remind the Western reader that traditional Chinese script reads from top to bottom and from left to right. Therefore, the last line is the fifth line from the right edge of the painting.
7. Peirce developed a triadic system instead of the traditional dichotomy. The third category in his second trichotomy of signs is that of the "index", whose vehicle is existentially or causally related to its referent, as an outstretched finger pointing at a house or smoke pointing at fire (cf. Peirce 9-19).
8. From his *Lidai minghuaji [Record of Famous Paintings of All the Dynasties]*, rpt. in Yu Jianhua, ed., *Zhongguo* 1:27.

9. The earliest texts concerning the legend of Changjie are the *Lushi chunqiu (Lu's Chronicles of Spring and Autumn),* the *Hanfei zi,* and the *Xun zi.* The same legend is also found in the *Shangshu (Book of Shang)* and the *Yijing (Book of Changes),* though Changjie is changed to Fu Xi or Bao Xi there (see Yu Jianhua, ed., *Zhongguo* 1:27).

10. According to current archeological records, the use of the brush was actually found as early as in the neolithic pottery of Yangshao culture (5000-3000 B.C.).

11. It has become a general consensus among Chinese linguists that only the first four principles concern character construction and that the last two merely involve applications of the previous ones. James Liu's classifications may derive from this consensus. Further, it is interesting to note that the principle of *zhishi* (pointing at the thing) was translated by the anthropologist and historian Ping-ti Ho as "indexical symbols" (255). For a useful account of the Six Principles, see his book, 253-55.

12. This branch of linguistics is traditionally called *xiaoxue* (primary learning). There had already been some studies listed in the section of "Records of Art and Literature" of "The History of the Han" compiled by Ban Gu (32-92 A.D.). Since the sixteenth century, though the term sometimes also includes phonetics *(yinyunxue)* and philology (*xunguxue*), the study centering on the character's visual structure has remained the core of traditional linguistics and has occupied a more important position than the other studies.

13. Chinese phonograms usually consist of a phonetic and a radical, which themselves are pictograms, ideograms, or phonograms. For example, in the composite phonogram *zhong* (忠 loyalty), the phonetic is *zhong* (中 middle: a simple ideogram showing a line across the middle of a square) and the radical, *xin* (心 heart; a pictogram of the heart). While the radical signifies that loyalty is associated with the heart, the phonetic may also serve a semantic function, to suggest that being loyal means keeping one's heart centered (Liu 5). This is why many "phonetic elements" of Chinese characters have become non-phonetic: the ideogrammic form of phonetics simply could not be adapted to the change of pronunciation in history. For details, see Yang 24-33.

14. This statement is actually reiterated thrice in his *Lidai minghuaji.* Rpt. in Yu Jianhua, ed., *Zhongguo* 1:35-36.

15. From Zhao Xigu (1225-79), *Dongtian Qingluji guhuabian [Collections from the Pure Emolument and Grotto Heaven: the Section of Ancient Paintings].* In Yu Jianhua, ed., *Zhongguo* 1:87; English in Bush, 115.

16. Zong Dian, ed., *Ke Jiusi shiliao* 54; translation modified from Sutherland, 1.

17. For a more detailed analysis of Zhao's statement, see Shi 90.

18. The inscription on the upper left was done by the Emperor Qianlong (1736-1795) of the Qing dynasty, who inscribed many of his tasteless poems in the imperial collections and whose changeless calligraphic style is generally viewed by connoisseurs as spoiling the paintings.

19. For a detailed account of the various symbolic meanings of the flower, see Bickford 17-33.

20. This reading was partly inspired by the catalogue explanation in Capon and Pang, 152.

REFERENCES

Barthes, Roland. *Eléments de sémiologie.* 1964. Rpt. in *L'aventure sémiologique.* Paris: Seuil, 1985.

Bickford, Maggie. *Bones of Jade, Soul of Ice: The Flowering Plum in Chinese Art.* New Haven: Yale UP, 1985.

Bush, *Susan. The Chinese Literati on Painting: Su Shih (1073-1101) to Tung Ch'i-ch'ang (1555-1636).* Cambridge, MA: Harvard UP, 1971.

Cahill, James. *Chinese Painting.* Cleveland: World, 1978.

Capon, Edmund and Mae Anna Pang, eds. *Chinese Painting of the Ming and Qing Dynasties.* Clayton, Australia: Wilke, 1981.

Driscoll, Lucy and Kenji Toda. *Chinese Calligraphy.* New York: Paragon, 1964.

Fan Ren'an, ed. *Zhongguo shufa dazidian [The Dictionary of Chinese Calligraphy].* Shanghai: Shanghai shuhua, 1991.

Fenollosa, Ernest. *The Chinese Written Character as a Medium for Poetry.* Ed. Ezra Pound. 1908/1918. Rpt. San Francisco: City Lights Books, 1969.

Ho, Ping-ti. *Cradle of the East.* Chicago: University of Chicago Press, 1975.

Liu, James. *The Art of Chinese Poetry.* Chicago: University of Chicago Press, 1962.

Nanjing Bowu Yuan changhua [Paintings Collected in the Nanjing Museum]. Shanghai: Shanghai renmin, 1981.

Peirce, Charles S. "Logic as Semiotic: The Theory of Signs". In *Semiotics: An Introductory Anthology.* Ed. Robert E. Innis. Bloomington: Indiana UP, 1978. 4-23.

Saussure, Ferdinand de. "On the Nature of Language". Extracts from *Course in General Linguistics.* 1916. Trans. Wade Bakin. New York: Philosophical Library, 1959. Rpt. in *Introduction to Structuralism.* Ed. Michael Lane. New York: Basic Books, 1970. 43-56.

Shi Mingfei. "An Image Beyond the Image: The Chinese Painter As Poet-Calligrapher – Zheng Xie's *Bamboos in Wind". Yearbook of Comparative and General Literature* 38 (1989): 79-99.

Sutherland, Martha. "K'o Chiu-ssu, a Bamboo Painter of the Yuan Dynasty: A Brief Introduction". *NPM Bulletin* 15 (1981): 1-13.

Wang Boming. *Zhongguo huihua shi [The History of Chinese Painting].* Shanghai: Renmin meishu, 1982.

Wimsatt, William K. and Cleanth Brooks. *Literary Criticism: A Short History.* New York: Vantage Books, 1957.

Yang Wuming. *Wenzi xue. [Study of Written Characters].* Changsha: Hunan renmin, 1986.

Yu Jianhua, ed. *Zhongguo hualun leibian [A Collection of Chinese Theories of Painting].* Beijing: Renmin meishu, 1986.

Zhongguo meixueshi ziliao xuanbian [Selected Materials for the History of Chinese Aesthetics]. Ed. Department of Philosophy at Beijing University. Beijing: Beijing UP, 1983.

Zong Dian, ed. *Ke Jiusi shiliao [Collection of Historical Data on Ke Jiusi].* Shanghai: Renmin meishu, 1963.

Interacting Signs in the *Genji Scrolls*

Aiko Okamoto-MacPhail

Nelson Goodman observes in *Languages of Art* that all modes of representation are dependent on a socially given frame of reference which is conventionally relative to another frame of reference (36-7). Such a frame exists not only between artistic representations and the real world, as Goodman shows in his analysis of realism, but also between different art forms. Any interarts phenomenon can therefore also be discussed as a field governed by conventions in which the bridge linking one artistic system with another is culturally and historically determined. This paper will examine conventions of interartistic reference observed in Heian-Period Japan at the beginning of the 12th century.

An outstanding example of the then prevaling conventions for linking visual signs with the literary signs of the genre called "monogatari" or fictive tale is offered by the *Scrolls* of the *Tale of Genji*, the oldest extant (though incomplete) version of the *Tale*, which was written in the 11th century.[1] In these *Scrolls* it is not only the illustrations and the calligraphy by which aspects of the literary text are rendered visually; as we shall see, the decoration of the types of paper on which the calligraphy has been executed is likewise a constituent of the complex scheme of visual signs interacting with each other and with the poetry and prose passages that make up the literary text. Such modes of interaction can be demonstrated in an analysis of the chapter "Minori" or "The Law" from the *Scrolls* that consists of poetry and a portion of prose narrative excerpted from the original *Tale of Genji*. In order to explain adequately the relationship between the two verbal systems of poetry and prose on the one hand and the relationships between illustration, calligraphy, and paper decoration on the other, it will be useful first to explain briefly the cultural background of the evolution of narrative and poetry in Heian Japan.

At the dawn of Japanese literature, painting and prose narrative seem to share a similar function in relation to poetry. "Waka" (the label for Japanese poetry in distinction from Chinese poetry) is a chain of 5-7-5-7-7 syllables forming one complete poem written in one to two lines. This poetry seems to be the expression of a pure lyrical movement of mind voiced like an exclamation at the height of emotion. Uttered in isolation, it lacks an indication of the context that engendered it; it appears that prose and painting developed as two separate but parallel and spontaneous modes of support to account for the situation that gave rise to the poetic utterance. This parallel development seems to have occurred typically in screen painting, and scrolls are a more refined and elaborate version of the artistic and literary tendencies of screen painting. In a book about the *Scrolls*, Akiyama Terukazu argues that by around 900 AD Japanese painting had become independent from Chinese influence in screen and sliding door painting. At around the same period, Japanese poetry and narrative tale emerged, distinct from the practice of Chinese poetry, along with the invention of Japanese calligraphy and the phonetical alphabet (Akiyama, *Ocho* 24). In screen painting, the written text of poetry is transcribed in calligraphy in order to place letter shapes on the same footing as painted images. If the painting is executed first, space is reserved for the calligraphy so as to render the whole screen artistically beautiful. The screen painting shows protagonists or painted scenery while screen poetry renders the voices of protagonists painted on the screen. According to Tamagami Takuya, the first fictive tale originated as a verbal explanation of how poems and drawings work together, for the benefit of children or uneducated adults. Consequently, Tamagami claims that the first fictive prose narratives, called "tsukuri monogatari" or "made-up stories", were told in front of screens in order to complement the information provided by the paintings and the short poems (199). *The Tale of Genji* is the most developed form of that kind of made-up tale. Prose has another more practical and technical function in the process of screen making. According to Shimizu Yoshiko's account, the patron who commissions the screen also supervises the whole process of screen making, including the composition of the poem to be attached to or inscribed in the screen painting. The patron does not make poems himself, but commissions them from professional poets or amateurs famous for their poetical skill. However, the poet does not actually get to see the screen painting; instead, he works from written notes which explain the painting he is supposed to write about. Shimizu quotes various notes dispatched to professional poets and reports that some are very short while others are long enough to be a prose description of the things going on in the paintings (246-47). Those notes were transcribed and conserved as headnotes in books of poetry in the same way as other headnotes which do not refer to painting but also explain the situations in which the poems were written. This function of headnotes as an explanation of events and of the circumstances of poetic composition is considered to be another origin of fictive tales. In extended form, headnotes gave birth to the prose narrative called "monogatari", exemplified by *The Tale of Genji.*

The Tale of Genji is a fictional narrative written continuously from about 1008 to 1014 by Murasaki Shikibu (ca. 973-1014) who served as lady-in-waiting to the Empress Shoshi. It is thought to have been accompanied by paintings from the very beginning, but the earliest extant illustrations are those of the *Scrolls*, which date from the first half of the 12th century. Today these *Scrolls* are no longer preserved as scrolls. For the sake of conservation, paintings and calligraphied texts have been separated by unpasting the paper joints and are kept separately (Tokugawa 150). However, Akiyama's meticulous studies of paper condition and calligraphy and his x-ray pictures of the paintings allow us to assume that this oldest extant version of *The Tale of Genji* originally consisted of ten scrolls (Akiyama, "Genji" 5; Ito 31). A scroll here means a sequence of sheets of paper pasted together and alternating between written text and illustration to form a roll which the reader/beholder can roll out with the left hand to open a new section of text while the right hand rolls up the portion already viewed;[2] the sheets containing verbal text were narrower, and several of them were combined to form a text that was then followed by a wider sheet with the illustration, to be followed again by text passages and their illustration.[3] In their original form the *Scrolls* supposedly followed the chapter order of *The Tale of Genji* and presented from each of the fifty-four chapters one to three written excerpts, with illustrations. However, only portions of the ten scrolls have survived. Akiyama supposes that what we have left is one fourth of the complete original. The remnants consist of nineteen paintings, some of which have lost their matching texts, and twenty text excerpts, one of which without its illustration (Sano 132). In many more cases both texts and illustrations are lost altogether.

Luckily, one scroll seems to have been conserved and reconstituted in an almost flawless original sequence from beginning to end, with only some lines missing at the very beginning of the scroll (Akiyama, "Genji" 4-6). Upon examining all ten perfect and imperfect scrolls, Akiyama speculates that five different ateliers of painters and calligraphers worked as five different teams to produce the *Scrolls* ("Genji" 3). The best preserved scroll was apparently executed by the team working in the oldest style and with the best knowledge of the previous century when the *Tale* was written. From this best conserved and best executed scroll, we have selected for analysis the last chapter which corresponds to chapter forty of *The Tale of Genji*, entitled "The Law". The choice is not arbitrary. First, this chapter contains three poems embedded in the prose narrative, and we have the matching painting that was attached after the verbal text. So we can fully examine the relationship between painting and both types of verbal text, as well as the calligraphic rendition of the verbal text on decorated paper. Second, the "Law" chapter describes one of the most important climaxes in *The Tale of Genji*, which is the death of Murasaki no Ue or Lady Murasaki, a major character. Therefore, on the basis of both its artistic skill and emotional value, this chapter is worthy of its conspicuous position at the end of a scroll and therefore particularly attractive for analysis.

Before going to the "Law" chapter, however, we will take a small detour and discuss the first picture from another chapter, entitled "Azumaya" or "The ably also a reference to the moon in the ancient legend of the princess Kaguya Hime[4]; as we have seen, it furthermore corresponds to the paper decoration in which Genji's appearance is symbolized by clouds in moonlight.

Genji looks isolated, because of the space between him and Murasaki no Ue and because the Empress Akashi, respecting the code of etiquette, puts a standing screen between Genji and herself and retreats behind it. Genji's solitude is probably stressed more by the mismatch of perspective. The direction of two beams indicates that the view of this room is open to the lower left, and that is the position to which the beholder is moving as the scroll unrolls. However, Genji is seen from the back of his right shoulder and does not move with the beholder, and thus his position creates a conflict between the point of view at the right from which he is drawn and the point of view at the left toward which the beholder is directed. Then the isolation of his figure becomes definitive by an abbreviation in the painting. The vertical pillar drawn on Genji's left opens the room to an autumn-grey garden, and Genji's back looks almost exposed to the outside. Between him and the garden, just enough of a very narrow balcony has been drawn to show that the whole room is not directly exposed to the windy garden. But the size of the balcony is kept exaggeratedly narrow in order to stress the closeness of the room to the garden. Furthermore, the painter seems to have used a bold abbreviation to draw the inside of the house. Considering the custom of the day and also the architectural room disposition of the house, it is not possible that the dying Murasaki no Ue and the Empress, who is the noblest lady and should thus be carefully hidden deep inside the house protected by many screens, could see Genji in such an outer edge of the house with so few protective screens. They are almost exposed to the garden. The distance from the inside of the house where the three protagonists are sitting to the garden has been reduced, and Genji is sitting at the limit of this abbreviated space to show symbolically that he himself is exposed to the chilly wind which is about to blow out the candle of his life. With the roof missing, the autumn wind blowing so strongly outside seems to blow, not only on Genji's back, but throughout the whole room, and just as the wind is bending the bush clover in the garden it seems to curb the posture of the three protagonists. This loss of distance between the inside and outside of the house creates a psychological sense of closeness between the three people and the garden plants.

The visual closeness of people and plants is emphasized by the poems in the text. In fact, the three protagonists are exchanging poems in which they compare their lives with the dewdrops on the blades of autumn grass. Because of the damage to the painted surface, we cannot judge if dewdrops were drawn, but the bush clover leaves on which the dewdrops are posed in the poems are drawn very clearly. The frail plants and human beings which divide the picture screen into two large blocks on the right and the left are but two forms of one and the same thing which is life symbolized by dewdrops. Since the three protagonists recognize their plight in the forms of nature it is even possible to say that these people are truly portrayed by the plants which express their hearts, and that their human figures are mere ephemeral shapes.

Heian Japanese nobles do not seem to trust their bodily presence as an adequate means of self-expression in pictorial representation. Their body is always buried in many layers of clothes, and the convention of "a line for an eye and a hook for the nose" to represent a face makes all faces the same regardless of gender or age. Thus their exterior appearance can hardly serve to express their internal state. That state, such as made evident in a lament for a dying loved one, is symbolized by objects placed outside in the garden, and since that outside object is not obviously an inner feeling or thought, poems are shaped to form a bridge. In a sense the western and modern Japanese distinction of the inside and the outside of a person does not exist here, just as the distinction of the inside and the outside of the house does not exist visually in this "Law" chapter illustration. The inside is lodged in any outside objects, and to indicate the connection, poems and sometimes prose are used. Helped by poetry, the strong wind which makes eulalia and bush clovers bend in the garden and which seems to stir the inside air of the house with anguish, acquires an emotional significance. The connection between the painting and the poems is established and explained by narrative prose, and the verbal figures of ephemeral plants and especially the clusters of dewdrops on plants are echoed by the clusters of fine gold and silver sand and flakes in the paper decoration.

Thus all sign systems gather and create a receptacle which is to be filled by the readers' and beholders' empathy. As mentioned earlier, in order to appreciate screen paintings duly, it was the custom of that time to compose poems in the voice of the protagonists drawn in the paintings, and to explain the poem-painting relation orally in prose. That activity in turn encouraged the beholders to identify themselves with fictive protagonists and to empathize with them. Ikeda writes as follows:

> That movement of the beholder's mind to get as close as possible to the protagonists in the painting and even to identify with them made the beholder see each protagonist or the scenery surrounding him or her in close-up, and that close-up view by the beholder made possible the birth of 'woman's painting.' (174, my transl.)

This is the kind of painting encountered in the Genji *Scrolls*. The abrupt juxtaposition of the garden and the innermost room of the house by reducing all other things in between is then a juxtaposition of two close-ups as a result of this inner eye which perceives the connection of plants to men and empathizes with them.

The Assertion of Heterodoxy in Kyoden's Verbal-Visual Texts

Fumiko T. Togasaki[1]

Santo Kyoden (1761-1816), merchant-class artist and writer, began composing in the Japanese genre of "yellow-cover" fiction *(kibyoshi)* in 1778 and continued working in the genre until 1806. His career came to a peak in 1785 with the publication of *Playboy, Grilled Edo-Style (Edomumare uwaki no kabayaki).* Kyoden was a champion of Edo urban culture, especially in the "heterodox" art-literary circle that included some warrior-class intellectuals. Maintaining a careful equilibrium between the visual and verbal elements of his narratives, he used the dichotomy of image and word as a tool to signal a protest against orthodox social dogma.

The then current regime had kept Japan secluded from the rest of the world since 1603, a seclusion that was to last until 1867. Domestically, its feudalistic society was stratified into four classes, with warrior-intellectuals at the top, followed by farmers, craftsmen, and merchants, in that order. The class of the warrior-intellectuals, ruling the country in accordance with Confucian doctrines, represented authority and orthodox traditional culture, while the merchant class contributed to the emergence of a non-traditional heterodox culture that was reflected in the mixed media style of the *kibyoshi,* which consisted of pictorial and verbal texts and emphasized contemporary themes.

During this period, even publishers were divided into two categories. Orthodox publishers, called "honya", published books on the "high" art and literature *[ga]* of traditional culture in Kyoto, the capital of Japan for the past millennium. Their publications covered topics such as Confucianism, Buddhism, Shintoism, and medicine, as well as Japanese classic waka-poetry (Kimura 511). Except for the technical illustrations in medical texts, they contained very few images. On the other hand, the heterodox publishers, called "jihon-toiya", published only the art and literature native to Edo, such as *ukiyo-e* prints and "yellow-cover" fiction or *kibyoshi.* Edo, now Tokyo, was the new metropolis, headquarters for the feudal Tokugawa regime where warrior-class officials gathered from all over Japan. *Kibyoshi* flourished there for thirty years, from 1775 till 1806, but found little official recognition; according to Kimura Yaeko, because of the inclusion of pictures "the genre of 'yellow-cover' fiction used to be considered 'valueless' books, in comparison to the academic and orthodox types of books" (511; all translations from the Japanese are mine).

The development of advanced hand-carving and hand-printing techniques of woodblock printing made it possible to carve both image and script in the same block. The simultaneous printing of visual and verbal text in the same space gave the non-verbal communication by image a co-equal role in "yellow-cover" fiction, the only mixed-media genre then in existence. Since word and image carry equal weight in the development of the fictional narrative, I refuse to categorize the image by the customary label "illustration", which assigns an inferior status to the picture in relation to the written text; instead, I shall refer to the images created by Kyoden side by side with the verbal texts as "visual texts".

A work of *kibyoshi* took the format of small booklets and was published in two or three volumes, each volume consisting of ten pages of pictures which provided a frame, within which appeared written text presenting verbal narrative and dialogue. We can trace the ancestry of "yellow-cover" fiction to the children's books called (by their covers) red-books (beginning in the 1660s), black-books, and blue-books (c. 1750-1774). In 1775, an elite warrior-intellectual artist-writer whose pen-name was Koikawa Harumachi (River of Love in the Town of Spring) (1744-1789; Yoshida 3: 54), utilizing the style of this mixed-media genre, created a new type of fiction which included pictures and verbal text in an equilibrium: thus, the "yellow-cover" genre was born. Dealing with current topics to appeal to the contemporary viewer-reader, it began to attract an audience of mature people with its witty style and its playful and often absurd content. Sometimes, however, a silent code was hidden, visually or verbally, in the fictional text to communicate a different message to the viewer-reader capable of deciphering it.

By Kyoden's time, Japan had already been ruled for one and a half centuries by the highly orthodox and feudalistic polity of the Tokugawa shogunate. The first decades of Kyoden's lifetime were marked by two politicians who successively dominated public policy and whose names are used to designate two periods. The Tanuma Period, which lasted from 1767 to 1786, was marked by a liberal cultural and economic policy and represented the high point of Edo culture; during the following six years (1787-1793), Matsudaira, heading a conservative reaction, tried to reverse Tanuma's policies. Kyoden's first success as an artist-writer of "yellow-cover" fiction came in 1782 at the tail-end of the Tanuma Period, and his career continued through the Matsudaira Period until the "yellow-cover" genre died away around 1806. Thus, Kyoden, a staunch liberal and heterodox artist-writer, having begun in a favorable social climate, subsequently had to survive an era of repression.

The Tanuma Period produced a culturally active circle of elite warrior-class intellectuals who affiliated themselves with merchant-class intellectuals like Kyoden to create the "yellow-cover" fiction movement at the fringe of the feudal power structure. In their fiction those intellectuals, including Kyoden, openly ridiculed the policy of the young Matsudaira when he came to power in 1787 as a new conservative Confucian politician. Matsudaira stood against those intellectual samurai, whom he "condemned as commercially corrupted warriors" (Kitahara 212). In order to enforce his feudalistic system, Matsudaira published in 1790 the Kansei Reform Edict, which subjected all types of "yellow-cover" fiction and each and every *ukiyo-e* woodblock print to censorship. As a result, the warrior-class intellectuals were forced into inactivity, and one, Harumachi, even committed suicide (Yoshida 3: 54). Kyoden was punished twice, once in 1789 as an artist, and again in 1791 as the author of a pleasure-quarter novelette. The sentence obliged him to stop writing such novelettes, but he did not give up working on "yellow-cover" fiction until the genre disappeared. He used his work to protest against feudalistic social dogma and a dominant cultural orthodoxy that worshipped the supremacy of the written word and classic literature.

In order to voice his protest in his chosen genre under conditions of censorship, Kyoden exploited the interaction of word and image by adapting the model of the children's book to his own purposes in a number of ways. Even children's books could use visual communication to contradict the verbal text. The following two figures are from a black-book by two *ukiyo-e* woodblock printmakers, Torii Kiyomasu and Torii Kiyomitsu, entitled *I-ro-ha Letters: Verses for Temple School Children,* which was published in Edo in 1762 and again in the 1780s. The first page-spread demonstrates how a school lesson is conducted; the ostensible objective of the lesson and the book is to promote the superiority of the word and of writing. In the black-book genre, the interaction between image and word is still rather naive, compared to that of the "yellow-cover". However, we can discern a basic dichotomy between image and word, in terms of their use as communication tools. The two-page spread is divided into two areas, its upper part being occupied by short poems, and its lower part filled with pictures. Dialogue is inscribed beside each figure in the empty space within the picture. Each page-spread contains five out of forty-six short poems, each beginning with one of the fifty-one Japanese syllables, with the initial character also set off in a circle. Each of the poems, composed in the traditional *waka* style, is didactic, telling children how to obey their parents and teachers. Furthermore, they teach the children the importance of "reading", "calligraphy", "arithmetic", "music", and "dancing" (see figs. 1a and 1b, overleaf), while pictures are treated as *graffiti,* or as useless and forbidden objects.

Even though school children love to draw pictures, pictures are excluded from the curriculum. Consequently, those who draw pictures become the target of the teacher's anger and are punished in the classroom (see fig. 2a, overleaf). One of the poems, illustrating the syllable *to,* relates to the punishment shown in the picture:

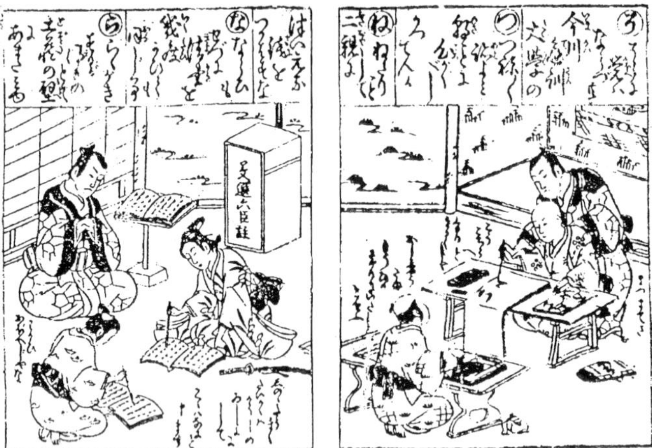

Figure 1b. Figure 1a.

Figure 1: Page-spread from *Iroha moji: Terako Tanka* [*I-ro-ha Letters: Verses For Temple School-Children*], by Torii Kiyomasu and Torii Kiyomitsu, *ukiyo-e* woodblock print-makers. Edo: Urokogataya 1762. [1b: classroom scene, calligraphy lesson; 1a: classroom scene, learning to read and write.] Y. Kimura, "The World of Red-Books".

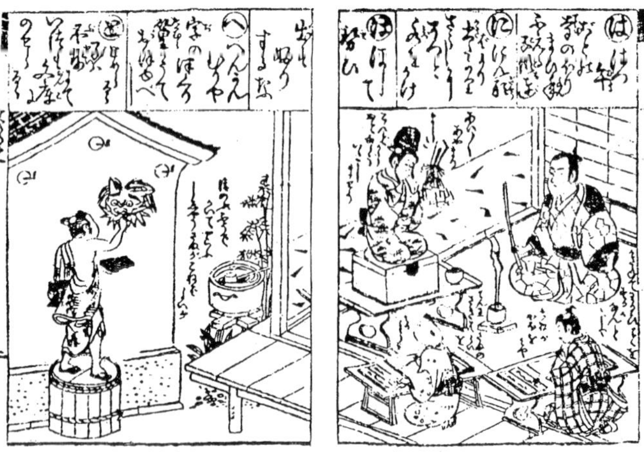

Figure 2b. Figure 2a.

Figure 2: Page-spread from *Iroha moji: Terako Tanka.* [2b: Pupil drawing *graffito* after being punished in class; 2a: classroom scene in which a pupil is punished.] Kaga Rare Book Collection, Tokyo Metropolitan Library.

Tomeraruru	A schoolboy who is punished
Ko ha busei nite	Is a lazy pupil,
Itsu mo bunko ni	Who is always forced to sit
Noseraruru	On a book-box placed on a desk.

The next scene shows the offender, on his way home from school, drawing a real *graffito* of a monster's head on the pure white wall of a treasure-house (fig. 2b). His natural desire to draw pictures makes him act out a kind of blasphemy, because it is forbidden. This scene even intensifies the crucial paradox of the picture devaluation set forth in this book. Pictures themselves articulate a discourse that condemns pictures. First, despite the anti-visual bias of the Confucian educational system, the picture is employed to teach a moral lesson. Second, the message to condemn pictures is presented through the combined media of word and image – a presentation that implies an affirmation of the value of pictures. This presentation by image and word contains the potential for the elevation of the image to the status granted by the orthodox system to words, or for the destruction of the superiority of words.

The next example depicts a theme similar to that presented in the children's book, but handled in a far more sophisticated manner. It was taken from a "yellow-cover" fiction with text and images by Kyoden, *Confucian Stripes, Timely Dye of Blue (Koshizima Toki ni Aizome),* produced twenty-seven years after the original publication of the children's book, but much closer to the date of its re-publication. *Confucian Stripes* appeared in the infamous year of 1789 when the conservative warrior-class scholar Matsudaira had just begun his policy to promote the "reading" of the Confucian classics and the dual virtue of "the Brush and the Sword" (Jones 57-59 and Yamaguchi 37-38; cf. Nakamura 130-64). Kyoden scoffs at Matsudaira's feudalistic idealism. The visual-verbal text of our example (fig. 3) is filled with his wittily ironical signs, interwoven so as to ridicule the official promotion of Confucianism. It refers in numerous ways to the subtitle taken from the Confucian *Analects* that Kyoden added to the work: "Do not teach any one whose ability is below average" (Mizuno 178-179). The visual text shows a quiet scene on a public bridge or in an open social space where beggars and outcasts are intently reading Confucian texts. Beggars' outfits, including straw-coats, as well as the Chinese character "woman" tattooed on one individual's arm, are incongruous with a serious subject such as the study of Confucian texts. In contrast, the verbal text discusses animatedly but absurdly how eagerly all classes in society, from top to bottom, are studying Confucian doctrine, with phrases like "carpenters' loyalty" and "potato-peddlers' filial piety" (Mizuno 179): both groups invade the moral territory especially monopolized by the warrior-class alone.

Furthermore, the word "woman" has a different effect from the words that appear in the black-book pictures (see fig 2a), where it is made so clear that

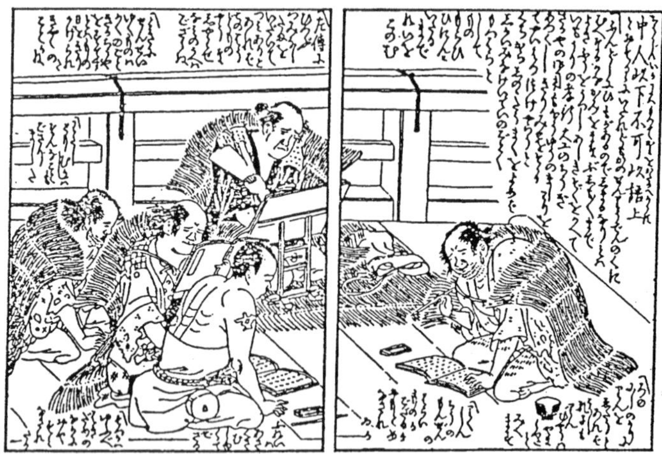

Fig. 3: Page-spread from *Koshijima Toki ni Aizome* (*Confucian Stripes, Timely Dye of Blue*) by Santo Kyoden, artist-writer. Edo: Owada, 1789. 1: 1-2. U. Nakamura, "Edo Fiction Picture Book".

these words have been written down – not drawn or tattooed – and thus have a privilege among the pictorial figures. The tattooed "woman", on the other hand, is part of the image: it is on a man's skin, not on special paper; it is a decoration, not pure communication; and it was not created by a writing-brush. Is decorating your skin with a word not as blasphemous, in a different way, as using a writing brush to draw a monster on a pure white wall? And does Kyoden not manage to get away with his blasphemy?

Kyoden uses Chinese characters or words within a picture again in another "yellow-cover" with the title *Longevity, Extended Measure, Long-Life Fabric to Order (Enmei nagajaku on'atsuraezome choju komon),* published in 1802. *Longevity* depicts twenty-seven topics, with verbal text by Kyoden and visual text by Utamaro,[2] and contains both a preface and a postscript. In our example (fig. 4a) Kyoden dramatizes one of the topics, concerned with life and loyalty; utilizing the Chinese character "Life" in a variety of ways, he fully exploits the mixture of verbal and visual signs. Interestingly, this figure indicates a striking disparity between the messages conveyed by the two kinds of texts. The verbal text expresses an officially sanctioned viewpoint, while the visual text states the author's anti-official conviction.

In the background, the Chinese character for "Life", hung from a pole, is being used as a target by two archers. A sign next to the pole says "Fight at the risk of your own Life." In the foreground, a handsome warrior-official is weighing "Life" against "Loyalty" on a balance-scale. A sign near him says, "Loyalty is heavy but Life is light". The verbal texts thus clearly proclaim the values supported by authority and tradition. The inscription above the pole states,

> A warrior's Life is like a lunch-box carrier's lunch,
> and also a spear-carrier's spear,
> because neither lunch nor spear belongs to its carrier.
> Lunch and spear are used only for one's master in time of need.
>
> Once the warrior's Life has been dedicated to his master,
> that Life doesn't belong to the warrior himself any more,
> even though it is still his own Life.
> If you don't fight at the risk of your own Life in an emergency,
> You cannot be considered a man of Loyalty.

The inscription near that handsome warrior official says,

> There is a proverb stating,
> "You should not desert your Life until Loyalty demands it."
> Life is precious, but it is not heavy if compared to Loyalty.
> Nothing in the world is as heavy as Loyalty.

Nowadays few would accept at face value the verbal text's dicta and proverbs in support of loyalty's supreme moral value. Even so, when I show people this page of Kyoden's *kibyoshi* and ask whether it is Life or Loyalty that is repre-

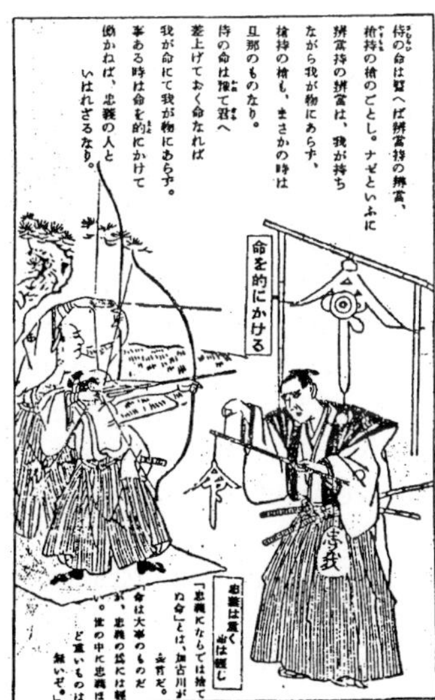

Figure 4a. "A Letter of 'Life'". From *Enmei nagajaku on'atsuraezome choju komon* (*Longevity, Extended Measure, Long-Life Fabric to Order*), by Kyoden, author, and Utamaro, artist. Edo: Tsutaya, 1802. 3: 3. Kaga Rare Book Collection, Tokyo Metropolitan Library.

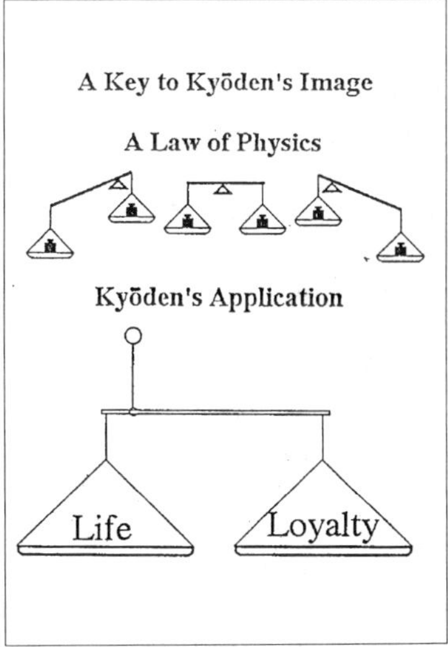

Figure 4b. A scale: A law of physics and Kyoden's application. (Drawing: F. Togasaki).

sented as more important here, many answer, "Of course Loyalty is shown to be more important than Life". Asked why they think so, they reply that it is written in the text that Loyalty is heavy, but not Life. If they would look more carefully at the picture or, more precisely, if they would read the scale properly, they would receive a very different message.

Figure 4b gives a visual representation of weights on a scale according to a simple law of physics, and of Kyoden's application of that law. On the scale held by the official the size of Life and Loyalty is similar, but the fulcrum is far to the left, very close to Life. Yet the scale remains horizontal, which we can tell from its being parallel to the horizontal pole beam and the edge of the mat holding the archers (whereas a superficial glance might trick us into thinking that Loyalty is indeed hanging lower). We must conclude that Life is much, much heavier than Loyalty. Thus a careful reading of the images (which would also include the treatment of "Life" as a target) reveals the interaction of verbal and visual texts as profoundly satirical, and the entire page as a silent cry of protest against the feudalistic and orthodox Tokugawa polity.

A scene from *Playboy, Grilled Edo-Style,* published in 1785, confirms the location of Kyoden's political protest in his visual text (see fig. 5). Here again, alongside the verbal text proper, words exist within the picture. Chinese characters appear, first, on the lid of a book-box placed in the gathering-room alcove; the titles are legible and name *The Tale of Ise* and *The Tale of Genji,* the great classics of Japanese literature. Second, they form an artist's name, Hanabusa Itcho (1652 to 1724), that appears conspicuously on a screen painting of the "King of Hell" situated behind two "bad" playboys. As for the verbal text proper, it fills almost all the empty space in the pictorial scene of the page-spread. And yet there is not a single line to explain the book-box and the screen with their inscriptions. Therefore, the viewer-reader has to figure out for himself why Kyoden chose to put such a tragic name as Hanabusa Itcho's on a screen painting.

Playboy is the most celebrated of all the "yellow-cover" fiction published in the thirty years of this genre's existence. However, to my knowledge no specialist has until now tried to listen to Kyoden's silent cry. I shall analyse the visual text's two inscribed objects in terms of what I will call Kyoden's "reduction mechanism".

This mechanism is clearly exemplified in the verbal text. The visual text indicates animated chatting among three playboys. The verbal text reproduces the entire fluent speech by one of the senior fellows who is trying to seduce the rich young fellow on the right into visiting the pleasure-quarters for the night. The senior insists that, to be well accepted there, it is best to familiarize oneself with contemporary popular ballads and songs. Then he simply lists the titles of sixty-eight ballads; each title, however, evokes a complex world of tragic stories with lyrical overtones. Here, Kyoden reduces a universe of words and

Fig. 5: Page-spread from *Edo mumare uwaki no kabayaki* (*Playboy, Grilled Edo-Style*) by Santo Kyoden, artist-writer. Edo: Tsutaya, 1785. Kaga Rare Book Collection, Tokyo Metropolitan Library.

melodies to the titles, which function almost as arbitrary signs. This is what I call Kyoden's "reduction mechanism", which is also at work in the two objects represented: the book-box and the screen painting.

The titles written on the book-box can be interpreted as signifying the world of classic and aristocratic literature of the tenth and eleventh centuries. Reduction of the classic world to those titles and their placement in the remote background space or an alcove implies belittlement of the classic world. In contrast, on the screen painting emphatically placed next to the two experienced playboys, we cannot overlook the name of the artist who was exiled because of his own painting. The two Chinese characters forming the artist's pen-name Itcho, meaning "Lone Butterfly", become a sign for the lonely life he was forced to lead. Itcho had portrayed a harlot in a boat wearing an aristocratic courtier's costume, in a picture accompanied by a poem on the harlot in a pathetic tone. Since this painting caused officials to suspect that Itcho might be alluding to the fifth Tokugawa Shogun's favorite concubine, he was jailed in 1693 and later exiled for twelve years to a tiny far-away island (cf. Yoshida 1: 18, 59). Itcho's name has been placed by Kyoden next to a humorous picture of the King of Hell, or Enma, who rules the underworld but also judges men's misdeeds in this world and punishes them in their afterlife. Here in the screen Enma's big eyes are observing the follies of the three playboys. The allusion to the artist's "crime" and his punishment by the inclusion of his name takes on ironic overtones through this juxtaposition, and the effect is further complicated by the relation of the screen texts to the scene depicted, which reinforces Kyoden's satire of the follies of a certain contemporary lifestyle.

In accordance with Kyoden's "reduction mechanism", the name Itcho inscribed in the representation of the screen signifies his tragedy and simultaneously Kyoden's sympathy with Itcho as an artist. It may signify even more. *Playboy* satirizes the Edo aesthetic and the lifestyle of Edo society at a time of apparent prosperity but also of social strain as reflected in the increasing number of farmers' uprisings. By picking the name of Itcho, an artist in a previous period of prosperity, the Genroku period, who was punished for his satirizing work, Kyoden may have suggested the potential danger for such work in his own time. *Playboy* was published in 1785, just prior to the conservative Matsudaira's ascent to power and the imposition of tight control over the publication of *kibyoshi* fiction and texts in similar genres. Later, Kyoden himself was to be punished twice. The invocation of Itcho's name may suggest the sense of foreboding felt by Kyoden and his attempt to communicate it to anyone who could decipher his coded word and image combinations.

Kyoden often conceals within the discrepancies, or heterodoxies, in the interplay between the verbal and the visual texts his silent but vital protests against the authoritarian power which condemns an artist and an artist's creativity. The availability of a medium mixing word and image made it possible for him to keep his passion and spirit alive. His "reduction mechanism", brought to prominence by the verbal text, reapplies to the words embedded in the visual text. The book-box titles evoke the courtly world of the classics in ironic counterpoint to the song titles' evocation of the pleasure-quarter world. Likewise, Itcho's name points to a world – strange intersection of the other two – where harlots are courtiers, or courtiers are harlots. Any viewer-reader who attends closely to the visual text and works from the premise that pictures and written texts are interdependent equals, will sense these pages' tone of subversion and silent protest. Conversely, it may be impossible to decipher the intermedia code without first adopting this anti-orthodox visual-verbal approach.

My conclusion is that the interpenetration of letters and images that conveyed Kyoden's subversive protests was itself a subversive protest. The message may have an authority like the government for its target, but the interpenetration of the media of words and images that creates the message is simultaneously subverting the authority of a written text held to be superior. We have seen, in four examples, several acts of visual-verbal blasphemy ridiculing various authorities of the time. The curious fact is that this blasphemy was somehow usually invisible to the censors.

Notes

1. The author wishes to thank Dr. Claus Clüver and Mr. Lewis Dibble, Comparative Literature, Indiana University, for their expert editorial advice. She gratefully acknowledges the financial support received from the office of Dr. Carol Y. Lucchesi, Head of Professional Enrichment Grants at Wittenberg University, which made her participation in the IAWIS Conference in Ottawa, Canada, possible.

2. In *Longevity*, Kyoden collaborated with Kitagawa Utamaro (1753-1806) who drew the pictures. However, the author of a yellow-cover fiction would nearly always draft the images himself. The artist then usually executed the pictures according to the author's pictorial drafts, received with instructions.

References

Jones, Sumie A. "Aspects of Gesaku Fiction: Comic Fiction in Japan During The Later Edo Period." Diss. University of Washington, 1979. Ann Arbor: UMI (7927813), 1979.

Kimura Yaeko."Aka-hon no sekai" [The World of Red-Books]. In *Kinsei Kodomo no E-hon-shu: Edo-hen [Anthology of Picture-Books For Early-Modern Children: Edo Version]*. Ed. Suzuki Juzo and Kimura Yaeko. Tokyo: Iwanami-shoten, 1985. 511-19.

Kitahara Susumu. "Kaikaku no arashi ni taeru chonin" [Townspeople Weathering the Storm of Reform]. In *Zusetsu: Nihon no koten: Kyoden, Ikku and Shunsui. [Classics of Japan in Graphics: Kyoden, Ikku and Shunsui]*. Ed. Jinbo Kazuya et al. Tokyo: Shueisha, 1980, 204-15.

Koike Togoro. *Santo Kyoden no kenkyu [Study of Santo Kyoden]*. Tokyo: Iwanami, 1935. 2nd printing 1986.

Mizuno Minoru. *Kibyoshi Sharebon shu [Kibyoshi and Sharebon Collection]*. Nihon Koten Bungaku Taikei 59. Tokyo: Iwanami Shoten, 1982.

Nakamura Usho, ed. *Edo no Gesaku-Ehon [Edo Fiction Picture Books]*. Kyoyo Bunko 1108 D 227. Tokyo: Shakai Shiso-Sha, 1985.

Santo Kyoden, writer and artist. *Edomumare uwaki no kabayaki [Playboy, Grilled Edo-Style]*. 3 vols. Edo, 1785. Rpt. in Jones, "Aspects of Gesaku Fiction", 82-92. Also rpt. in Yamaguchi, ed. Kibyoshi Nijugo-shu, 151-182.

-----. *Koshijima Toki ni Aizome [Confucian Stripes, Timely Dye of Blue]*. 3 vols. Edo, 1789. Rpt. in Nakamura, ed. *Edo no Gesaku-Ehon*, 5: 130-147. Also rpt. in Yamaguchi, ed. *Kibyoshi Nijugo-shu*, 243-274.

Santo Kyoden, author and Kitagawa Utamaro, artist. *Enmei nagajaku on'atsuraezome choju komon [Longevity, Extended Measure, Long-Life Fabric to Order]*. 3 vols. Edo, 1802. Rpt. in Yamaguchi Go, ed. *Kibyoshi Nijugo-shu*. 617-48.

Torii Kiyomasu and Torii Kiyomitsu, *ukiyo-e* print-makers. *Iroha moji: Terako Tanka [I-ro-ha Letters: Verses For Temple School-Children]*. 2 vols. Edo, 1762. Rpt. in *Kinsei Kodomo no E-hon-shu: Edo-hen. [Anthology of Picture-Books For Early-Modern Children: Edo*

Version]. Ed. Suzuki Juzo and Kimura Yaeko. Tokyo: Iwanami-shoten, 1985. 352-62.

Yamaguchi Go, ed. *Kibyoshi Nijugo-shu [Twenty-Five Works of Kibyoshi Fiction]*. Nihon Meicho Zenshu 11. Tokyo: Edo Bungei: Nihon Meicho Zenshu Kankokai. 1926.

Yoshida Teruji. *Ukiyo-e Jiten [Dictionary of Ukiyo-e]*. Tokyo: Gabun-Do, 1972. Vols. 1 and 3.

Beyond Conventional Boundaries

Semiotics and Ideology in Mixed Messages: The Postage Stamp

David Scott

The difficulty of precisely defining the structure of signs is well illustrated in the semiotic ambiguity of the postage stamp, particularly in relation to its multiple functions. In what follows, I use the categories of sign classified in Peirce's Second Trichotomy of Signs – *Icons, Indices* and *Symbols* – in an attempt to underline some of these difficulties.[1] Whereas the stamp functions primarily as an *indexical* sign, as an object it englobes *iconic* and *symbolic* elements. So, although the visual images the stamp adapts – portraits, monuments or landscapes – , can as objects, be classed as *icons*, they may, like the maps, diagrams, logos or other schematic representations the stamp incorporates, also function *indexically;* in addition the stamp uses *symbols* in the form of numbers, letters, names, acronyms or other linguistic elements incorporated into its design. But as with other classes of sign, these are far from straightforward: context and interaction exert pressures on individual semiotic elements, causing them to take on functions that, in isolation, they would not adopt. A *symbol,* for example, can become an *icon* when it receives a noticeable degree of typographical definition or is placed in a prominent and isolated position. On the level of theoretical definition, Peirce of course allows for the shifting of semiotic functions: thus *symbols,* he concedes, involve "a sort of index" while *indices* involve "a sort of icon".[2] He adds further that "it would be difficult if not impossible, to instance an absolutely pure index, or to find any sign absolutely devoid of the indexical quality".[3]

In his chapter on the Ten Classes of Signs in the *Collected Papers,* Peirce combines the categories singled out in his three Trichotomies of Signs. In this way, he pinpoints and defines the semiotic mix constituting each category of sign. The fourth and fifth categories are of particular interest here since they confront the problem of the degree of *indexicality* of *iconic* signs. The fourth class – the *Dicent Sinsign* – is illuminating in relation to the semiotic status of the postage stamp.[4] A weathercock is cited as an example of this set, but a postage stamp might also be classed thus since a "*Dicent Sinsign* is any object of direct experience, in so far as it is a sign, and, as such, affords information concerning its Object. This it can only do by being really affected by its Object; so that it is necessarily an Index. The only information it can afford is of actual fact. Such a sign must involve an Iconic Sinsign to indicate the object to which the information refers. But the mode of combination, or *Syntax,* of these two must also be significant".[5] The role of the *Iconic Sinsign* in "embodying information" in the stamp and the *syntactical* relationship between *Indexical Sinsign* and *Iconic Sinsign* are particularly relevant to an understanding of the semiotic functions of the postage stamp. The problematizing of the stamp's functions as a sign communicating "information [...] of actual fact" is explored in the second part of this paper.

The stamp's first function is to identify a country, that is to play an *indexical* role. This is the role of the *definitive* stamp, which is the stamp that is normally used for regular mail and which, usually of a small format, is issued over a number of years. It is moreover the role of the stamp in general which is to *indicate* from which country the mail to which it is attached comes: the letter and the stamp affixed to it standing in a contiguous relation with the country of origin, and to that extent being "really affected by it"; the stamp also functions as an index of the cost of postage of the letter or parcel; and the fact that the price of postage has indeed been paid. The role of conventional *symbols* (numbers and letters primarily) in clarifying the *indexical* function of stamps is of course paramount. The Universal Postal Union was set up in 1874 with the express purpose of agreeing, legislating and monitoring international conventions in relation to the postage stamp's indexical functions.

But as well as *indicating* a country, the stamp has, as a second general function, also to *represent* that country, to "afford information about its Object", that is, to offer a symbolic representation of it in traditionally recognisable terms. This it often does, as I shall show, by incorporating an *icon* – the profile of a reigning monarch, the national flag, an allegorical figure or national figurehead (as in the French Marianne) or even an abbreviation of the country's name in some acronymic or logo-like form. This is the second function of the *definitive* stamp. The pattern for it – format, iconic content, textual message – was established in 1840 with Sir Roland Hill's famous Penny Black stamp showing the profile of Queen Victoria, the device "Postage" and the face value of one penny (fig. 1).

Figure 1. *Penny Black*

Figure 2. Elizabeth II definitive

The current British definitive stamp, displaying the portrait bust of Elizabeth II by Arnold Machin, continues this convention almost without change (fig. 2).

A third function of the stamp is that of representing an *aspect* of a country. This is a more specific function, one that operates within the more general representative function of the stamp in its definitive role. Here the stamp appears to operate primarily *iconically;* indeed, it may in incorporate *two sets* of *Iconic Sinsigns.* This is the function of the *commemorative* stamp, which though a secondary, has become increasingly important in recent stamps. In this case, the stamp, usually pictorial, offers a memento, a souvenir, the *icon* of an event, an anniversary of an object of national or international importance. If the event being commemorated is contemporary to the stamp's issue, the *indexical* role of the commemorative image is also significant. Today by far the largest majority of stamps are commemorative and are issued in a vast range of formats, colours and designs.

However, even when the stamp represents an aspect of a country (for example, a monument or site), it represents at the same time the country itself. For the image reproduced on the stamp is accompanied by the signs which establish the identity of the country. The postage stamp is therefore, strictly speaking, never, as Peirce would say, "merely an Icon" or a picture: while representing an aspect of the reality of a country or a culture, it continues at the same time to represent the country as a national unit. This is its primary function. That is why the stamp – even when it incorporates *iconic* or pictorial elements on two or more semiotic levels, or when these elements seem almost to eclipse all other signs – remains, at bottom an *indexical* sign. It is this tension between *iconic* and *indexical* functions that will be explored in what follows, particularly in so far as it reflects the relationship between word and image in postage stamp design.

Many countries, anxious to capitalize on the *iconic* potential of what is essentially an *indexical* function in stamps, have adopted a number of strategies calculated to *iconize indexical* elements in the stamp design. One strategy is to transform the essential symbolic element clarifying the stamp's indexical function – the naming of the country of origin – into an *icon* of sorts. Thus the acronym *RF* has often replaced the longer device *République française* on French stamps, turning it in fact into the *logo* of the country. In Edmund Dulac's design – *La Marianne de Londres* – of 1945, for example (fig. 3), the acronym *RF* appears discreetly in the top left-hand corner of the stamp, balanced to the top right by the Cross of Lorraine, while the main part of the stamp is devoted to the profile of Marianne, symbol of Liberty, the French Republic and the country France. The borders to either side of the Marianne figure are the olive branches symbolising the peace which followed the liberation of France in 1944.

In this way, the strictly *symbolic* sign *RF,* while maintaining its essential *indexical* function, also becomes a significant element in an *iconic syntax,* relaying a specific ideological message: namely the liberation of France and the re-establishment of Peace, Liberty and French Republican values after the national humiliation suffered during the Second World War.

A second strategy used to *iconize indexical* elements in the stamp is that of pleonasm – the repetition of the *indexical* message in terms of *icons*. In the current French definitive stamp, the *Marianne du Bicentenaire*, created by Briat to commemorate the Bicentenary of the French Revolution in 1989 (fig. 4), the *symbolic* elements indicating the stamp's country of origin (*République française*) and function (*La Poste*) are both aligned with and complemented by purely *iconic* motifs.

Figure 3.
Dulac: *Marianne.*

Figure 4.
Briat: *Marianne.*

So the Marianne of 1989, with her Phrygian bonnet and Revolutionary *cocarde*, looks out at the viewer through three vertical bands of tone representing the French national flag, the *tricolore*. The stamp's, message is thus first read as a *diagram of icons,* only secondarily confirmed by the textual elements clarifying the stamp's indexical function (the *verticality* of the text, making it more difficult to read at a glance, confirms this). The *flag* motif is a common manifestation of semiotic pleonasm in stamps, and can see in many designs.

In the Ghana stamp of 1961 (fig. 5, attributed to Michael Goaman), the textual message confined by the stamp's designer to the margins of the frame, is rendered more or less superfluous by the iconic elements – map of Africa showing Ghana, profile of Elisabeth II, the national flag – which convey the essential message of the stamp in visual terms. (The fact that the text is embossed in dull gold means that in certain lights it disappears.)

Figure 5. Goaman:
Royal Visit to Ghana.

If ideological messages often prefer iconic signs to symbolic signs, images to words, it is because they appeal to irrational or unconscious impulses and are therefore less susceptible to criticism and objective analysis by the unalert viewer. As Peirce would say, they permit a greater degree of ambiguity in their presentation of "information concerning [their] Object". This tendency is evident in the commemorative stamp in its role as a medium of cultural promotion.

Despite its small size and relatively discreet *support* (letter or parcel), the stamp probably has an ideological density per square centimetre more concentrated than any other cultural form. Many countries, have grasped this fact and some have created a stamp industry whose function is the production of a range of seductive images aimed at the collector. The issue of a triangular stamp, for example, is a certain sign that a country depends on philately for an important part of its revenue. It is often the smallest countries that produce the largest number of stamps, often extravagant in their colour, format and imagery. Their aim is to create the illusion of a rich cultural identity. So the stamps of Andorra, Monaco, Liechtenstein and San Marino give the impression that the cultural life of these little principalities is an endless succession of sports events, flower festivals or motor shows. Other small countries, such as the old British colonies, offer the collector a range of poetic visions of exotic flora and fauna, ceremonial rites and customs of primitive civilizations.

To the charms of theme and image must be added the seductions of form. The stamps's tiny format works like a microcosm, offering a vision of the universe in which cultural and natural essences are concentrated. Sets of stamps offer the opportunity of creating a *musée imaginaire* of pictures, an anthology of poetic images. The stamp album becomes a kind of encyclopaedia, testifying to the splendour and diversity of the world; it is knowledge encapsulated in an idealized, one might almost say *imaginary* form. Similarly, stuck onto the envelope or parcel and franked by a distant mail office, the stamp offers the charm of a mysterious and exotic message, a fragment of another time and place sent to join us in our banal world.

In investigating the *imaginary* stamps of two artists, I aim to clarify both the potential of the stamp as a means of genuine cultural expression and for ideological propaganda. First, the American artist Donald Evans (1945-1977) who began to invent stamps from the age of ten. He stopped at 15 to take it up again when, disillusioned with his career as an architect, he decided to become an artist – *of stamps.* He sold his stamp collection to support himself in his new artistic career and began to work seriously on his imaginary stamps from 1972. Imitating the formats, the issues in sets and even postmarks and envelopes, he succeeded in integrating into his stamp designs many autobiographical or imaginary elements. His stamps represent not only imaginary countries but also his real life. The country of *Achterdijk* (fig. 6a), for example – which means *Behind the Dyke* – is a reconstruction of the part of the Netherlands in which Evans lived in the later 1960s. Sets from islands of *Fauna and Flora* (fig. 6h) imitate the number, valuations and format of typical British colonial stamps (except for the absence of the royal head or crown) and exhibit the usual encyclopaedic approach to exotic flora and fauna associated with them. Overall, Evans painted the plants, animals and landscapes of 42 imaginary countries and created a set of stamps for issue for every year from 1852 to

1973. He also explored the documentary side of philately – an area of absorbing interest to collectors – producing an exhaustive catalogue of his philatelic works, indicating the refinements relative to colour, format, value, dates, sets, perforation, etc. that one finds in the catalogues of Stanley Gibbons or Yvert et Tellier. In surveying Donald Evans's stamps, I will focus primarily on the semiotic issues they raise, choosing examples which seem, consciously or unconsciously, to explore the tensions between the indexical and iconic functions of the postage stamp that I indicated earlier.[6]

In his set depicting *Achterdijk* (fig. 6a), Evans adopts the triangular format, so popular with young philatelists, to concentrate the viewer's attention on the small aircraft visible in the upper part or apex of the stamp.

Figure 6a. Evans: *Achterdijk.*

This addition of aeroplane images to the otherwise banal views of the Dutch landscape is sufficient to transform the stamps into *airmail* issue, a ploy adopted in many real stamps. The refinement of Evan's style as a designer is evident in the way the two textual elements of the stamp *Achterdijk* and *Luchtpost* are, like the landscape/skyscape of the pictorial image, divided by a horizon and, thus, in effect, *iconized.*

The next three examples show how Evans's stamps literally *point to* the *indexical* functions of the stamp. In the Tropides *Islands* issue (fig. 6b), Evans adapts the convention of designing stamps in *se-tenant* blocks to transform the individual stamps into segments of a larger diagram, in this case indicating the geography of some imaginary Caribbean islands (probably based on the Caymans). The flight-paths of the aircraft that hop from island to island are indicated in the higher values by itineraries that likewise hop from stamp to stamp. The stamps designed for the imaginary country *Domino* (fig. 6c) are mounted on an authentic-looking envelope. This set beautifully illustrates the iconic pleonasms that strengthen the indexical messages of the stamps. Here the *Etat Domino* is embodied in the domino images, the face values of the stamps in francs coinciding with the numerical value of the domino that constitutes the image of each.

Figure 6b. Evans: *Tropides Islands.*

Figure 6c. Evans: *Domino.*

a word in Dutch. The scope for deconstruction is not lost on Evans here as he places on equal footing signs from different functional categories – punctuation marks and shadow, mist and numbers, abstract forms and figurative images. In some of the stamps he includes a stamp and a stamped letter, creating an effect of semiotic *mise en abîme.*

In the stamps issued by *Fauna and Flora* (fig. 6h), Evans restores a *definitive* role to the *commemorative* stamp by giving an apparently *iconic* theme a specifically *indexical* role.

Figure 6h. Evans: *Fauna & Flora.*

In an ingenious semiotic reversal, *Fauna and Flora,* a commonplace *theme* in many colonial stamps, becomes *the name of the country;* the latter thus *takes on the function of the stamp,* existing, as Donald Evans stamps themselves do, as pure signifiers, not referring to any signified in the real world. Here Evans identifies a ploy adopted by many stamps ostensibly referring to real countries or to aspects of real countries, that of proposing a message that is pictorially or ideologically satisfying but which in fact does not give a true account of the phenomena to which it claims to refer. Collin-Thiébaut's stamps, though lacking the visual seductiveness of Evans's, adopt a similar strategy.

Born in France in 1946, Gérard Collin-Thiébaut is a conceptual and installation artist, whose work ceaselessly interrogates art's strategies, especially those mobilised in the reception of the supposedly "aesthetic" object by the observer – and, in the case of his multi-media works, the listener. In 1986, in Dunkirk, he presented his first set of *Characters.* In this series, a number of seriographed plaques displaying various type-faces were hung on the walls of the gallery. Each plaque incorporated a word – such as *Arts, Messages, Palimpsest, Monuments,* etc – with, beneath, a label indicating the type of type-face, always different, used for each.

Naturally, viewers tended first to *read* the brief messages, trying to take the sign for the object, the message for the medium or, to use Peircean terminology, reading *icons* as *symbols.* For Collin-Thiébaut, as for many conceptual artists since Marcel Duchamp, the artist should problematize or abandon the analogical codes that have operated in the world of art – and of cultural communication – for so long that we are no longer aware of them.

In his stampbooks, exhibited from 1988, Collin-Thiébaut problematizes or subverts the seductive process activated when the stamp image attracts the viewer's attention. Like Evans, he is aware of the arbitrariness of the postage stamp, but instead of exploiting it to produce images even more flagrantly seductive, he prefers rather to empty philatelic images of their latent symbolic content. For him, those little squares of paper that seem to open perspectives onto (sometimes exotic) phenomena, in fact often have little to do with reality – cultural or political. The stamp is an empty sign, susceptible to signifying any object or "reality" its issuing agency decides to impose. Collin-Thiébaut's stamps emphasize this semiotic arbitrariness by foregrounding the "readymade" aspect. So, his stamps at exhibitions can be purchased from stamp machines exactly like those found at the post office or in the streets of Paris and London. Also like Evans, Collin-Thiébaut uses the accessories of philately to both seduce and disconcert his public. Part of his exhibitions includes cases display-

Figure 7a-c. Collin-Thiébaut: *Charles Rennie Mackintosh; Audio-visual device; The Fall of the Angel.*

ing sets of stamps presented in polythene envelopes – just like those used by the post office when promoting First Day Issue covers – which can be set in albums bound and printed, ready to accommodate the stamps. Specialist collectors can buy custom-made sheets of stamps perforated with their buyers' initials. Marketing is of course through the publisher/issuer, Collin-Thiébaut himself. The aim of this is to make the viewer distinguish between the "natural" and the constructed. The message is that all images are constructed.

I conclude this article with a brief review of the stamps exhibited in 1990 in Glasgow (European Cultural Capital that year). In the *Charles Rennie Mackintosh* stamp (fig. 7a), Collin-Thiébaut parodies the conventional commemorative stamp by showing the prestigious site (the Glasgow Museum) with, in an oval as though he were the monarch of the place, the great Scottish architect and designer, Mackintosh. Like the stamps issued at the ARC show, the *Audio-Visual Device 1981-1986* series (fig. 7b) refers to the medium (in this case a slide projector) used by the artist in some of his installations of the 1981-86 period. The stamp's *indexical* function here is to *indicate* and commemorate *means* previously used by the artist. In *The Fall of the Angel* (fig. 7c) a Christmas card image is used to indicate an earlier work, *Audio-Visual Device,* whose aim was precisely that of deconstructing the process of seduction by the image.

As important as patrons of the past are present gallery directors: it is they who promote the work of modern artists and who have in their hands the power to create reputations. In *Tramway Glasgow 1990: Three Gallery Curators* (fig. 7d), Nicholas Serrota, director of the Tate Gallery, is commemorated, his profile framed in an oval like that of a monarch on a British definitive stamp. To deconstruct the process, the artist reminds us – like Magritte in his famous painting *Ceci n'est pas une pipe* – that *this is not a stamp.* Likewise, in *1990 Art*

Figure 7d-f. Collin-Thiébaut: *Tramway Glasgow 1990: Three Gallery Curators; 1990 Art Collectors; Glasgow Cultural Capital of Europe 1990: Three Plaques.*

Collectors (fig. 7e), Saatchi and Saatchi make their appearance as commercial gallery directors: the kings of English publicity, the Saatchis became picture buyers as a result of selling seductive images. Their collection of paintings notably includes the work of Andy Warhol, the artist who, more than any other, stressed the link between the commercial image and the work of art. Finally, *Glasgow Cultural Capital of Europe 1990: Three Plaques* (fig. 7f), in the black blanks of their surface, represent the *degré zéro* of the philatelic image. Here Collin-Thiébaut reminds us that the first stamp ever, issued exactly 150 years before, was nothing but a little black oblong carrying the portrait of Queen Victoria.

Notes

1 Charles Sanders Peirce, *Collected Papers*, Vol. II *Elements of Logic*, (ed. Ch. Hartshorne and P. Weiss), Cambridge, Mass.: Belknap Press of University of Harvard, 1960, 143-44.

2 *Collected Papers*, 143.

3 *Collected Papers*, 172.

4 Gérard Deledalle is the first semiotician to have tackled the problem of the postage stamp's semiotic status; see Ch. II of *Théorie et pratique du signe. Introduction à la sémiotique de Charles S. Peirce* (Paris: Payot, 1979), 95-116.

5 *Collected Papers*, 147.

6 Donald Evans's stamps reproduced from *The World of Donald Evans* (ed. Willy Eisenart), New York: Harlin Quist, 1980.

Illustrations

1 Henry Corbould: *Penny Black* 1840.

2 Arnold Machin: Elizabeth II definitive (Great Britain from 1967).

3 Edmund Dulac: *Marianne* (France, 1945).

4 Louis Briat: *Marianne* (France 1989).

5 Michael Goaman: *Royal Visit to Ghana* (Ghana, 1961).

6a-h Donald Evans *Achterdijk* (1974); *Tropides Islands* (1977); *Domino* (1974); *Iles des Sourds* (1975); *Tricentenaire de l'Ile montagne des Sourds* (1974); *Republica de Banana* (1975); *Nadorp* (1972, 1973); *Fauna & Flora* (1975). Copyright 1994 Estate of Donald Charles Evans.

Art reprinted from *The Worl of Donald Evans* by Willy Eisenhart, with the kind permission of Judy Fireman, agent of author and estate.

7a-f Gérard Collin-Thiébaut *Charles Rennie Mackintosh; Audio-visual device;The Fall of the Angel; Tramway Glasgow 1990: Three Gallery Curators;1990 Art Collectors; Glasgow Cultural Capital of Europe 1990: Three Plaques* (1990). Reproduced by permission of the artist.

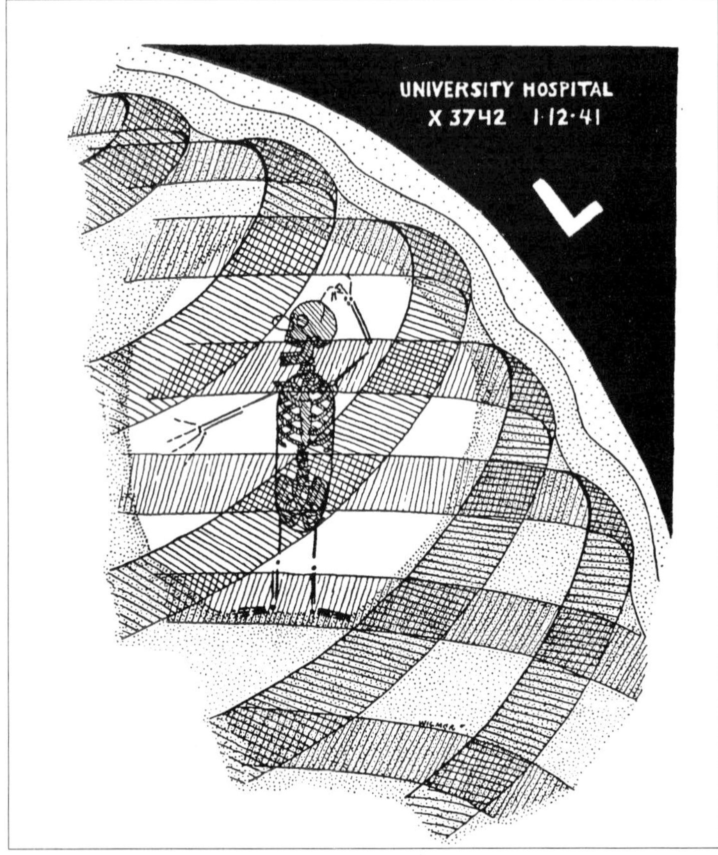

Figure 2. *Huber the Tuber*, 34.

fingers? Or are the "its" and "yous" supposed to be as entangled as the ribs-on-ribs-on-ribs in Wilmer's x-ray cartoon (fig. 2)?

My notion is that Wilmer forges the necessary link from intractable dilemma to imperative conclusions by exploiting the potential weaknesses of his chosen media and style of expression. In the case of his cartoonish drawings, the weakness lies in the fragile conventionality with which they encode three-dimensional space – perhaps in collusion with weaknesses in Wilmer's own draftsmanship that incline him towards the violation of conventions. One effect of these drawings is to lend plausibility to linguistic absurdities: a wayward line that confounds inside and outside unmakes distinctions that syntax and signification inherently respect. But Wilmer also exploits the fuzziness of language itself, especially its way of making sense through vagueness of reference, oxymoron, ambiguity, and paradox. I do not think there is any "master code" behind this confusion. Rather, what I would like to show is just how Wilmer manages to use the attenuated representationalism of "cartoon" outline-drawings to lay out a quirky spatiality within which we reader-viewers are to seek our own paths of interpretation.

Wilmer, a physician-psychiatrist, has also dealt with the mental disorders brought on by lengthy hospitalization (*This is Your World*, 1952, also a verbal-visual text), the therapeutic management of penal institutions *(The Correctional Community),* the psychic and social trauma of the Vietnam war's aftermath ("War Nightmares", *Vietnam in Remission*), and even the problem of evil itself *(Facing Evil)* – sometimes as author, sometimes as editor or conference chairperson. Always, the problem confronted involves the inward persistence of some ineradicable, undesirable, trace. And always the moral is, and must be, something like "acknowledge affliction and live on accordingly". But, as our introductory example has suggested, there is something interesting and out-of-the-ordinary about Wilmer's characteristic route from stubborn problem to comforting bromide.

Wilmer recommends an inner change that is something like religious conversion, but tightly bound to the mundane particulars of one's special situation. There is no faking it: you can't simply declare your intention to stop having nightmares, or wilfully intervene between your mental agony and your physical disease. This message demands a lot from its media. Wilmer's scheme encompasses verbal/visual art, and more. *This Is Your World,* an extreme case that we will look at in more detail, achieves a sort of total modal promiscuity. It includes a review of related scholarship with illustrative charts etc., some texts intended for distribution to patients, and the words of a recorded "Ballad" to be played to them, a number of related drawings by the author "portraying the patient's quandaries" (xi), several "psychodramas" (some available as audio recordings and some developed into short films) for presentation in patient therapy groups, and a scholarly essay explaining Wilmer's mixed approach, apparently designed to "sell" it to skeptical physicians and psychiatrists. The "moral" is: the institutionalized TB patient *must,* if he is to live, understand that confinement is the route to freedom. In the Foreword, Adelaide Johnson indicates the "leap of faith" that such an act of understanding can entail. Even for her, we note, the intractable facts confront the patient in the guise of a picture that speaks.

> To many patients it seems an impossible paradox to be expected to relax into complete serenity and yet maintain hopes and plans for a far future. . . .
>
> Cooperative for nearly a year, you rest and rest. And then, you produce an x-ray showing a recent spread, an x-ray which threatens, "Maybe you will never be able to sit up in a chair" (x-xi).

This Is Your World is addressed in part to patients, in part to the doctors who are expected to treat them; now encouraging the patient to produce, by a heroic act of interpretation, hope out of desperation, now trying to persuade the doctor to adopt new psychiatric modes of treatment that cannot, by their very nature, be empirically tested. Wilmer approaches this second audience by way of a verbal image that connects the apparent "leap of faith" he demands of the patient with the speculative rationality proposed to the doctor. In his concluding essay, Wilmer is reflecting on how scientific thought, applied to human reality, becomes weak and conjectural:

> It used to be a belief that the road between original observations and final conclusions –even final causes – was a rather short and pleasant one, and one that could be traveled very rapidly if one had rather obvious mechanical vehicles. Of course actually it is an almost pathless field; the development of science does not proceed like the driving of a vehicle along a road which can be assumed *a priori.*
>
> It is, rather, the advance of a large number of individuals, some running swiftly, some going with plodding steps over a field full of obstacles and pitfalls, in which the labors of many in the company will be lost or their gains rather small. Eventually we arrive at a point which is not narrowed to one simple, clear pathway, but one from which, perhaps, the number of paths is discernible. (151-2)

Of course a metaphor is getting out of control. A road becomes an almost pathless field in which, it turns out, some run while others fall or labor; somehow all these endeavors map, tread, and alter this "field" until it reveals a discernible number of paths. There is something sardonically realistic about this muddle: it *does* rather suggest the characteristically messy course of real-world inquiry.

There is a close correspondence between this "road" from observations to conclusions and the "road to health" that the hospitalized patient must follow (and which actually appears on the page 11 "map" of the sanatorium experience). TB's typical course, like that of conjectural thought, is neither short nor direct: it is not a matter of clear crisis followed by complete recovery. The hospitalized patient does not know whether he will live, whether he will ever be released, or whether release will be followed by a permanent remission. All that is really certain here is that if a patient does not believe that his long-term hospitalization is the only road to health, the resulting despair can kill him. Wilmer's psychotherapeutic strategy is first to induce the patient to acknowledge the real senselessness of his dilemma, then to encourage him to find his own sources of hope within this fabric of uncertainties. Like the road of interpretation, the road to health guarantees nothing; indeed the book is peppered with warnings that its materials are liable to demoralize patients if used injudiciously.

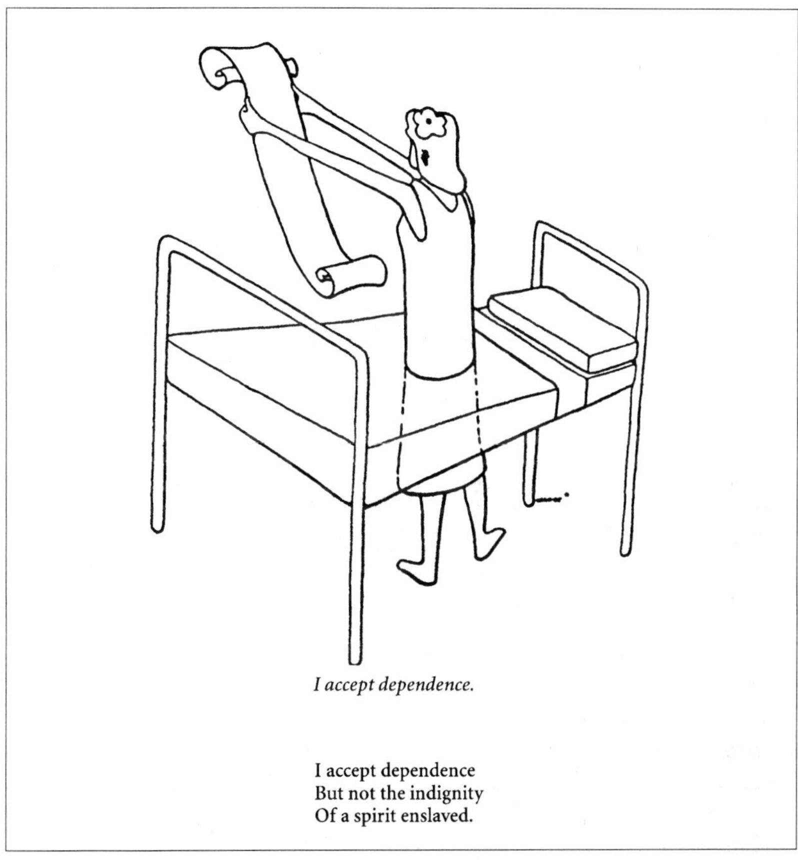

I accept dependence.
I accept dependence
But not the indignity
Of a spirit enslaved.

Figure 3. Harry Wilmer, M.D., *This Is Your World* (1952), 69.

Let us see how Wilmer pictures acknowledgment of one's dilemma, and then hope born of uncertainty, in the drawings entitled *"I accept dependence"* and *"Someone conquered, / Someone rose to victory"* (figs. 3, 4).

The first, illustrating a firmly cadenced "declaration of dependence", shows a patient defiantly erect, a flower in her hair. Her impossible intersection with the bed parallels the declaration's impossible "shadow" rhetorical construction, from "dependence", plus the "in" of the next line's "in dignity", of the word [in]dependence. And there is something about the heavy stylization of the tubular dress, folded bedclothes and curling scroll that predisposes one to accept the apparent co-extensiveness of thighs and mattress as part of some as-yet-unlearned graphic convention. The "Ballad"'s claim is that even in accepting dependence a patient retains the rights to self-defense and to flight; these

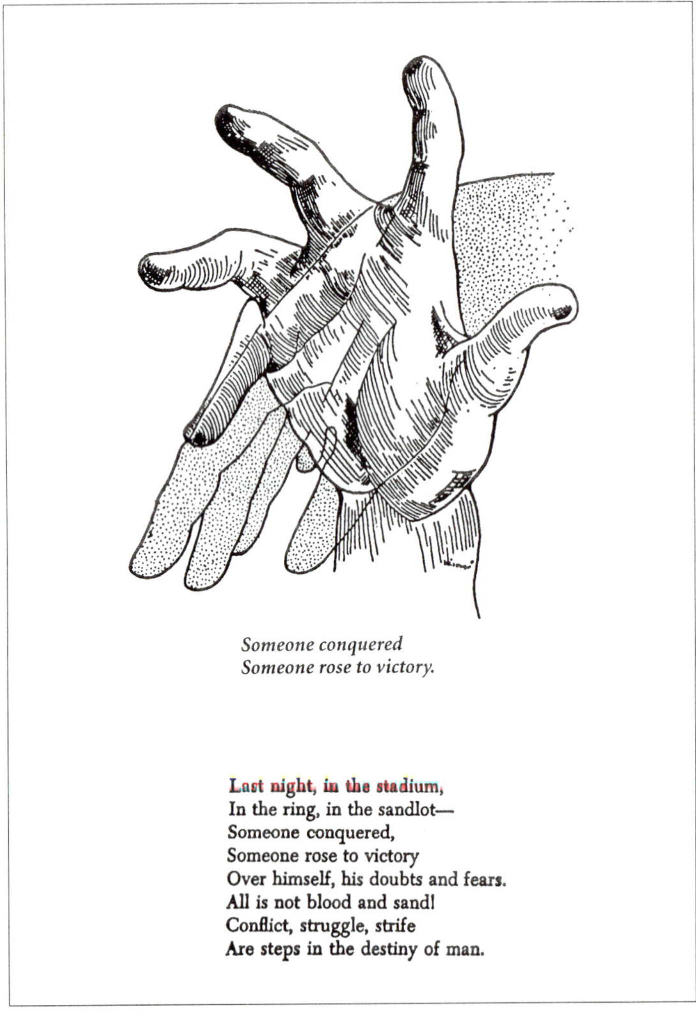

Figure 4. *This Is Your World*, 96.

attributes appear mingled in the metaphor, "camouflage of feathers", and in "Still, breathless fright / Or soaring flight". Accordingly, Wilmer's stretching and outright violation of the outline conventions that govern the compression of three dimensions into two serves to express, almost to schematize, the violations of verbal conventions – semantic, morphological, even phonemic (the near-perfect overlap of "flight" and "fright") – that convey his paradoxical verbal message.

Outline contours can also misbehave by simply refusing to efface other outlines, weakening the sense of "in front" and "behind", as in *"Someone conquered, / Someone rose to victory"* (fig. 4). Is "conquered" here an active verb or a past participle? Do the two occurrences of "someone" have different referents? Does the contour of a raised thumb supply the outline for a drooping shadow wrist? Outlines, contours, and shading compose an unsettling but suggestive image: perhaps a shadow hand infecting the volume of a real hand, or a real hand bursting out of an empty shadow. Yet somehow the "shadow" hand seems to be a more natural image than the laboriously contoured one, which itself seems close kin to the crossed fingers from *Huber's* ambiguous "Don't think it can't happen to you!" This time, perhaps, it is the tormented tension in the "victorious" raised hand that sparks ambivalence: one can imagine it stretching upwards from a drowning person.

These images are not subtle. Each merely unseats the viewer from his good-faith attempt to determine a three-space referent for the printed lines into a paradoxical and personal act of interpretation. Yet, artless as they seem, their message is lucid and controlled: even though dependence and freedom can be as one, victory and defeat, for all their interconnections, remain opposites.

> This is the world I have waited for,
> So wondrous, so monstrous,
> So full of love withheld but for the loving. (*World* 101)

The "Ballad"'s final image, *"This is the world I've waited for"*, suggests depth, but its perspective is vague (fig. 5). The recovered patient walks home across a field. Her outline falls across that of a big almost-dead tree, and echoes in the curve of an adjoining smaller forked tree. Since the woman would seem to be walking past the dead tree and toward the living one, the image would seem to signify a positive "final conclusion". But doesn't the visual rhythm of the composition point up as much as in? Up there, the branch of the small tree is dead. The vagueness of the picture's implied depth encourages the viewer to conflate and reconnect outlines. The position of the smaller tree's base and the greater detail with which it is rendered make it seem near to the picture plane; but its upper branch passes behind the larger, less distinct tree. Distances and depth are only weakly specified. This picture's collapsing space can do no more than place us, with the patient, at a point "from which, perhaps, the number of paths is discernible".

This image, even though it does not overtly flout outline conventions, tempts the viewer to regard them as violated. This implicit and conjectural violation evokes the uncertain future of the TB patient whose disease is in remission – even as, by dissolving its implicit dimensionality, it reduces the image itself to a tangled analog of Wilmer's contorted verbal figure of the

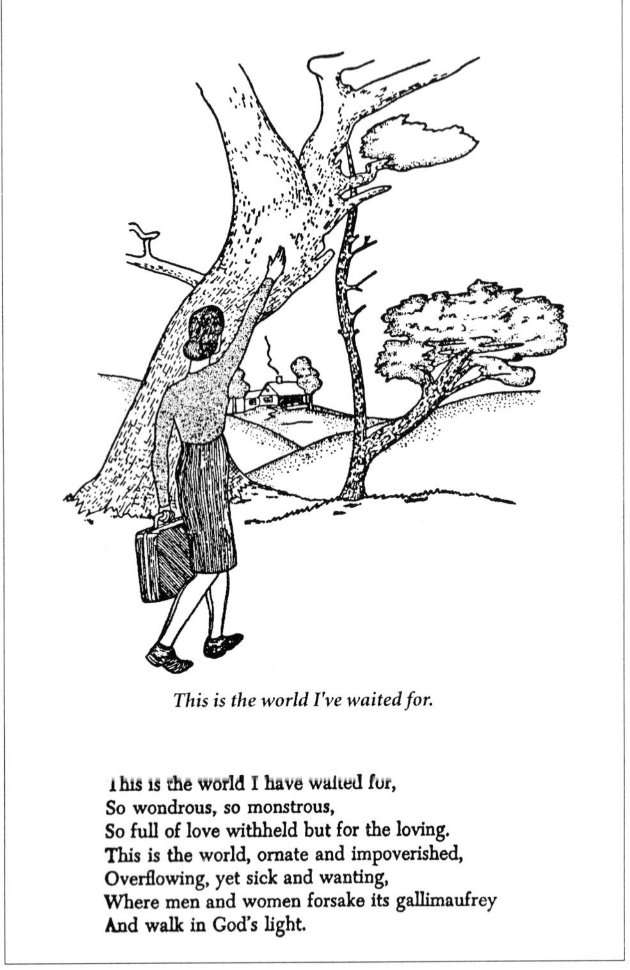
This is the world I've waited for.

This is the world I have waited for,
So wondrous, so monstrous,
So full of love withheld but for the loving.
This is the world, ornate and impoverished,
Overflowing, yet sick and wanting,
Where men and women forsake its gallimaufrey
And walk in God's light.

Figure 5. *This Is Your World,* 102.

path-that-is-not-a-path from scientific observation to conclusions. Perhaps we can reread the resultant composite figure, now both verbal-visual and scientific-therapeutic, in terms of the patterned violations of visual conventions we've encountered in the preceding pictures. The outlines of rolling hills could be, like those of the patient and bed, indices of objects that impossibly penetrate one another. And what about that heavily contoured tree passing awkwardly *behind* a lightly contoured one that seems to be rooted no nearer to us – and in front of *that,* lightly stippled like the shadow-hand, the woman's sweater. Do they represent neatly layered three-space objects, or an impossible involution like that of the shadow hand wrapping its way back into and around the contoured one?

Certainly, something that weakens the conventional construal of the spatiality of *"This is the world I've waited for"* is the absence of a path, of the one or two lines that would freeze this unsettled dimensionality into a vista, lead our gaze, with the woman's steps, to the door of the inviting, distant house, foil the linear composition's insistence on climaxing not in the foreground or the "vanishing point" but overhead in a forking nest of dead tree limbs. But there is something else for us to see in this vitiated representation, if we leave its outlines empty of the rounded objects they might represent. The teardrop-shape of the light central area is recurrent in Wilmer's pictures; compare the stylized *"Why do you live?"* (fig. 6) and the photographic plate in

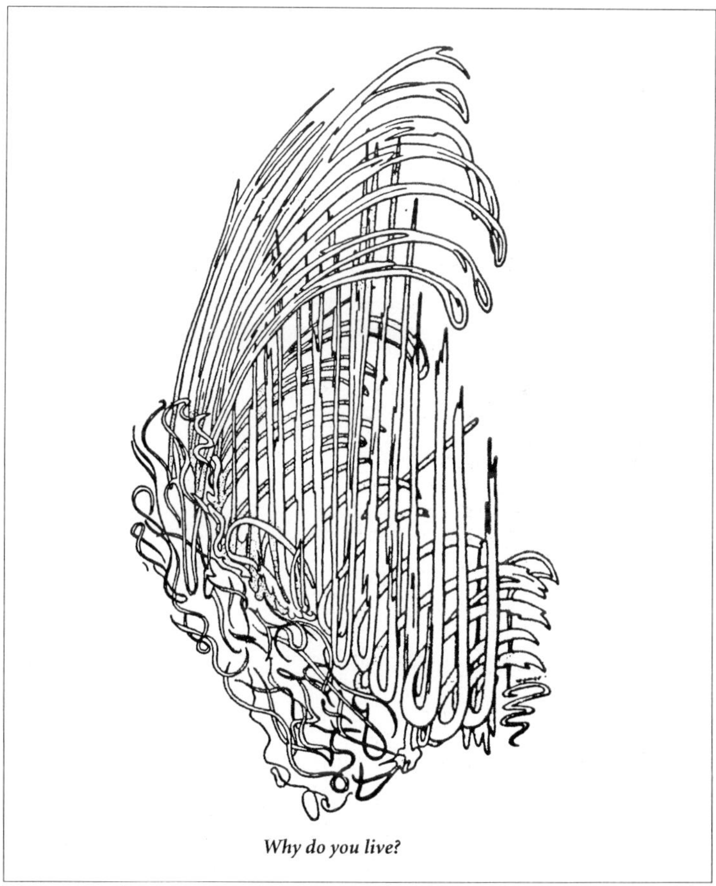

Figure 6. *This Is Your World*, 94.

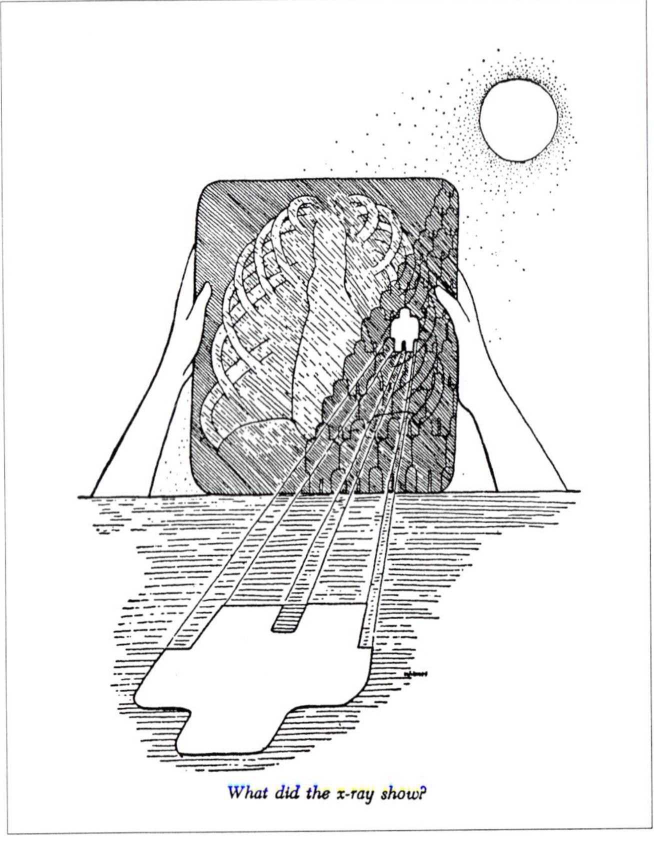

Figure 7. *This Is Your World*, 63.

"What did the x-ray show?" (fig. 7): the shape can be a chest-cavity. Cheeringly, the last picture fills this outline with light and air. But looking closely at "the world we've waited for", we begin to worry about the "shadow" on the porch there: after all, "our world" was the one we got sick in the first place. And a closer look shows us something more disturbing: that the scene's overall layout is practically a duplicate of that of the "x-ray" picture (fig. 8), the main thing absent being the converging lines that lead the earlier image all too clearly from "observations" to grim "conclusions".

What, actually, *did* the x-ray show? It showed the doctor a two-space image from which to reconstruct a three-space form. It showed the patient the special uncertainty of his own future. The drawing shows its viewer a vaguely anthropomorphic outline *projected* from a tiling of intersecting, overlapping shapes onto a diverging plane. What we, as doctors or patients, find meaning-

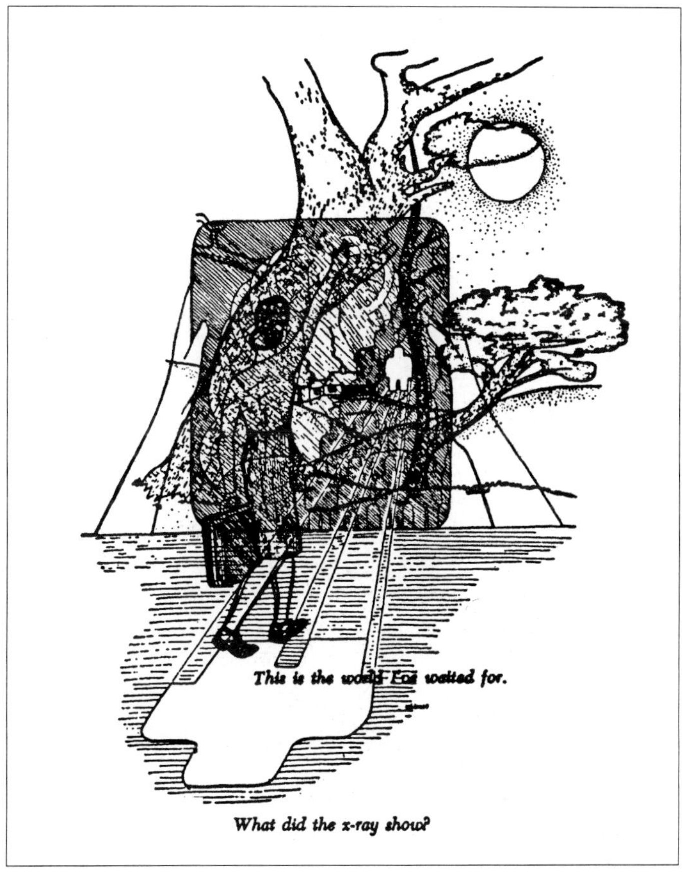

This is the
waited for.
What did the x-ray show?

Figure 8. The images of figs. 5 and 7 "double-exposed".

ful is here being brought to "our plane" via the attenuating template of a film negative. In that it inherently lacks the same representational conventions that Wilmer flouts, the x-ray negative takes its place as a sort of referent or original for his drawing style.

Wilmer's drawings are not exactly illustrations, nor do they function precisely in compensation for insufficiencies of written language. Rather, they seem to conspire with the verbal text in the articulation of complex and uncertain figures, such as that of the path that is not a path. How do we make progress without a path? joins with: what do we do with lines if they don't "outline"? Any answer we arrive at will, like the "leaps" of interpretation Wilmer demands of afflicted patients, be conditioned by the unusual fixity his chosen topics impose on interpretive beginnings and endings. It will also, it would seem, have something to do with "projection". Lines *project* from x-ray film plane to interpretive plane, and accordingly from the recovered patient across the rolling field; finally, in interpreting these images and texts together we *project* a likeness linking the "x-ray" picture and the "world" picture. The characteristic of this "projection" process is to work, within the interpretive process, from a plane of representation such as the x-ray plate, that is merely "mechanical" or devoid of meaning, to a plane that can at least bear meaning.

I believe, with Nelson Goodman and C. S. Peirce, that "likeness" is part of the interpretive process, and not a relation that holds all-on-its-own between bits of the world and bits of representation. The trick spatiality of Wilmer's drawings fits in with this notion. But these drawings also, and more interestingly, exploit the fact that likeness, if it is to exist at all, can and must be found among *representations:* it is a relationship that holds not so much thing-to-thing as image-to-image. The world is not congenial to its representations: few objects are in reality circumscribed by anything like an outline, while practically all proper drawings of objects are. But interpretable connections become possible among fabricated images: x-rays don't "look like" people, but do resemble other x-rays in meaningful ways. Thus, working from mechanically or conventionally fixed images, we can have what I am calling "projection", an interpretive process that works among representations in space. Lured or trapped into interpreting some baffling collection of representations, one essays projections among such fixed elements as a spiral line that denotes a curled parchment, a lightened area resembling an exposed bit of photo negative, the dot-stippling that indicates fuzzy cloth, or shadow – until these brittle portrayals cease merely to relay a set of fixed observations, and begin, in harmony with verbal figures such as that of the path of interpretation, to support the inner gesture that makes, for instance, a way from despair into hope.

References

Wilmer, Harry A., M.D. *Huber the Tuber.* New York: NTA, 1943 (1942).

-----. *This is Your World.* Springfield IL: Charles C. Thomas, 1952.

-----. "Vietnam and Madness". *The Journal of the American Academy of Psychoanalysis* 10.1 (1982): 47-65.

-----. "War Nightmares: A Decade after Vietnam". *Vietnam in Remission.* Ed. James F. Veninga and Harry A. Wilmer. Salado, TX: Texas Committee for the Humanities, 1985. 91-106.

Wilmer, Harry A., M.D., and Paul Woodruff, eds. *Facing Evil: Light at the Core of Darkness.* LaSalle, IL: Open Court, 1988.

From Epigraph to Iconic Epigram: The Interaction between Buildings and Their Inscriptions in the Urban Space

Hans Lund

Some years ago, the head office of Bank of Norway moved into a new building in Oslo. The old building, which had become too small and uncomfortable, was taken over by the Museum of Modern Art. The palace of finance was transformed into a palace of visual art (fig. 1). The former bank building is constructed of rough granite blocks with a symmetrical and strictly axial façade. Above the portal, flanked by lions' heads, there is a window with two heavy pillars, accentuating the vertical movement across the front. At the top we see Norway's coat of arms in relief, framed by two carved figures. The structure can be summed up in concepts such as centrality, symmetry, balance, order, weight and enclosure. According to a conventional way of reading architecture within our interpretative community, the sum of the architectural elements, combined with the sculptural pictures on the façade, lends to the building an authoritarian appearance.

Today the Norwegian words *Museet for samtidskunst – Museum of Contemporary Art* – are written above the grandiose main portal. The old exterior of the bank building, however, is protected by law. No change of any details of the exterior is allowed, not even of the old text on the façade. As a consequence, the Norwegian words *Norges Bank – Bank of Norway* – are still there, quite visible under the inscription *Museet for samtidskunst.* Thus we have a building identified by two totally different labels, one stressing the concept of bank, the other stressing that of modern art.

As the façade text is to the building what a title is to a painting, we might read both texts on the old bank building in Oslo as titles and read the architecture in the light of its two alternative "titles". Some scholars argue that the title has no aesthetic relevance. Marcelin Pleynet says that "the critic rarely sees the title of a work as being anything more than a handy way of designating a picture which would otherwise be hard to identify".[1] Other scholars, however, claim that the title or the label is an integral part of the painting itself and that a work differently titled will invariably be aesthetically different. Another frequent claim among art theorists is that in interaction between word and image, the word will normally be hierarchically dominant. The reason, Gombrich argues, is that language can specify while images cannot. "It is an observation which stands in curious contrast to the fact that images are concrete, vivid and

Figure 1. Museum of Modern Art, Oslo (Photograph: Morten Thorkildsen, Museum of Modern Art, Oslo).

inexhaustibly rich in sensory qualities, while language is abstract and purely conventional".[2] Norman Bryson talks about the supremacy of the discursive over the figural and J. Hillis Miller accepts the view of Mark Twain: "A painting presents something, but what that something is cannot be known for sure unless the picture is labelled".[3] The words *Norges Bank* may confirm the conventional reading of the building in Oslo as a sign of authority and centre of power, whereas the new text *Museet for samtidskunst* may influence some observers to read the architectural units as post-modern and ironic signs, anachronisms or even kitsch.

The label influences our reading of the picture. That is obvious. But the contrary is obvious, too: the picture and its context will always influence our reading of the label. As Michel Foucault stresses, an order always hierarchizes the verbal and the visual signs, "running from the figure to discourse or from the discourse to the figure". It is very rare that subordination remains stable.[4]

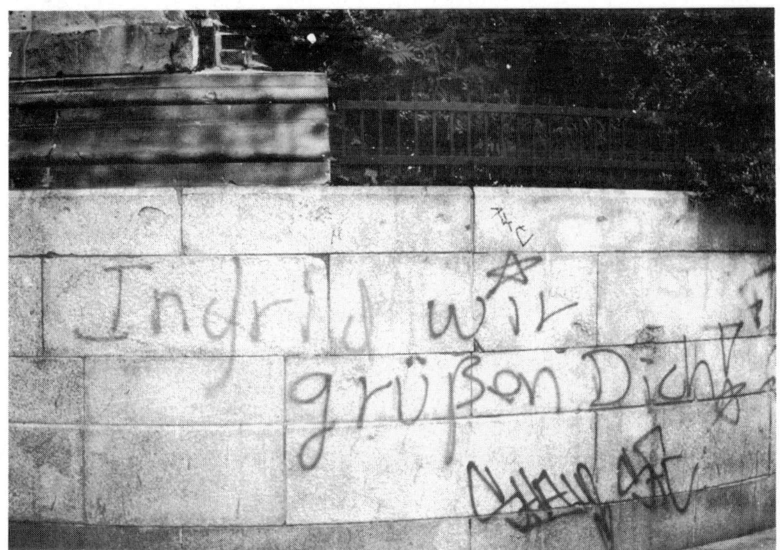

Figure 2. Graffiti, Berlin 1990 (Photograph: H. Lund).

The strict design of the Oslo building influences our reading of the new label. Within our interpretative community it somehow lends a special meaning to the words "contemporary art" and indirectly also to the art exhibited in the building. Thus the architecture seems to signal a view of modern art which is far from today's anti-authoritarian conception of art, as expressed for example in the rollicking exterior of the Centre Pompidou or in the equally playful interior of the Picasso Museum, both of them in Paris. A photo of the façade of Museet for samtidskunst, distributed by the Museum itself, shows an effort to rhetorically reduce the building's centrality and weight, i.e. its authority – and with that the polarization between building and façade text – by showing the building from an oblique angle, viewed through a modern sculpture (see figure 1). The effect of the architectural signs on our reading of the words on the wall is evident from the two following graffiti texts, one in Berlin, and the other in Paris.

In the spring of 1990, the words "Ingrid, wir grüssen dich!" – Ingrid, we greet you – could be read on a wall of the Memorial Church, the *Gedächtniskirche,* in Berlin (fig. 2). The design of the graffiti is not without a certain aesthetic finesse and pictorial expressiveness. The greeting is written in green with a conspicuous orange decoration added to the name of the addressee. The plural form "wir" suggests that it is not a matter of a relationship between two individuals, but rather of group solidarity. "Wir" is adorned with a star which seems to emphasize the group as essential. The greeting could also be said to have a certain literariness as the sentence consists of two dactyls, and the vowel *i* appears as many as four times. What makes the writing in Berlin

Figure 3. Graffiti, Paris 1992 (Photograph: H. Lund).

interesting is its architectural context. Above the words on the wall towers the *Gedächtniskirche.* The ruined church is standing there as an alarming sculptural reminder of the insanity of the Second World War. For the historically well-informed observer the message of the text can therefore take on a strong note of defiant political willpower with overtones of destruction and terror. The reader is very likely to connect the verbal message with the political violence which brutalized Berlin up to the time when the wall was pulled down. Ingrid might be one of the imprisoned German terrorists who are heirs to the notorious Rote Armee Fraktion. Whether that is really the case, we cannot know, but we can argue that the building interacts hermeneutically with the green text and thus helps the onlooker and interpreter to create a possible meaning.

From one of the windows of the Picasso Museum in Paris can be seen a white wall which is part of a neighbouring house. Last spring the words "Hélène, je t'aime!" could be read on the wall (fig. 3). Here the interpretation is more obvious than in Berlin, because we all know the code. The bold letters of the

Figure 4. Patrick Raynaud, "Voyelles" (Photograph: H. Lund).

name *Hélène* are painted in the primary colours blue and yellow and in the secondary colours green and orange. The expressionism of the polychrome letters are telling us about the writer's enthusiasm and amorous passion. Again, it is the architectural context, the inscription's proximity to the Picasso Museum, which makes the written text so interesting. The iridescent declaration of love is not easily seen from the street, whereas it is very easy to see it from one of the windows of the Picasso Museum. The writer could not have found a more suitable place for his tribute. The newly renovated and rebuilt mansion has unconventional exhibition rooms, grouped in a surprising and playful

there is also an influence in the opposite direction. The building and its urban surroundings load the text with meaning. Standing in front of this epigraph on the Bishop's square, we become very much aware of the fact that we are present in the city of Hans Christian Andersen. In contrast to my Rimbaud example, the text in Copenhagen was written directly for the location on which it is displayed. That is the case with my last example, too. In the 70s Jenny Holzer placed her electronic epigraphs in the urban landscape where people move and where advertisements are exposed on walls and roofs – as in Times Square in New York :"Protect me from what I want" (fig. 6). Holzer's laconic texts operate in the field of tension created by the opposites of aphoristic sayings and truistic banalities. The architectonic context almost makes us read the text as a picture epigram. Other texts of Holzer's are: "Action causes more trouble than thought", "Money creates taste", and "Decadence can be an end in itself". One may ask if this is avant-garde visual poetry or if it is conceptual

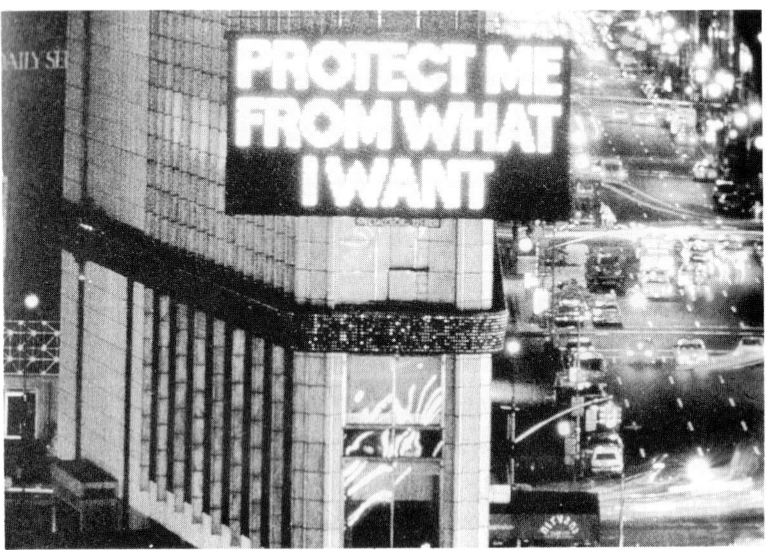

Figure 6. Jenny Holzer, "Protect me from what I want".

art. "I am an installation artist. I am not a poet", Holzer claims. "I knew the Truisms weren't poetry, so they shouldn't go into a little book. ... I realized that they had to go outside. They were useless as a list on a desk. I hoped that people would get something from reading them on the street".[5]

Somehow, Jenny Holzer's texts have an affinity with the city guerilla's spontaneous social criticism expressed in graffiti. But visually they are designed in accordance with the iconic aesthetics of outdoor advertisements, and thus they act as a kind of fifth column inside one of the commercial centres of United States. Holzer makes use of the very rhetorical means employed in advertising in order to unmask the advertisements and to make their aims and strategies visible. At the same time her truisms are meant to be a representative sampling of opinion. Their character is anonymous, just as most of the city buildings and people in the crowd are anonymous. The words interpret the cityscape but on the other hand the meanings of the words are hermeneutically dependent on the cityscape. The city and the texts refer to each other, accentuating each other in an epigrammatic way.

*

Like architecture, writing is a visual medium. It is object-like and static, permanent and surveyable and much more dependent on physical context than speech is. In the urban space a continuous dialogue is going on between architectural and verbal signs, between buildings and epigraphs, a dialogue realized by the hermeneutic participation of the reader/observer. In other words, the effect of epigraphic text is not isolated from the architectural and urban context. When we read the text on the building, the architectural signs influence our reading of the text, and thus the texts become part of multimedial manifestations. They are involved in the complex sign production that constitutes the city.

Notes

1. Marcelin Pleynet, *Art and Literature: Robert Motherwell's 'Riverrun'*, in *Interpreting Contemporary Art,* ed. Stephen Bann and William Allen, London 1991, 15.
2. E. H. Gombrich, *Topics of Our Time. Twentieth-Century Issues in Learning and in Art,* London 1991, 167.
3 Norman Bryson, *Word and Image. French Painting of the Ancien Régime,* Cambridge 1981, 167; J. Hillis Miller, *Illustration,* London 1992, 61.
4. Michel Foucault, *This is not a Pipe,* Berkeley, Los Angeles and London 1983, 33.
5. Michael Auping, *Jenny Holzer,* New York 1992, 74 and 78.

Images du corps et communication non verbale dans l'écriture de Franz Kafka

Monique Moser-Verrey

En littérature les images du corps sont innombrables et multiformes. Il est donc fort difficile de les apprécier de façon systématique et de comprendre comment elles permettent au texte de déployer des enjeux culturels, sociaux mais aussi individuels et intimes. Dans la réalité même le corps parle de multiples façons. Il se donne à voir selon des codes de représentation qui intéressent bien sûr l'anthropologie, la sociologie, la psychologie et plus récemment la linguistique, alors qu'elle tente de leur faire une place dans l'étude de ce que l'on peut appeler avec Catherine Kerbrat-Orecchioni *Les Interactions verbales.*[1] La communication en face à face ne se réduit certes pas à un échange de mots et de phrases, mais orchestre de nombreux messages simultanés perceptibles par tous les sens.

Lorsque le texte littéraire rend compte d'interactions, il évoque généralement de façon sélective les données somatiques signifiantes. Aussi les spécialistes de la communication non verbale illustrent-ils parfois les catégories qu'ils établissent en citant des auteurs célèbres dont les observations font alors autorité. C'est ainsi que Erving Goffman[2] et Edward Hall[3] se réfèrent par exemple à Franz Kafka, car certains passages de son œuvre illustrent bien la question des distances interpersonnelles ou encore celle de l'interdépendance de l'environnement et de la façade sociale de l'individu. En tant que spécialistes du texte littéraire il nous faut bien sûr retourner la question. Si, en effet, certains passages de l'œuvre kafkaïenne peuvent illustrer les thèses des spécialistes de la nouvelle communication, il est clair que ces mêmes thèses peuvent alimenter utilement une réflexion sur les fonctions des images du corps dans le texte littéraire et leur signification particulière dans l'œuvre de Franz Kafka.

La critique littéraire a de tout temps été sensible à la présence du corps dans les œuvres de langage, mais, depuis peu seulement, un intérêt pour les rapports interculturels et l'anthropologie en général lui ont inspiré des approches tenant compte de la valeur communicative des signes non verbaux, tant corporo-visuels que voco-acoustiques. Ainsi, le sémioticien Fernando Poyatos explore, par exemple, l'inscription de signes paralinguistiques et kinésiques dans plus d'une trentaine de textes épiques et romanesques tant européens qu'américains, dans le but de proposer un modèle de compréhension du processus de communication entre l'auteur et le lecteur et de souligner l'effet de réalisme généré par ce type d'inscription.[4] Du côté de la narratologie l'observation de la parole romanesque mène, par ailleurs, Gillian Lane-Mercier à signaler certains mécanismes compensatoires permettant de récupérer dans l'écriture les éléments non verbaux de la communication qui sont soit mimés au niveau du préconstruit générique discursif qu'elle étudie, soit verbalisés dans les composantes narratives et descriptives du texte. Là aussi, la prise en compte par l'écriture de signes non verbaux propres aux échanges oraux est comprise dans le cadre des effets de réel microdiscursifs produits par le texte.[5]

La question du réalisme, très généralement associée aux images du corps et de la communication non verbale dans le texte littéraire, peut être dépassée et une interprétation de ces données peut être proposée, lorsqu'on les étudie dans l'ensemble d'une œuvre, comme le fait, par exemple, Gaétan Brulotte dans son "Gestuaire de Nathalie Sarraute". Empruntant à l'anthropologie une grille d'analyse, il peut classer les gestes présents dans l'œuvre de Sarraute selon les registres des techniques du corps, de la gestuelle d'interaction, particulièrement importante, de l'expression des émotions, de la socialité infracorporelle, soit le domaine de la sensorialité et enfin de la socialité corporelle d'inconduite, soit l'anormalité, la folie, la maladie. Cette approche globale de l'œuvre permet d'évaluer les angles aveugles de l'auteur, ses intérêts et ses obsessions, de sorte qu'on en arrive en fin de parcours à l'énonciation d'une logique de la création littéraire chez Sarraute dont le cogito serait: "Je communique donc je suis", et l'écriture le moyen de régler un conflit proxémique personnel entre le désir de se rapprocher des autres et le besoin de les tenir à distance.[6]

Que l'on étudie les images du corps et la communication non verbale dans le texte romanesque comme indices culturels, comme effets de réel ou comme symptômes d'un malaise particulier à l'auteur, il semble aller de soi que ces détails s'offrent à la lecture comme des signes intelligibles. Tel n'est pas nécessairement le cas dans la prose de Franz Kafka.

Kafka ou l'image du corps énigmatique

L'image du corps est au contraire souvent énigmatique chez Kafka. C'est là sans doute une des particularités de son écriture qui a été reconnue comme unique dans le contexte de l'histoire littéraire du visage humain, par exemple. Pour comprendre ce fait, Peter von Matt étudie les portraits inclus dans les journaux de Kafka et suggère que la fonction de l'aspect énigmatique de ces descriptions physiques est de permettre à l'auteur de se détacher de l'autre dont paradoxalement il veut s'approcher par l'écriture.[7] Comme chez Nathalie Sarraute, on retrouve là, de toute évidence, la marque d'une ambivalence en ce qui concerne la rencontre de l'autre, à la fois désirée et crainte. Von Matt observe finement qu'une double tentative de décrire Felice Bauer est deux fois suspendue à la faveur, sans doute, de la relation avec cette femme qui sera plus tard la fiancée de Kafka. Ce qui étonne en général dans les portaits du journal, c'est qu'ils renversent les règles du genre, trompent les attentes du lecteur sans offrir pour autant une nouvelle clé de lecture. Souvent un détail physionomique de la personne décrite prend une importance démesurée sans rien révéler sur l'individu concerné qui disparaît alors derrière l'image de sa bouche, de son front et ainsi de suite. Ce procédé de démembrement peut être mis en rapport avec ceux de l'avant-garde cubiste de l'époque mais il fait aussi apparaître avec netteté une propriété essentielle de l'image textuelle. Comme le dit Kafka lui-même, le fait de décomposer une vision fugitive en détails la rend "improbable". Dès lors elle n'appartient plus au monde de la réalité, mais bien à celui de l'art.[8]

On voit que même si l'image textuelle est censée figurer quelqu'un que Kafka a rencontré, elle ne ressemble pas à cette personne mais opère dans l'ordre des "systèmes symboliques" que sont les *Langages de l'art* pour y référer.[9] La conscience aiguë de cet écart semble détacher Kafka de tout souci de réalisme ou de vraisemblance dans l'utilisation poétique qu'il fait des images du corps dans ses récits et ses romans. Chaque détail demeure cependant très précisément observé et immédiatement reconnaissable, mais il ne s'inscrit pas toujours dans des schémas de compréhension attendus. Il peut être sidérant ou paraître absurde, voire comique. Les spécialistes de Kafka, qui ont étudié la présence insistante d'images gestuelles dans son œuvre, ont montré qu'elles ne se laissent pas ramener à un système signifiant immédiatement décodable. Walter Benjamin et Theodor Adorno avaient les premiers été sensibles à cette particularité qu'il est convenu de comprendre aujourd'hui comme un effet d'indécidabilité.[10] Joan Ramon Resina va même jusqu'à soutenir que pour Kafka le geste n'est pas tant un moyen de communiquer qu'un moyen de faire silence[11]. À son idée, le geste kafkaïen défie toute rationalisation et s'impose tout bonnement en tant qu'image concrète de la vie.[12]

Il est sans doute faux de ramener les images énigmatiques du corps proposées par Kafka à une sorte de cratylisme. Si elles sont porteuses d'un sens éclairant la vie, celui-ci n'est pas immédiatement saisissable mais artistement construit. En étudiant de près les contextes dans lesquels s'inscrivent ces images énigmatiques, on s'aperçoit qu'elles participent à des chorégraphies concertées qui ne proposent pas des images concrètes de la vie, mais en élucident les mystères par le truchement de systèmes symboliques propres à l'art tels ceux du mime et de la danse, par exemple. Comme le montre Nelson Goodman, les langages de l'art se réfèrent à la réalité d'une façon dense. Ainsi, dans l'œuvre visuelle, la signification se décode par la mise en rapport de tous les points du système les uns avec les autres, plutôt que selon une grille d'unités de sens distinctes et librement combinables.[13] De telles œuvres visuelles, dont les divers points construisent ensemble un sens, sous-tendent selon mon hypothèse les romans et récits de Kafka.

Les contextes de l'énigme ou l'éloquence de l'art

Pour démontrer que l'image kafkaïenne du corps s'inscrit dans des réseaux d'éléments chorégraphiques signifiants dans le contexte de la communication non verbale, je reprendrai ici l'exemple textuel principal à partir duquel Ramon Resina développe sa réflexion sur l'usage énigmatique du geste chez Kafka. Il s'agit des derniers moments de Joseph K. avant son exécution à la fin du *Procès.*

> Ses regards tombèrent sur le dernier étage de la maison attenante à la carrière. Les battants d'une fenêtre s'y ouvrirent à la volée comme jaillit une lumière, un être humain que la distance et la hauteur rendaient vague et mince se pencha d'un coup en avant et étendit les bras. Qui était-ce? Un ami? Un homme bon? Quelqu'un qui prenait part? Quelqu'un qui voulait porter secours? Était-il seul? Étaient-ce tous? Y avait-il encore un secours? Existait-il des objections oubliées? Il y en avait sûrement. La logique est certes inébranlable mais elle ne résiste pas à un homme qui veut vivre. Où était le juge qu'il n'avait jamais vu? Où était le haut tribunal jusqu'où il n'était jamais arrivé? Il leva les mains et écarta les doigts.[14]

Un des principes fondamentaux qui a guidé les recherches américaines sur la kinésique est de tenir compte avant tout du contexte des gestes. Pour Birdwhistell la signification d'un geste isolé n'existe pas.[15] Il faut donc se demander quel est le contexte des gestes décrits dans le texte cité. Si l'on se place à l'intérieur de la diégèse, l'approche de la mort fixe un cadre existentiel clair. Les questions que se pose Joseph K. de même que l'aphorisme selon lequel la logique "ne résiste pas à un homme qui veut vivre" confirment la pertinence de ce cadre plus métaphysique que concret. La valeur prégnante de l'image des mains levées aux doigts écartés a donc suscité quelques discussions sur le sens du dernier geste de Joseph K. Des critiques distingués ont voulu le comprendre comme un geste de bénédiction, une marque de refus, de désespoir ou encore le dernier soubresaut d'un chien écrasé.[16] L'hétérogénéité étonnante de ces explications montre bien que le geste en lui-même ne signifie rien mais que sa forme et le moment fatal de sa réalisation en font un signe éloquent qui trouve son sens dans le contexte des visions du monde les plus variées. C'est bien sûr grâce à un effet d'indécidabilité comme celui-là que les romans et récits de Kafka intéressent tant de lecteurs.

Pour étudier les stratégies d'écriture qui produisent l'énigme, il faut maintenant se détacher du contexte diégétique et analyser la façon dont le geste s'inscrit dans le discours du récit. En fait, la mort de Joseph K. donne lieu à deux récits fort différents, l'un publié du vivant de Kafka dans le recueil *Un médecin de campagne* sous le titre "Un rêve", l'autre paru de façon posthume comme dixième chapitre du roman *le Procès.* Il est bien évident qu'un récit de rêve et la conclusion d'un roman, qui tient de la parabole, constituent des contextes génériques différents qui modifient la lecture des gestes, bien que les mondes oniriques et fictifs se rejoignent souvent. En l'occurrence un détail important pour mon enquête sur l'image du corps et de la communication non verbale dans le texte est commun aux deux récits : l'essentiel de l'interaction entre les personnages est muette. Ils se comprennent sans se parler. Dans un cas comme dans l'autre on est bien éloigné de l'interaction verbale de nos échanges quotidiens. Seule l'éloquence du corps, formant une sorte de ballet, est mise en récit.

Le rêve de Joseph K.

Dans son rêve Joseph K. est très attiré par une tombe fraîchement creusée dans un cimetière plein de réjouissances. Il glisse sur une allée tortueuse et saute dans l'herbe tout à côté du monticule qu'il reluquait, tombe à genoux et voit là deux hommes planter solidement une grande pierre tombale. Apparaît alors un troisième homme en qui il reconnaît un artiste. Celui-ci vient pour écrire sur la pierre tombale "Ci-gît Joseph K." non sans avoir de sérieux scrupules qui désolent Joseph K., car son bonheur sera de voir enfin briller son nom sur cette pierre. L'interaction qui se déroule entre l'artiste et Joseph K. est faite de gestes (G), de données proxémiques (X), de postures (P), de jeux de regards (R) et de pleurs, seul signe à la fois corporo-visuel et voco-acoustique, affectant et la mimique (M) et la voix (V). Mise en tableau, cette interaction se déroule de la façon suivante :

	L'artiste	Joseph K.
G	il traçait des figures en l'air	
X	en s'approchant pour écrire sur la pierre tombale de l'autre côté du tertre	
P	Il se tenait donc sur la pointe des pieds et s'appuyait de la main gauche sur la surface de la pierre	

Tableau 1. *L'arrivée de l'artiste.*

L'artiste		Joseph K.	
X	il se retourna vers K.	R	n'avait d'yeux que pour la pierre
G	il abaissa son crayon		
X	se retourna de nouveau vers K.	R	K. regarda alors l'artiste
R	ils échangèrent des regards de désarroi	R	ils échangèrent…
	pour faire taire la petite cloche de la chapelle		
G	fit d'une main de grands gestes en l'air		
		M et V	se mit à pleurer
		G	en se cachant le visage derrière ses main

Tableau 2. *Les hésitations de l'artiste.*

L'artiste		Joseph K.	
G	tapa furieusement du pied dans la terre du tertre		
G	de tous ses doigts il creusa dans le sol		
		P	retourné sur le dos
		X	K. s'enfonça [dans la tombe]
		G	se tordant encore le cou pour redresser la tête [pour voir les lettres d'or] [17]

Tableau 3. *L'élimination de Joseph K.*

Comme le soulignait Freud, les pensées du rêve sont figurées le plus souvent dans le contenu du rêve par des situations visualisables.[18] Ainsi les postures et les gestes de l'artiste et de Joseph K. montrent comment le premier finit par s'affirmer en éliminant le second qui est absolument consentant et se réjouit de disparaître au profit de l'œuvre qui le nomme. Sans commenter longuement chacune des images du corps apparaissant dans la narration de cette interaction rêvée, on peut distinguer trois phases dans la chorégraphie qu'elle propose, à savoir l'inconfort relativement heureux du début de l'écriture, visualisé par la posture de l'artiste, les hésitations et la crise, essentiellement visualisées par des jeux de regards, et enfin le coup de pied qui règle le sort de Joseph K., définitivement sacrifié à l'œuvre de l'artiste qui porte son nom.

La mort de Joseph K.

Le dernier chapitre du procès est beaucoup plus sinistre. Il ne s'agit pas du récit d'une petite mort, mais bien de celui de la vraie mort de Joseph K. Non pas une mort glorieuse, mais une mort honteuse. Elle est amenée selon le topos littéraire du dernier voyage. On sait que la Mort, quel que soit son déguisement, est une visite qui arrive à l'improviste, bien qu'elle soit attendue, et qui fait route avec le héros pour recueillir enfin ses dernières paroles. Deux messieurs vêtus de noir se présentent donc chez Joseph K. la veille de ses trente et un ans. Joseph K. s'avoue que ce ne sont pas eux qu'il attendait alors même que sa posture et ses gestes sont ceux de "quelqu'un qui attend des invités" (251). Si l'on s'arrête à la posture et au geste en question, cette explication étonne :

Joseph K.

P   était assis sur une chaise près de la porte
G   et mettait lentement des gants neufs très tendus sur les doigts (251).

La focalisation sur les mains et les doigts de Joseph K. dès le premier paragraphe du chapitre n'est sans doute pas sans rapport avec son dernier geste. Une mise en scène visuelle s'annonce, digne du théâtre expressionniste, si l'on s'imagine que torse nu, couché dans une carrière, Joseph K. lèvera les mains et écartera des doigts gantés avant d'être poignardé.

L'interaction de K. avec les deux messieurs est presque entièrement muette. Lorsque K. leur parle (D) ils répondent par gestes et par mimiques (M). Mise en tableau, cette interaction se présente ainsi :

Joseph K.		Messieurs	
D	"Vous m'êtes destinés?"	G	hochèrent la tête
		G	le haut-de-forme à la main
		G	l'un montra l'autre
D	"Vous jouez dans quel théâtre?"	D	"Un théâtre?"
		M	les coins de la bouche tremblants
		M	fit comme s'il était un muet incapable d'arriver à parler (251-252).

Tableau 4. *Joseph K. et ses bourreaux.*

Puis se constitue l'unité que vont former Joseph K. et ses bourreaux, qui incarnent la mort, "une unité comme ne peut en former que ce qui n'a pas de vie" (252) dit le texte. Cette pensée est visualisée ici par la description d'une posture insolite et d'un geste magique, tout comme dans le récit de rêve de tout à l'heure :

Les bourreaux

P Ils tenaient leurs épaules juste derrière celles de K., ne
pliaient pas les bras mais les utilisaient pour enlacer ceux de
K. sur toute leur longueur,
G par-dessous, ils prirent les mains de K. d'un geste étudié,
bien rodé et irrésistible (252).

Maintenant K. a perdu l'usage de ses mains et l'être monstrueux, dont il est le centre, chemine au hasard à travers les rues sombres de la ville. Ses bourreaux ne le lâchent pas mais c'est lui qui les mène. Ce sont de "vieux acteurs de niveau subalterne" (251), peut-être des ténors (252), trop polis et trop propres, en tout cas "des messieurs à demi muets et dépourvus d'intelligence" (253) dont les manières empesées et le visage gras dégoûtent K., mais il se prête à leur théâtre et le récit de son dernier voyage est en fait la représentation verbale d'une représentation visuelle, spectacle ou rituel inexorable. Pris dans cette machine infernale comme la mouche dans la glu du papier tue-mouches (253), K. conserve sa lucidité. Toute la différence entre le récit de rêve et le texte du roman est là. Alors que le Joseph K. du rêve est entièrement conduit par ses élans affectifs, le Joseph K. du roman s'accroche à sa conscience et rationalise ce qui lui arrive.

Dans le dernier chapitre du *Procès*, Kafka conjugue avec art la narration du rituel avec le monologue intérieur du héros et la description des visions qui arrêtent son regard. Les images du corps investissent bien sûr tous ces préconstruits génériques du texte, de sorte qu'on trouve dans les pauses descriptives et les monologues intérieurs des images de mains et des gestes qui éclairent à leur manière l'énigme de la fin. Au cœur du chapitre K. évalue en pensée la conduite à suivre et s'avoue ses erreurs passées :

"La seule chose que je puisse faire", se dit-il, et la régularité de ses pas et des pas des deux autres confirma ses pensées, "la seule chose que je puisse faire est de garder jusqu'à la fin une intelligence qui évalue les choses calmement… Je voulais toujours avoir une vingtaine de mains à la fois pour empoigner le monde, et dans un but de plus discutable. C'était une erreur" (253).

Ici les rythmes mesurés de la phrase, de la marche et de la pensée illustrent la sagesse de K. et mettent en évidence sa folie passée, visualisée par la métaphore des vingt mains empoignant le monde. Cette image de l'excès fait ressortir l'économie extrême du jeu des mains de Joseph K., soigneusement gantées, puis immobilisées et enfin tendues et ouvertes sans rien pouvoir saisir.

La chorégraphie du jeu des mains inscrite dans la diégèse est doublée par les descriptions de ce que Joseph K. aperçoit aux fenêtres qui attirent son regard tant au début qu'à la fin du chapitre. Avant de quitter son appartement il jette un dernier regard par la fenêtre. Tout est sombre mais à une fenêtre de petits enfants jouent dans un parc :

P	incapables, encore, de bouger de leur place,
G	ils essayaient de s'attraper de leurs petites mains (251).

Entraîné par la Mort, il contemple là un geste vital dont il ne sera plus capable lui-même. Quand il voit sur sa route son amie, Mademoiselle Bürstner, il la suit sans vouloir la rattraper (253), et quand un policier qui pourrait le libérer s'approche de lui, il fuit à toutes jambes (254). Cependant, au dernier moment, incapable de bouger de sa place, l'homme à la fenêtre, qui se penche en avant et tend les bras lui fait lever les siens. Force est de reconnaître dans cette scène énigmatique les mêmes données proxémiques que dans la scène des petits enfants. Elles montrent une interaction difficile, car les participants ne peuvent pas bouger de leur place. Mais la jeunesse des uns et la volonté de vivre de l'autre confirment que le geste qui défie la Mort, c'est celui qui porte l'être humain vers son semblable.

Ces quelques remarques permettent d'apprécier le fait que, tout en paraissant énigmatique, le geste kafkaïen s'inscrit en fait dans des réseaux d'images du corps éloquentes sur le plan de la communication non verbale. Ces réseaux sont cohérents à tous les niveaux du texte, monologue intérieur, description et narration. Dans ses récits Kafka construit donc véritablement des œuvres d'art visuel inspirées de visions oniriques qu'il faut lire tantôt comme un spectacle de mime ou de ballet, tantôt comme un tableau ou encore comme un rituel social ou même sacré. L'ekphrasis de ces œuvres d'art visuel est entrecoupée de réflexions aiguës, voire d'aphorismes, de sorte que le récit surprend toutes les facultés du lecteur dont la sensibilité peut être touchée par la force des messages non verbaux et l'intelligence éveillée par la logique de leur enchaînement et la rigueur de l'argumentation verbale les accompagnant. C'est finalement en combinant les acquis de la recherche en communication non verbale avec la réflexion sur les langages de l'art et sur la poétique des genres que la critique peut espérer décrire avec justesse ce qui résiste à l'explication dans l'écriture de Kafka, mais fascine toujours à nouveau.

Notes

1 Catherine Kerbrat-Orecchioni, *Les Interactions verbales* (Paris: Armand Colin, 1990).

2 Erving Goffman, *La Mise en scène de la vie quotidienne: 1. La Présentation de soi* (Paris: Minuit, 1973) 95-96.

3 Edward T. Hall, *La Dimension cachée* (Paris: Seuil, 1971) 126.

4 Fernando Poyatos, *New Perspectives in Nonverbal Communication. Studies in Cultural Anthropology, Social Psychology, Linguistics, Literature and Semiotics* (Toronto: Pergamon Press, 1983) 277-314.

5 Gillian Lane-Mercier, *La Parole romanesque* (Paris: Klincksieck, 1989) 139-203.

6 Gaétan Brulotte, "Le Gestuaire de Nathalie Sarraute". *Revue des sciences humaines* 93/ 217 (1990) 75-95.

7 Peter von Matt, "Kafka der Porträtist"*....fertig ist das Angesicht. Zur Literaturgeschichte des menschlichen Gesichts* (Frankfurt am Main: Suhrkamp Taschenbuch Verlag 1989) 13-60.

8 Ibid., 46-47.

9 Nelson Goodman, *Langages de l'art.* Présenté et traduit de l'anglais par Jacques Morizot (Nîmes: Éditions Jacqueline Chambon, 1990) 28.

10 Régine Robin, *Kafka* (Paris: Belfond, 1989) 104 sq.

11 Joan Ramon Resina, "Gesture: Kafka's Means to Silence". *The International Fiction Review* 15/1 (1988) 14-20.

12 Ibid., 20.

13 Nelson Goodman, op. cit., 192 sq.

14 Franz Kafka, *Le Procès.* Traduction nouvelle et présentation de Georges-Arthur Goldschmidt (Paris: Presses Pocket, 1983) 256. Les références incluses dans le corps du texte renvoient à cette édition.

15 Bateson et al., *La Nouvelle communication.* Textes recueillis et présentés par Yves Winkin (Paris: Seuil, 1981) 74.

16 Joan Ramon Resina., op. cit., 16.

17 Toutes les citations sont tirées de Franz Kafka, *Dans la colonie pénitentiaire et autres nouvelles.* Préface et traduction de Bernard Lortholary (Paris: Flammarion, 1991) 180-183.

18 Sigmund Freud, *Sur le rêve* Traduit de l'allemand par Cornélius Heim (Paris: Gallimard, 1988) 91-92.

Video – or the Intermedial State of the Art

Jürgen E. Müller

1. Video and Intermediality[1]

1.1. Intermediality – or Some Theoretical Remarks

It is a commonplace of media-studies that the notions of *medium, media, multi- and intermediality* are used in different scientific contexts and that – according to these theoretical contexts – the meaning of the notion changes. Let me remind you of the concepts *medium/media* in mass-communication research, where media are reduced to their technical aspects and the notion of *media* in aesthetics, where media are defined in terms of fictional communication. Fortunately, today a growing number of scholars are aware of the fact that it is not sufficient to conceive *media* purely as a means of transmission, which transmit some kind of information from a "producer" to a "receiver" . This definition produces – as do the above mentioned positions – certain shortcomings, which we will have to question and to overcome.

Under these premises it seems less relevant to study technical aspects of information transmission. We should direct our attention towards the impact of this information transmission on the *structure* of that which is transferred, and towards the impact of this process on the *constitution of meaning* for the producer and the recipient. That is why I suggest a more comprehensive and pluri-dimensional concept of media. According to Hickethier, Bohn and others, I conceive as a *medium* "that which mediates on the basis of (meaningful) signs (or sign configurations), with the help of suitable transmitters for and between humans. And this takes place over spatial and historical distances" (10).

Following this proposal, I would like to emphasize the fact that media are embedded in *intentional patterns and contexts of action*; they are constructed on a dialogical and semiotic basis and they comprise several dimensions which interact in the process of semiosis, but which can be isolated for purposes of analysis.

If media (and also "media-texts") are to be located in changing relationships, if their function also depends on historical changes of these relationships, then we have to conclude that the idea of isolated media-monades or isolated sorts of media has to be abandoned. – And of course, this is also true for the media "word", "text" and "image". – On the other hand the concept of intermediality does not mean that media are to be found in a relationship of mutual plagiarism, but that they *integrate questions, concepts and principles,* which have been developed in their history and in the history of other media into their own context (Aumont). A media-product becomes an *inter*-media-product if a *multi*media coexistence of different media-quotations and elements is transformed into a *conceptual inter*media coexistence. The aesthetic refractions and faults (*Verwerfungen*) of intermedia processes open new dimensions of experience to the recipient (Müller, "Intermedialität" 15).

Media studies which direct their attention to the medial dynamics and fusions within certain media-texts and between different media and to their history must necessarily re-perspectivize broad fields of traditional media theory and media history (Müller, *Intermedialität: Formen*). But to be honest, my proposal of a theory and history of intermediality does not have the status of a "closed scientific paradigm" (which today will be very questionable, anyway) but of a theoretically and historically based perspective, which can be related to the works of Bakhtin (*Ästhetik des Wortes*), Kristeva (*La Révolution*), Higgins (*Poetics*), Prümm ("Multimedialität"), Albersmeier (*Theater*) and others. Nevertheless, it offers the opportunity to transgress and expand the traditional concepts of "multimedia" and their technical restrictions, because it is *not* primarily directed towards the "synchronized use of text, sound, picture, animation and video on the screen, with multimedia technology as the coordinating instance" (Negroponte), but on the *dynamics* and fusions of media patterns in certain productions and in the history of media.

In the following I would like to take a first glance at the central issue of this short article: the question of intermediality and video art.

1.2. Video and Intermediality

Video art as the hybrid post-modern media of transgression and transition *par excellence* has been for longer than twenty years a *scandalon* for every reductionist media theory and its corresponding methodology. Due to the dynamic and voracious qualities of this new media, our traditional aesthetics of the static are condemned to failure (Weibel). The video machinery makes use of words and images, of texts and pictures, of sounds and voices, of music, film, painting, photography, television, news(papers), sculpture, architecture, literature ... and it is able to constitute and generate digital realities. *Cyberspace* and *virtual reality* have opened a completely new chapter in the history of media and art which must bring about a revision of common and basic theories of so-called social reality and its media-representations (Rötzer).

But let me come back to one of the "characteristics" of video art. Even if it is correct to describe video as a *voracious* media, this voracity does not imply a simple "usage" or "addition" of all the media fragments and elements, which are put together, but their *transformation and integration into new intermedia processes*. That is why video and video art are, for example – even if they have to make use of the television machinery and some devices of the television-apparatus – always more than just a re-allocation or a compilation of some elements of television. Video creates an intermedia-labyrinth with new spatio-temporal "structures." In this sense video art is a very good test of, and a challenge to, any proposal of a concept of intermediality. (And, naturally, also of the proposal I have presented above.)

I suggest to proceed in the form of a short case study of the French-Canadian Video *GOD'S GREATEST GIFT*...[2] However, while studying our video-art-production, we must not forget the fact that intermedial structures are to be found in almost every audiovisual artefact and that *video* and *video-art* constitute just a very exciting "special case", which – with its dynamics and immateriality – has to be located in the historical context of our so-called post-modern age.[3]

2. God's Greatest Gift and Some Patterns of Intermediality

2.1. Some Initial, Pre-Scientific Impressions

A video-production of 58 shots (can we still talk about "shots" in this case?) of two minutes and 47 seconds. There are words and – naturally – images, sounds, music, signs, letters, written texts, stills and moving images. The video starts with beats of the drum coming from the dark, followed by a voice, the volume of which increases then decreases. The rhythm accelerates to the staccato of a machine gun, then slows to a verbal and vocal slow motion, only later getting the sound-quality of music. Is all this is effected by the synthesizing power of computerized post-production-machines?

In our ears (and in our mind) the paralinguistic and prosodic qualities of this voice have broken away and break away from the historical figure of its speaker, but they also return to that figure called Ronald Reagan. The second segment/"shot" of the video allows us to relate this voice to its speaker, to bring – at least for some seconds – word and image together. But this voice is not only doubled by its correlating image, it is also doubled by a written text, by an electronic subtitle which delivers some further superimpositions and surcharges of denotations and connotations. *GOD'S GREATEST GIFT ... IS HUMAN LIFE.* The pose of the speaker, voice and written text constitute a frame (Goffman 10) of the video. Voice, image and text explode with the final big bang of the nuclear bomb.

Even if it is difficult and strange to see, we can see a scenario of everyday-violence. Images in a state of flux turn out to be a collage of a ballet of death and a post-modern choreography of a *danse macabre.* Protagonists of that machinery are at the same time actors and victims. There are burned, mutilated, evaporized bodies and corpses which move according to the melody and rhythm of electronic music and to Reagan's changing voice repeatedly uttering only one sentence. There is a contrast between words and the visual kaleidoscope of horror and the quality of the relation between word, image, written text is permanently changing.

So far I have discussed some initial impressions of the video and what it "might do to me" (Grivel). In the following, I address some theses about the intermedial state of the art of *GOD'S GREATEST GIFT* and of video art.

2.2. Video, Audiovisions and Intermediality[4]

– *Our "chapter" from the Science-Fiction-Video-Opera "Out" represents media-patterns of different modern and traditional media: silent film and sound film, radio, painting, literature and print-media, television, news, – to mention just the most prominent.*[5] *It constitutes a collage of "visual raw material" (of "matière première visuelle",* (Virilio 119) *of so called T.V. documents and other audiovisual "sources', which are transformed and integrated into a new media-context. This transformation presupposes technical and operational possibilities for the television apparatus, which are left behind and which are opposed to the new images and sounds generated by the video-apparatus. The common and well known images of T.V. and other media are digitally and electronically remodelled; they have lost their stability and frames* (Goffman).

We can see and hear that the relationship between these two *frères ennemies,*[6] who – at first glance – are so close to each other, is in fact a very distant one. Even if the screen and the loudspeakers are identical, they make us see and hear two different media and genres, and it becomes evident that our example cannot be described by generic and aesthetic typologies of the medium "television".

– *The use of mass-media products, mass-media genres, of elements and structures of cinema, portrait-painting, spoken and written words, ... opens a staggering game with expectations, patterns of knowledge, or – to bring into play a more fashionable cognitive concept – "schemata"* (Bordwell) *of the spectator. From one unit (or "shot") to another and within the frame of these units, the consciousness of the spectator oscillates between different generic patterns and options. The viewer can never decide whether what is to be seen might be a "Video-Opera", a clip, a science-fiction film, a documentary, or news, ... because the status of the represented words and images is much too fluid to stick to one of those potential options of media- and genre frames.*

These aesthetic procedures direct our consciousness towards modes of reception and habits of perception of audiovisual products, which have been established centuries ago in western societies.[7] In this video, well known signs of power and violence (for example Ronald Reagan in the pose of a statesman and as a represented victim of an assault) are detached from their original referential context; they transgress their common denotations and connotations and allude to general mechanisms and procedures of representation.

– This effect is also reached through and supported by the electronic and digital transformation of sounds and colours, which are put into new spatial and rhythmic configurations.

GOD'S GREATEST GIFT presents an intermedial play with basic spatio-temporal factors of audiovisions and so adds another version to the many already existing representations of power, horror and violence and forces us – after a phase of reflection – into a new perception of those common media-texts, which we normally fail to realize.[8] (Actual war-images from Yugoslavia might be a good example of the kind of "every-day-reception" of such images.)

2.3. Word, Sound, Image and Intermediality

– GOD'S GREATEST GIFT shows us that, in principle, the name "Video" is wrong for this new medium and for its products. This video is not only a visual spectacle, it is also an audio spectacle *– and this impression can be tied back to its multi- and intermedial generic "characteristics", which are described by the producers as a Science-Fiction-Video-*Opera. *Sound is as relevant and functional as the images and visual material, and both take part in dynamic interactions. The spoken words vary according to the changing rhythms of electronic music and other types of sound, they move from the sound-quality of the staccato of a machine gun to an agonizing vocal (slow) motion, returning to the voice qualities of their speaker.*

This play with the spoken word and with its electronic and digital transformations and *Verfremdungen* can be seen as an indication of the central and independent role of the universe of sound in video art, which finds itself in an unstable and dynamic relation with the images. The permanent changes of the quality of the voice blur the common borderlines between spoken language, sound and music. Where and when do the words stop and where and when do sound and music start?

– Our video also breaks with some of the basic patterns and traditions of sound film and audiovisions. The ongoing instability of the spoken words makes them lose their traditional denotations and connotations and also their primarily intended function. Through this procedure our attention is directed towards some of the ideological components of their meaning.

But with regard to the relationship between word and image there is still another aspect I would like to mention. Having looked at the history of sound film, it becomes evident that one of the most crucial problems of its development was the question of how to achieve synchronicity between the spoken words and images.[9] *We all know the kind of standardized solutions, which have been offered by technicians and are permanently used in film- and T.V. productions. Today, there are very stable rules for the screening of spoken words (over-the-shoulder shots, reverse shots etc.) and all these rules are based on the (nowadays) almost unnoticed principle of synchronicity between spoken word and image of the speaker, which is taken for granted.*

The soundtrack of our video destroys these presuppositions and that stability, which were so difficult to achieve. The video and audio-machinery have transformed and manipulated the sounds (and also images) in such a way that their traditional relationship has been dismissed. The basic synchronicity between spoken words and represented speakers can no longer be taken for granted.

– We can find similar procedures with regard to the use of other traditional filmic procedures of showing spoken words which have lost their usual function. For example that kind of "voice over" (if we wish to apply a category of film studies to video), or electronic voice from the dark.

Could some possible effects of the temporary juxtaposition of a computerized *GOD'S GREATEST GIFT* with these alienated images of horror and violence (which have not yet lost their actuality in our days, even if – according to the temporal construction of the video – they are intended to be some sort of historical documentation of the year 1984) be related to common motives of audiovisual representation? But, this voice over cannot be an ordinary voice over of an omniscient narrator commenting upon certain aspects of a narration, which – in our case – does not exist. If we conceive – with Iser – irony as a rhetorical figure, where the opposite of what is being said is the intended and "real" meaning, then Reagan's sentence can not be regarded as irony.[10] The reason for this is, as I tried to make clear, that the spoken words have lost their common referential function and are juxtaposed with images of violence, which also have undergone a mutation and *Verfremdung*, but which, nevertheless, allude to that opposite. Can we read that constellation as a post-modern audiovisual irony?

– But there is another aspect of our audio-video example, which I have yet to deal with: The written text, that digital display of letters at the bottom of the Reagan-images, which shows us the written version of GOD'S GREATEST GIFT. This text is to be found at the beginning and at the end of our production, it interacts with the spoken words and the represented images and takes part in the central activities of our mind of the construction and de-construction of facets of meaning.

In some of these "shots" the *moving* image has undergone a mutation into a *still*, whereas the spoken words, sounds and the written text keep moving.

– The text constitutes a redundant subtitle of a silent *film in a* sound *production. It quotes procedures of the classical media and of the printed text, as well as those of the classical modern media of the silent film in order to mix these with the structures of computer displays, of television, portrait-painting and video and to negate them immediately.*

This is just another example of the intermedia-voracity of our example.

– Within the media "video" the written text forms a redundant means of transmission of a spoken sentence and even if – at the first glance – it seems to deliver a contribution to the construction of the meaning of that which is being said, it only deconstructs words, which are themselves already in a state of being electronically and digitally deconstructed.

The text is a sort of fake-documentation of the fugitive instant of speaking, of an instant which has undergone a change of its basic spatio-temporal coordinates and which has been exposed to the flux of the video-machinery.

It refers to speech in a typical situation of communication and to a typical political pose and suggests the underlying patterns of these situations. It labels the speaker and the quasi-informative character of that which is said, emphasizing the general possibilities of the interventions of the video machinery with regard to the flood of words/sounds and images with which we are confronted in everyday life.

– This "printed" text constitutes an electronic subtitle of the picture, an inscription of a mourning-crape, or a signature at the bottom of the image for our "album" of history. It crystallizes certain qualities of the words and images of our video and by looking at and looking through these crystals, we constitute new, fugitive and kaleidoscopic configurations of meaning of the production.

It is astonishing to see, how important a role the classical medium of "print-text" still plays in this post-modern production.[11]

3. Conclusion

Naturally, within the framework of this short article, and on the basis of our case study, I was able to discuss only a few aspects of the intermedia-dynamics of video art. There are still many processes we could and should analyse, for example the interaction between film, television and video (Zielinski), which also plays an important role in *GOD'S GREATEST GIFT*, or the intricate time configurations of this production. (It is conceived as a science-fiction-video-opera which plays in the year 2084.)

I hope that, in spite of all the inevitable shortcomings of my paper, I was able to illustrate at least some of the involved processes, processes, which I believe, cannot and should not be grasped by a comprehensive theory, but only through thorough analyses of specific cases in different media.[12] I cannot offer a super-theory of intermediality (who can?), but only a theoretical foundation for so called "post-(?) structural" and historical research. A perspective, which hopefully will have made clear that the fusion of media never means a simple *addition* of media, but a dynamic and intricate *interaction* of different media procedures, for example of words, printed texts and images.

Notes

1 I would like to thank Daniel Sayer very much for his help in the linguistic correction of this article.

2 *GOD'S GREATEST GIFT* is an extract from the production *OUT* by Alain Thibault, Miguel Raymond, Jacques Collin and Sylvie Panet-Raymond, Montréal 1985, *(P.R.I.M. – Productions Réalisations Indépendantes de Montréal).*

3 With regard to this question cf., for example, Bellour *(L'Entre-Images)* as well as Bellour and Duguet *(Vidéo, Communications).*

4 I use "audiovisions" according to Zielinski *(Audiovisionen).*

5 *GOD'S GREATEST GIFT* is one of the ten "chapters" of the *Science-Fiction-Video-Opera OUT.* Thibault and his colleagues describe their production as follows:

> Cette oeuvre musique/vidéo de science-fiction raconte l'histoire d'un être voyageant dans son cerveau à travers des univers simulés, appelés OUT-réalités pour les habitants de la terre. L'illusion et l'hallucination deviennent le quotidien et la route de la paix éternelle pour celui qui franchit le passage entre l'IN et l'OUT-realités.

As far as the relationship and interaction between different genres is concerned, I would like to refer to my article "Le bouleversement des images et des sons dans l'art vidéo – ou *God's Greatest Gift is ...* ".

6 As far as their history is concerned cf. Albert Abramson. "Video Recording 1922 to 1959"(Zielinski, *Video* 35-57).

7 For example towards the famous central perspective established in the Italian *Quattrocento.*

8 It is important to note that our *Science-Fiction-Video-Opera* takes place in the year 2084 (one hundred years after Orwell).

9 This is already true for the very first attempts of establishing a sound film, as Edison tried with his *Black Mary,* and can be followed throughout the decades of the early history of sound film.

10 According to a definition given by Wolfgang Iser in one of his lectures at the University of Constance.

11 It seems promising to follow that line and to dicuss these aspects against the background of Derrida's concept of *écriture.*

12 Here I agree with F. Albersmeier, who suggested a similar procedure in his book *Theater, Film, Literatur in Frankreich,* op. cit.

References

Abramson, Albert. "Video Recording 1922 to 1959". *Video – Apparat/Medium, Kunst, Kultur.* Ed. Siegfried Zielinski. Frankfurt a.M./Bern/New York: Peter D. Lang, 1992, 35-57.

Albersmeier, Franz-Josef. *Theater, Film, Literatur in Frankreich. Medienwechsel und Intermedialität.* Darmstadt: Wissenschaftliche Buchgesellschaft, 1992.

Aumont, Jacques. *L'oeil interminable. Cinéma et peinture.* Paris: Librairie Séguier, 1989.

Bachtin, Michail M. *Die Ästhetik des Wortes.* Frankfurt a. M.: Suhrkamp, 1979.

Bellour, Raymond. *L'Entre-Images. Photo. Cinéma. Vidéo.* Paris: La Différence,1990.

----- . and Anne-Marie Duguet, eds. *Vidéo, Communications 48.* Paris: Seuil, 1988.

Bohn, Rainer, Eggo Müller, Rainer Ruppert, eds. "Die Wirklichkeit im Zeitalter ihrer technischen Fingierbarkeit". *Ansichten einer künftigen Medienwissenschaft.* Berlin: Edition Sigma, 1988, 7-27.

Bordwell, David. *Narration in the Fiction Film.* Madison: Wisconsin University Press, 1985.

Goffman, Erving. *Frame Analysis.* Harmondsworth: Penguin, 1974.

Grivel, Charles. *Le Fantastique. Mannheimer Analytika.* Mannheim: MANA I, 1983.

Hess-Lüttich, Ernest W. B. "Multimedia Communication". *Towards a Pragmatics of the Audiovisual. Theory and History. Vol. 1.* Ed. J. E. Müller. Münster: Nodus, 1983, 47-60.

Higgins, Dick. *The Poetics and Theory of the Intermedia.* Carbondale and Edwardsville: Southern Illinois University Press, 1984.

Kristeva, Julia. *La révolution du langage poétique.* Paris: Editions du Seuil, 1967.

Müller, Jürgen E. "Le bouleversement des images et des sons dans l'art vidéo – ou *God's Greatest Gift is ..." Cinémas,* 1 (1991): 21-37.

-----. "Intermedialität als Provokation der Medienwissenschaft". *Eikon. Internationale Zeitschrift für Photographie & Medienkunst* 4 (1992): 12-21.

-----. Intermedialität: Formen moderner kultureller Kommunikation. Münster: NODUS, 1996.

Negroponte, Nicholas. "Multimedia" (Interview). *hightech* 68 (1991).

Prümm, Karl. "Multimedialität und Intermedialität". *Theaterzeitschrift* 22 (1987): 95-103.

Rötzer, Florian, ed. "Mediales und Digitales. Zerstreute Bemerkungen und Hinweise eines irritierten informationsverarbeitenden Systems". *Digitaler Schein. Ästhetik der elektronischen Medien.* Frankfurt a. M.: edition suhrkamp, 1991, 9-78.

Virilio, Paul. *Guerre et cinéma I. Logistique de la perception.* Paris: Editions de l'étoile, 1984.

Weibel, Peter. "Transformationen der Techno-Ästhetik". *Digitaler Schein. Ästhetik der elektronischen Medien.* Ed. Florian Rötzer. Frankfurt a. M.: edition suhrkamp, 1991, 205-246.

Zielinski, Siegfried. *Audiovisionen. Kino und Fernsehen als Zwischenspiele in der Geschichte.* Reinbek bei Hamburg: rororo, 1989.

-----, ed. "Einleitung". *Video-Apparat/Medium, Kunst, Kultur.* Frankfurt a. M./ Bern/ New York: Peter D. Lang, 1992, 9-20.